Photographs from Boyhood

This publication was made possible with support by

the National Research Foundation of South Africa, the Oppenheimer Memorial Trust,

the British Academy, and the University of the Western Cape.

J.M. Coetzee
Photographs from Boyhood

Edited and introduced by Hermann Wittenberg

PROTEA

"I believe I was interested in
being present at the moment
when truth revealed itself,
a moment which one half discovered
but also half created."

J.M. Coetzee
"Remembering Photography"

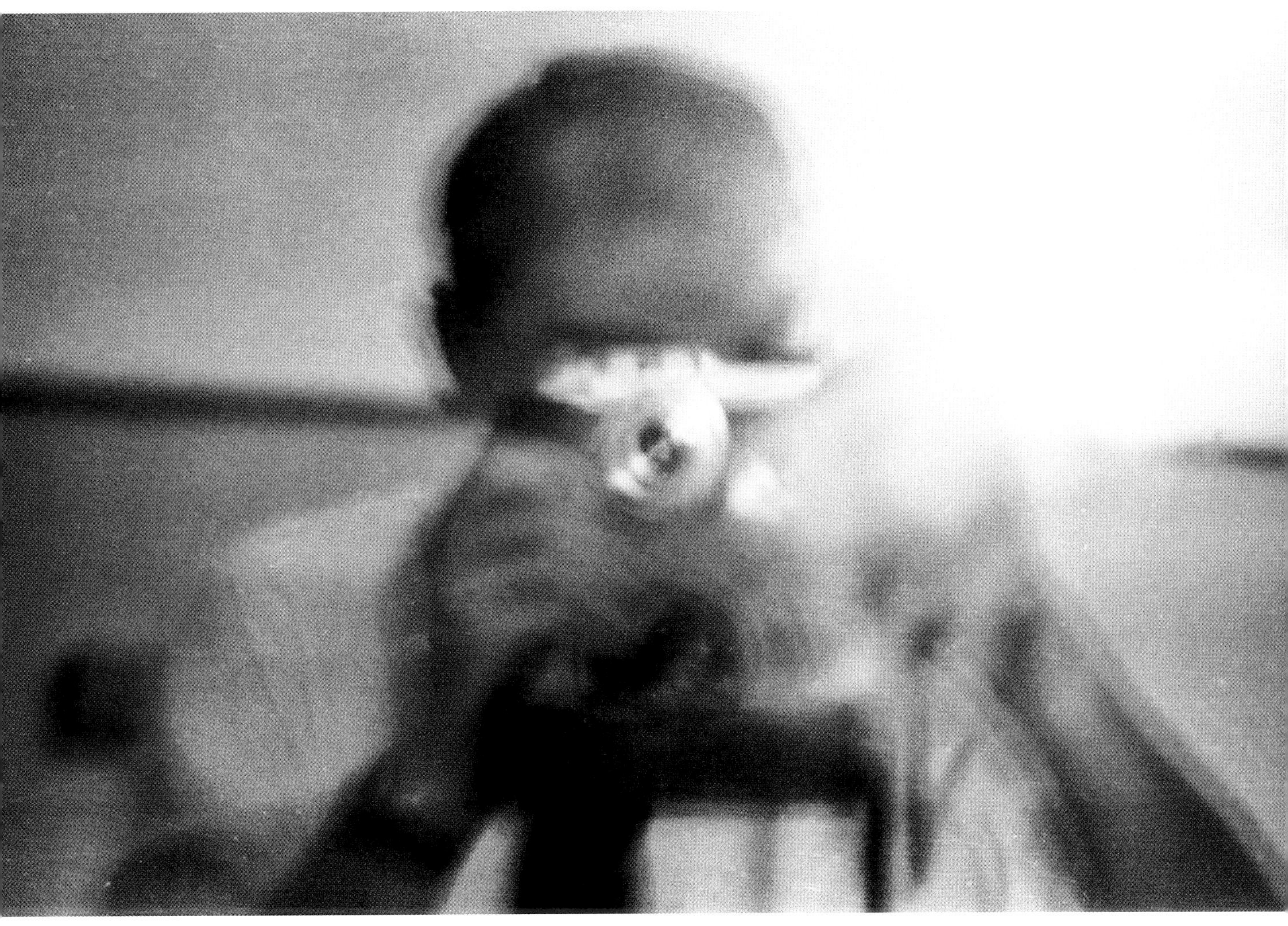

Contents

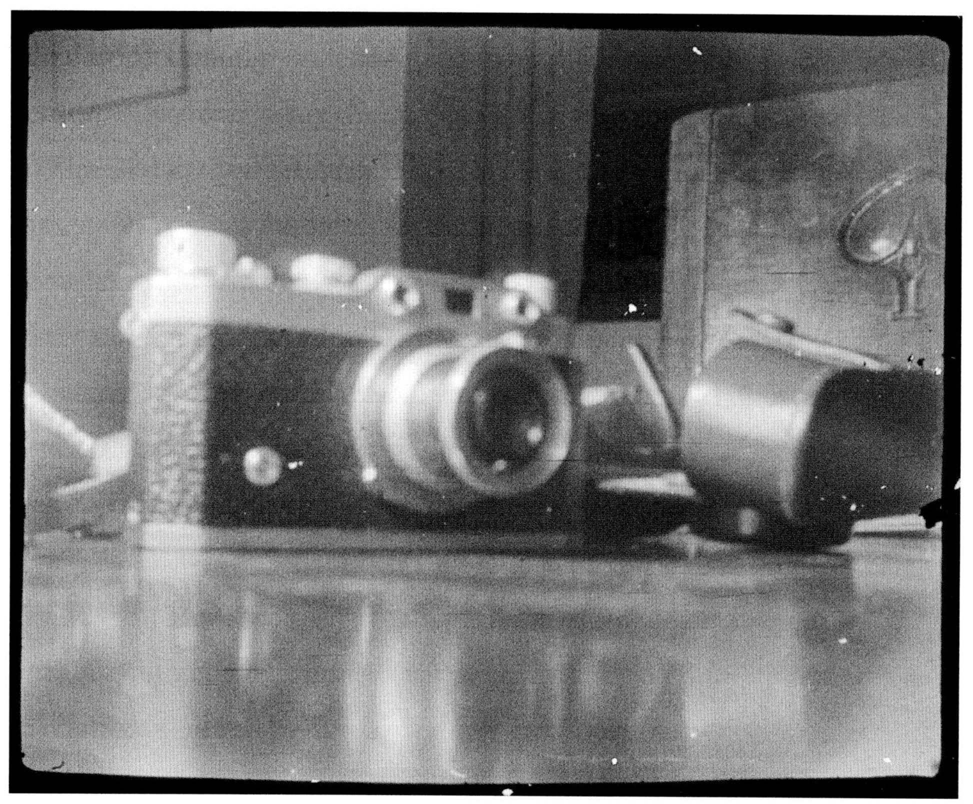

J.M. Coetzee's Wega camera, photographed circa 1955. The Wega was produced for a short period and in small numbers by the AFIOM company in Pordenone, Italy. It is now a rare collector's item.

1

A Note on Provenance

J.M. Coetzee's early photographs have only recently come to light, after being kept in storage for more than 60 years. After he emigrated to Australia in 2002, Coetzee still retained an apartment in Cape Town, and when the property was sold in 2014, a number of stored personal effects had to be disposed of.

Dorothy Driver, Coetzee's partner, came to Cape Town to sort through the belongings, and I was asked whether I had any interest in an old photographic enlarger and some assorted darkroom utensils. I had, at the time, worked with Coetzee on the publication of his film scripts (*Two Screenplays*, UCT Press). The enlarger arrived, together with an old-fashioned cardboard suitcase which contained a full set of darkroom equipment (development tanks, trays, filters, measuring jars, frames, and an assortment of chemicals and photographic paper), as well as a few photographic prints and some spools of developed film. These were rolls of 35 mm black and white negatives, stored in vintage aluminium film canisters. Judging from the expiry dates on the Ilford and Afrox tins (APRIL 1957, SEPT 1956, etc.), the film dated from the mid-1950s when the Coetzee family had moved from Worcester back to Cape Town, and John attended St Joseph's Marist College in Rondebosch.

I immediately emailed Coetzee about the photographs, suggesting that these were records that needed preservation, and that they might be of possible interest to scholarship. None of these materials had been used in J.C. Kannemeyer's major biography of Coetzee, which suggested that Coetzee may have overlooked these pictures when he gave Kannemeyer access to his personal records. Coetzee wrote back, giving me permission to work on the images, but also expressed some doubt that anyone would

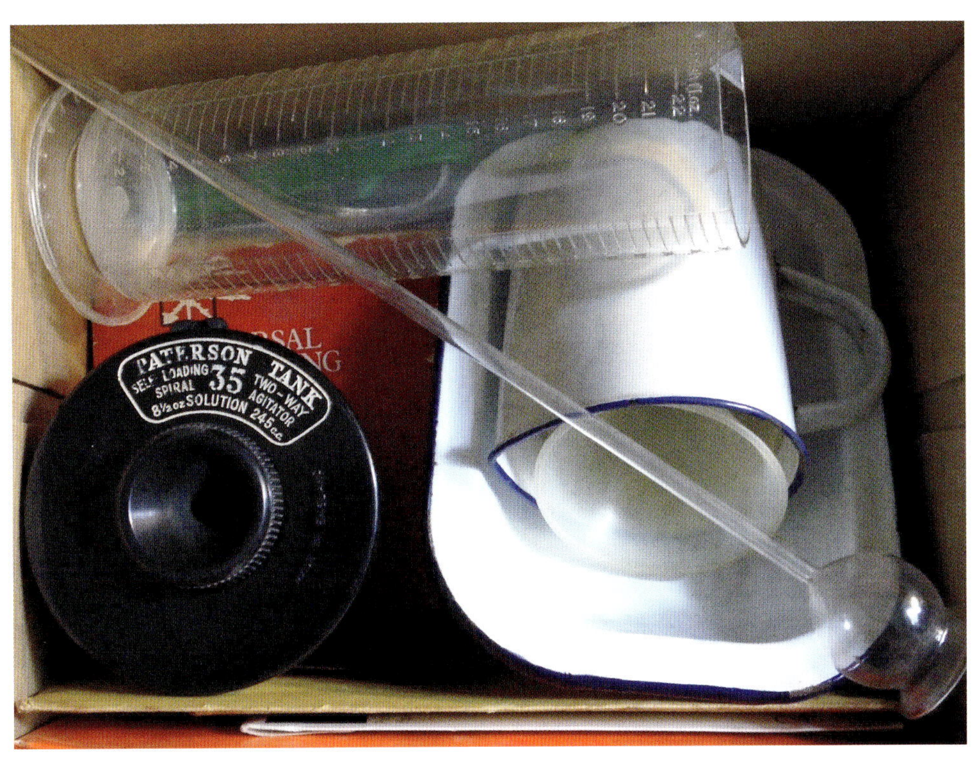
PATERSON TANK
SELF LOADING
SPIRAL 35 TWO-WAY
AGITATOR
8½ oz SOLUTION 245 c.c.

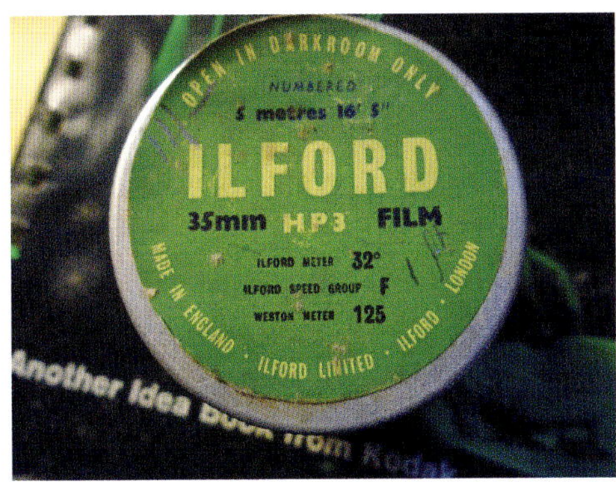
OPEN IN DARKROOM ONLY
NUMBERED
5 metres 16' 5"
ILFORD
35mm H.P.3 FILM
ILFORD METER 32°
ILFORD SPEED GROUP F
WESTON METER 125
MADE IN ENGLAND · ILFORD LIMITED · ILFORD · LONDON
Another Idea Book from Kodak

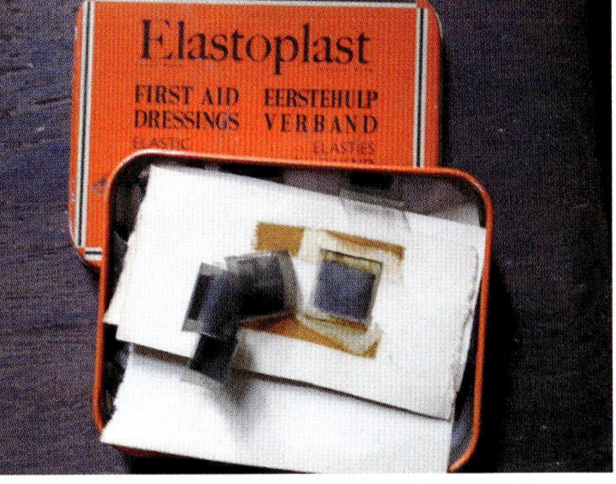
Elastoplast
FIRST AID   EERSTEHULP
DRESSINGS VERBAND
ELASTIC   ELASTIES

find amateur photographs snapped by a 16-year-old boy interesting.

The immediate challenge was that some of the original cellulose acetate film had begun to decay, producing a characteristic vinegar odour. The negatives were thus immediately digitally scanned by a professional photo lab, and the original film stock subsequently deposited at the Harry Ransom Center in Texas for expert preservation. The Ransom Center houses the substantive Coetzee Collection, a comprehensive archive of manuscripts, notes, drafts and correspondence that had earlier been sent to the US, when Coetzee left South Africa.

Opening the CD of digital images on my laptop for the first time was a revelation, like looking through a keyhole into a lost world. The photographs gave intimate glimpses into the world of *Boyhood*, Coetzee's poignant memoir of growing up in the Cape. The images were absorbing in their imperfections, but also revelatory about the boy who took the photographs and the people and scenes before his camera.

In 2016, I gave Coetzee a full set of the images in the form of contact sheets, and broached the idea of a public exhibition. He was cautiously supportive of these plans, and agreed to provide explanatory captions that would be complemented by excerpts from his published fictions. The photographs were exhibited at the Irma Stern Museum in Cape Town (November – January 2017/18), following an earlier limited preview at an international conference in Oxford (September 2017). This book reproduces these photographs, but also supplements them with previously unseen images. Some of the photographs are facsimiles of original prints which the young Coetzee had enlarged and printed in his darkroom at the time, but most images are reproductions of the digitised old black

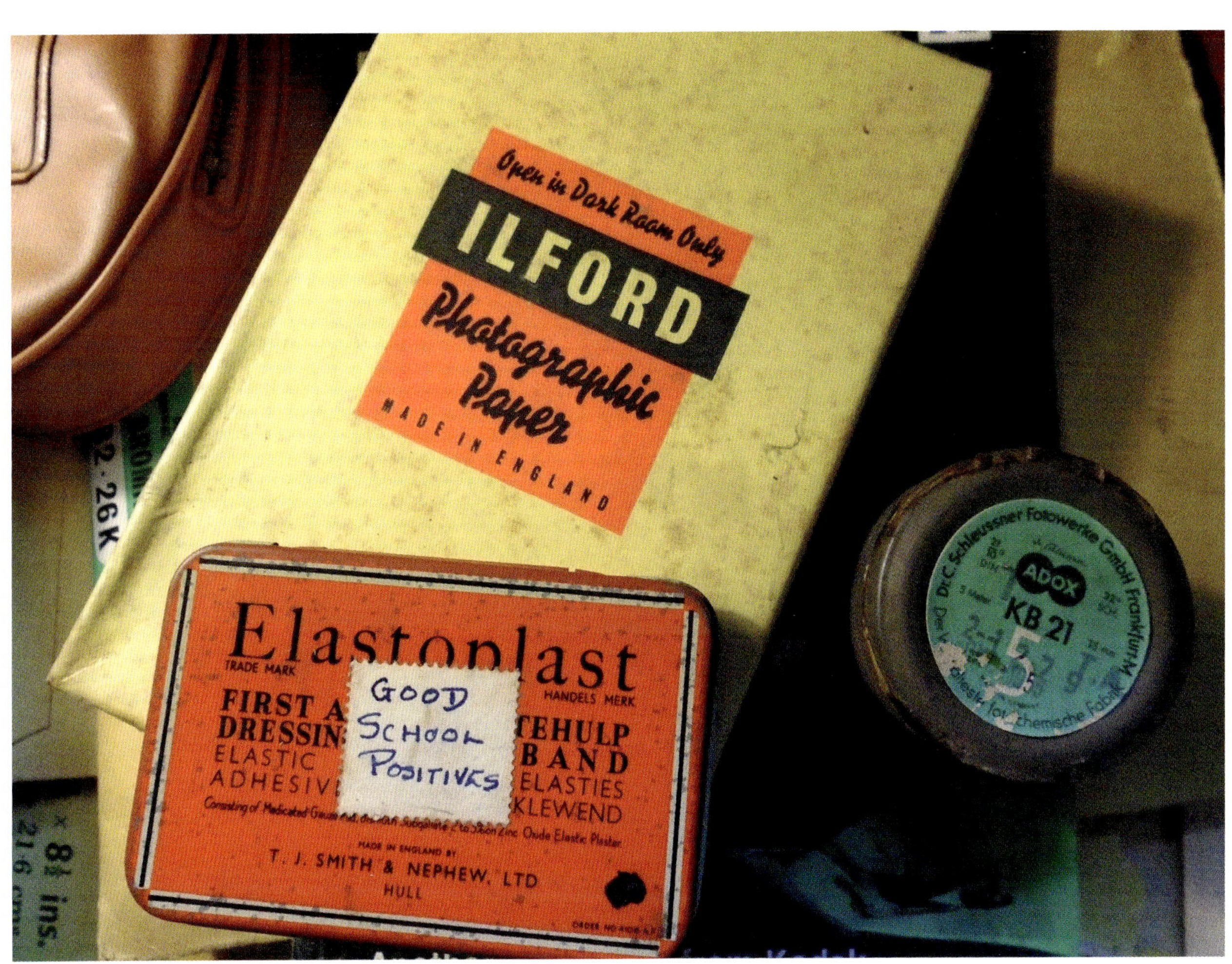

Open in Dark Room Only
ILFORD
Photographic Paper
MADE IN ENGLAND
Elastoplast
TRADE MARK
HANDELS MERK
FIRST AID
DRESSING
TEHULP
BAND
ELASTIC
ADHESIVE
ELASTIES
KLEWEND
MADE IN ENGLAND BY
T. J. SMITH & NEPHEW, LTD
HULL
GOOD
SCHOOL
POSITIVES
Dr. C. Schleussner Fotowerke GmbH Frankfurt-M.
ADOX
KB 21

and white film stock. A number of these photographs show traces of deterioration and aging, but in the interests of authenticity, a strategy of minimal digital retouching and editing was chosen. After more than 60 years, this publication is thus the first time that the full extent of Coetzee's early photographic experimentation has become public.

2

Before writing

J.M. Coetzee is one of the most significant writers of our times, but it is less well known that he had early ambitions to become a photographer. This collection of images records Coetzee's first experiments with the camera, documenting the beginnings of his encounter with photography. At a young age, Coetzee attained technical mastery and a considerable degree of formal proficiency in taking pictures, long before the poetry experiments of the student days and the choice of prose as the preferred creative medium when he was in his late 20s. He was a photographer before he became a writer.

The photographs, dating from the years 1955-56, allow us to look at Coetzee's adolescence through his eyes. He trained his camera at what was of interest to him, taking pictures of friends and teachers at school, sports events, Cape Town's natural and built environment, the ancestral Karoo farm, and family life at home. Many of the photographs are of a domestic and private nature that give us remarkably candid insights into the time of his youth, but some images also register the political situation of South Africa in the 1950s, as a policy of racial segregation increasingly pervaded the social order. This was a formative period of life that is also the subject of the autobiographical work *Boyhood* (1997), and readers may recognise parallels between characters and scenes in the semi-fictional memoir and some of the photographs. The images are also an archive of aesthetic development that reveals how he recorded and interpreted the world around him as a series of pictures, or "scenes of provincial life", to use the subtitle of *Boyhood*.

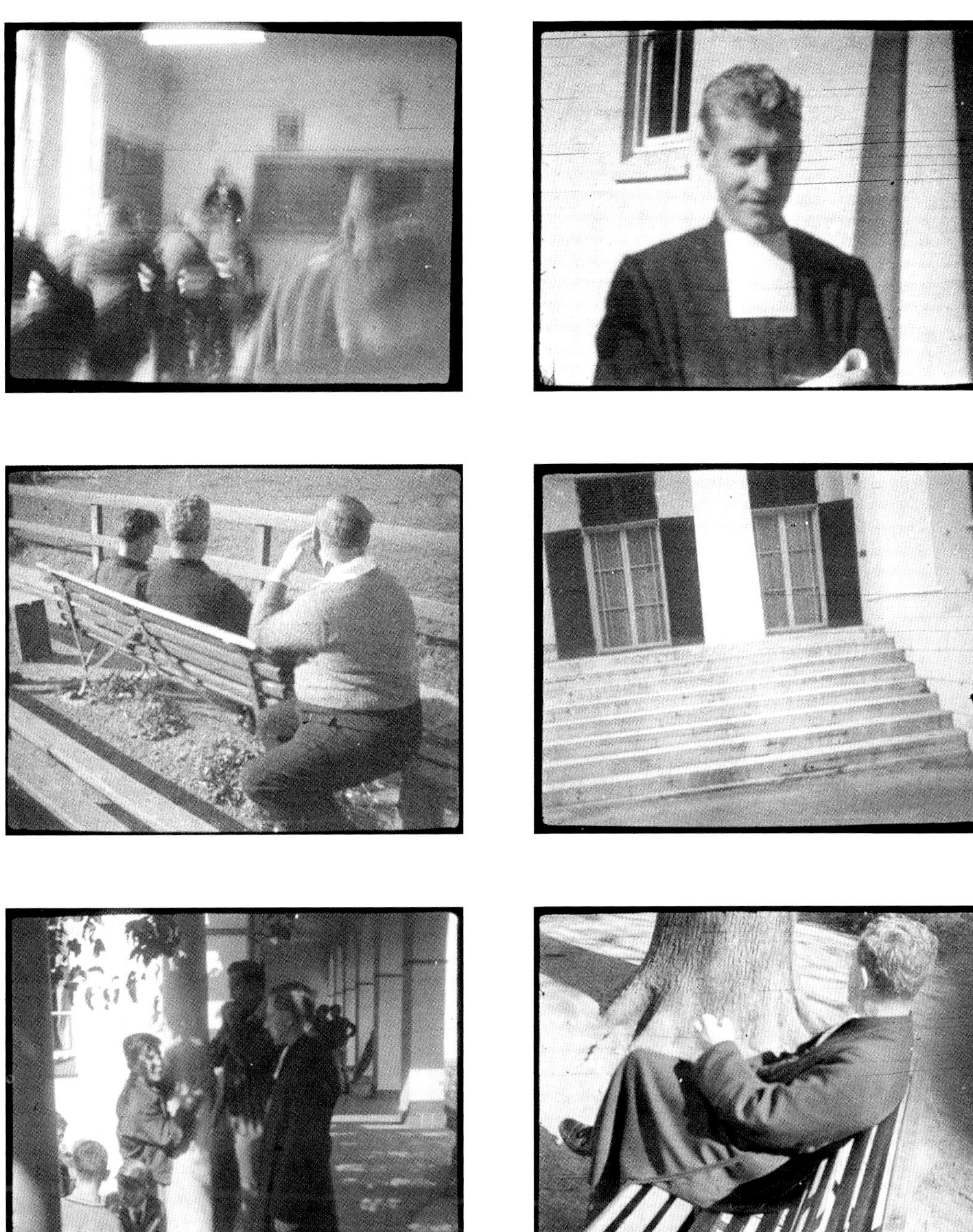

Various scenes from St Joseph's Marist College, taken by the spy camera.

The first camera that the young Coetzee acquired was a small, discreet "spy camera" that could be used to take clandestine pictures. He would have been about 15 years old at the time, attending St Joseph's Marist College, in Rondebosch, Cape Town. Coetzee recalls that he bought the camera by mail order: "It was a novelty, advertised as the sort of camera that spies used."[1] As recounted in J.C. Kannemeyer's biography, Coetzee's best friend at school, Nic Stathakis, remembered "how they had, between classes, mischievously taken photos in secret of teachers and schoolfellows."[2] Around 70 of these miniature photographs have survived, most of them as negatives. The images show his playful use of the new toy, taking illicit pictures of teachers who were mostly not aware of being photographed. One of his favourite teachers, the gentle and soft-spoken Brother Otto, soon appears to have realised what game Coetzee and his friends were up to, and in one of the pictures his hand is seen pushing away the lens. But he also took more risky pictures of his authoritarian English teacher, Mr Scully (given the name of Mr Whelan in *Boyhood*), who would not have taken kindly to being photographed by a schoolboy.

In *Boyhood*, we read how the young John was exceedingly anxious of getting into trouble with teachers during his primary school years in Worcester, but by the time he was a teenager in high school he was clearly no longer averse to transgressing rules. Several of the images taken of his friends at school reveal a teenage rebelliousness that was typical of strict public boys' schools at the time: mocking teachers' authority behind their backs, secretly smoking cigarettes in the

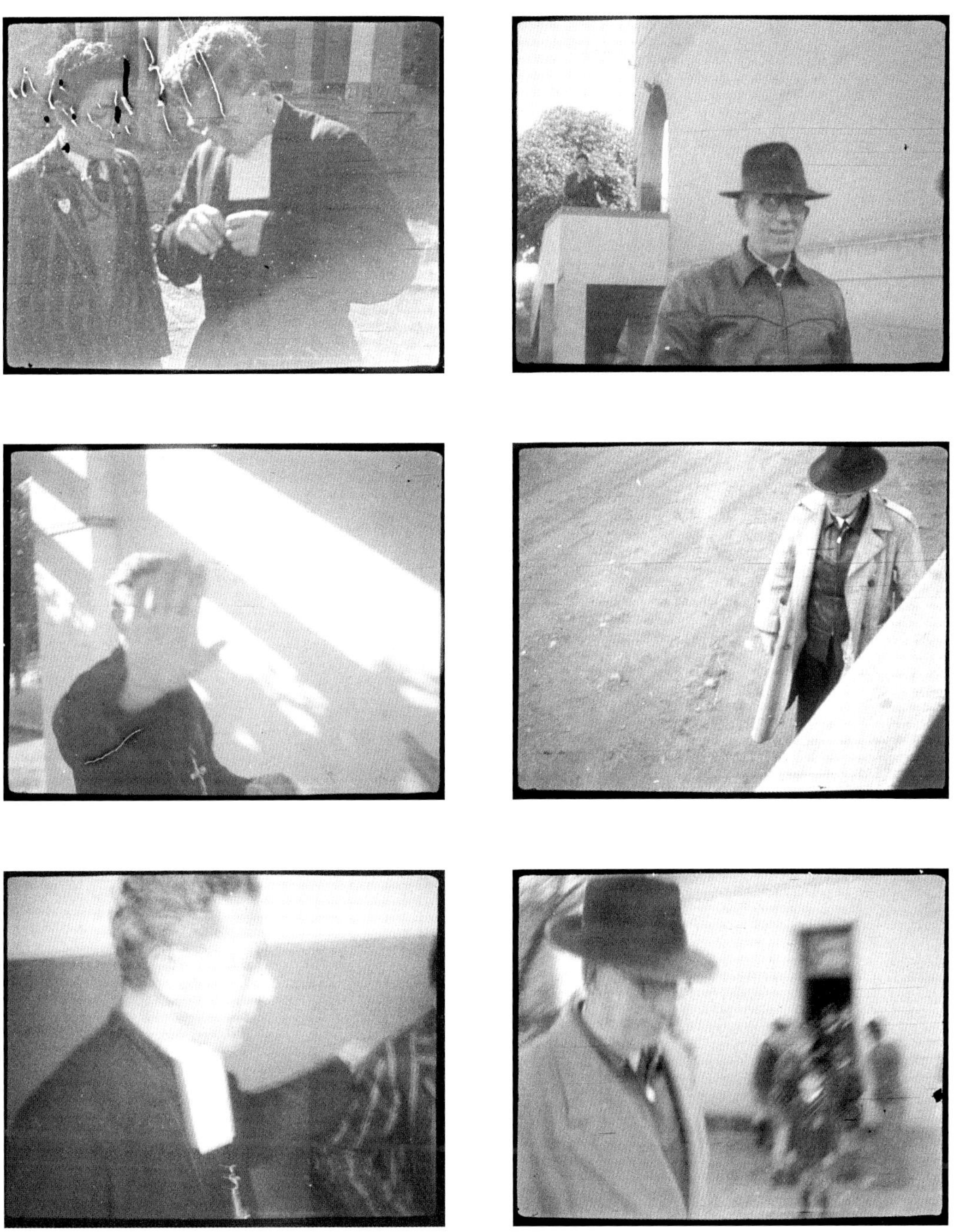

Left: Pictures of Brother Otto. Also visible is Nic Stathakis, Coetzee's best friend at school.

Right: Secretly taken photographs of Mr Scully, Coetzee's English teacher.

classroom, or even playing around with the teacher's cane, that fearful symbol of teacher authority (p. 119). It is not difficult to imagine the entertainment value of some of Coetzee's illicit photographs, as they were secretly passed around among the teenage boys.

But taking pictures was only part of being an aspiring photographer. From the beginning, Coetzee took the craft of photography seriously, and that meant setting up his own darkroom at home where he could develop his negatives and make his own prints. He purchased an enlarger, a second-hand Opemus 4x4 model, produced by the Czechoslovakian Meopta optical company, as well as other equipment such as a development tank and a fixing bath, measurement containers, a thermometer and an assortment of other tools and chemicals. He was largely self-taught, guided by *Kodak's Basic Developing, Printing, Enlarging* booklet that was among the material in the suitcase. The memory of the excitement and magic of these first experiments with light and chemistry probably underpins passages such as the following from *Slow Man*:

> The camera, with its power of taking in light and turning it into substance, has always seemed to him more a metaphysical than a mechanical device. His first real job was as a darkroom technician; his greatest pleasure was always in darkroom work. As the ghostly image emerged beneath the surface of the liquid, as veins of darkness on the paper began to knit together and grow visible, he would sometimes experience a little shiver of ecstasy, as though he were present at the day of creation.[3]

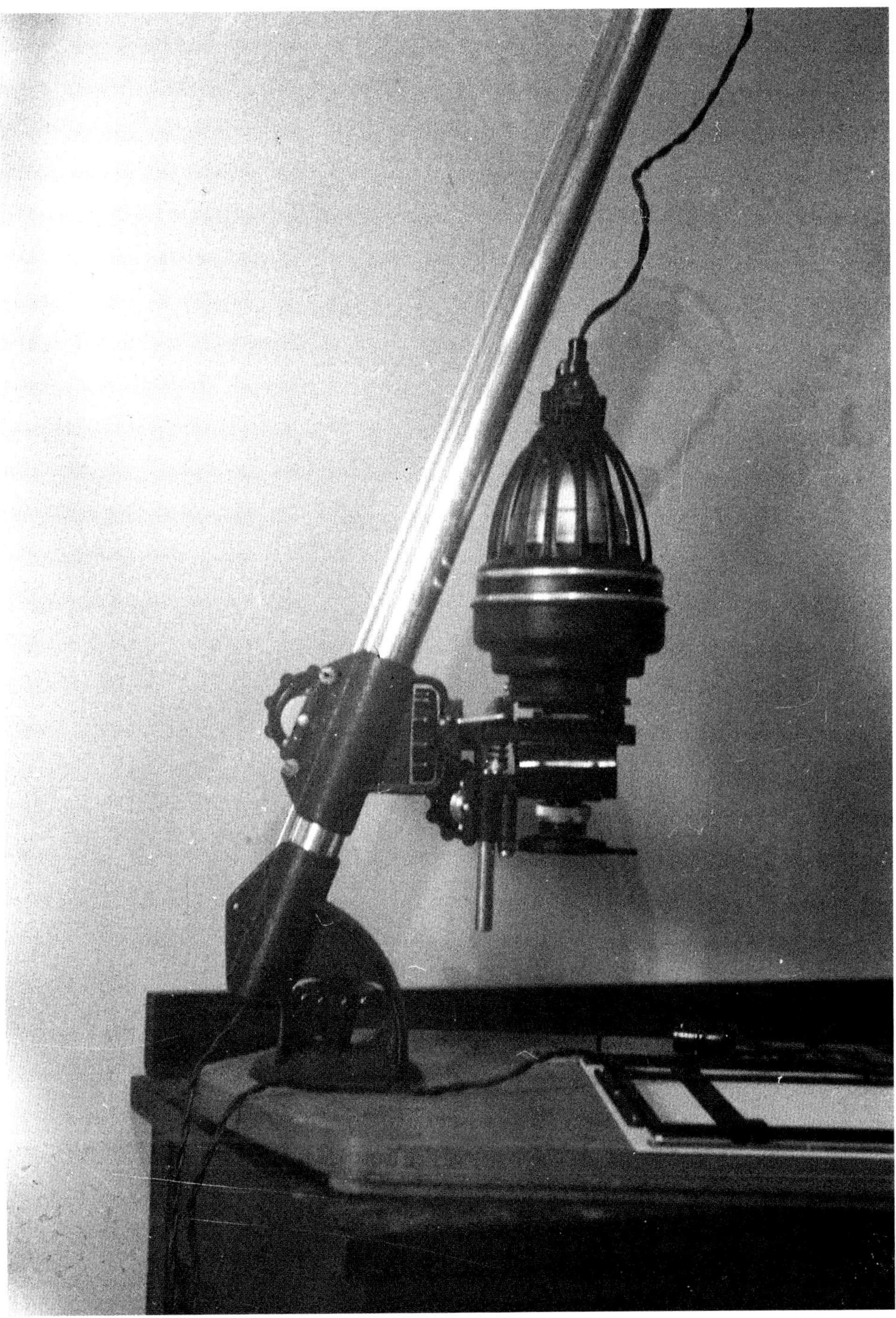

Coetzee's enlarger, an Opemus 4x4 model.

Coetzee's first simple point & shoot camera took inferior images, and the small negatives were difficult to enlarge and obtain satisfactory prints from. As Coetzee remembers, the spy camera "took images about 15 mm x 15 mm which had to be enlarged," and that there "was only one shop in Cape Town that stocked film for it."[4] Coetzee did not grow up in an affluent home, and unlike in our digital age, photography involved purchasing film, chemicals and photographic paper, besides the considerable investment in darkroom equipment. Although photography had become affordable to middle class families in the post-war era, it was not a cheap hobby for a boy whose family sometimes struggled to make ends meet. "I had to ration my shots," Coetzee remembers, and he consequently took pictures more sparingly than he might have wanted to, and once the film was developed, would only print out a few select photographs.[5]

Perhaps out of frustration with the limitations of the miniature spy camera, Coetzee soon upgraded to a more professional camera, a 35mm rangefinder Wega that allowed much more sophisticated control over the photographic process. The Wega was an Italian-made copy of the legendary Leica II, the camera that was used by many professional photographers at the time. Although the Wega was more affordable than the Leica, it cost Coetzee £40, which would have been a considerable sum for a schoolboy at the time. He was clearly becoming substantively invested in photography, and thinking back to this moment Coetzee recalls that "buying the Wega plus darkroom equipment marked the moment when I began to take photographs 'seriously'."[6] One of the spy camera pictures shows the newly acquired Wega, proudly displayed

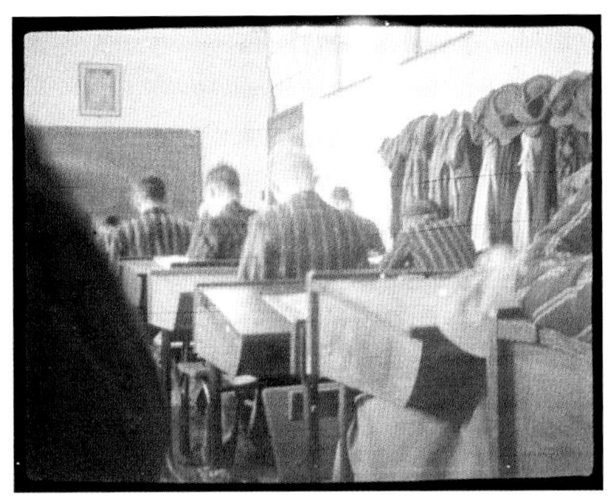
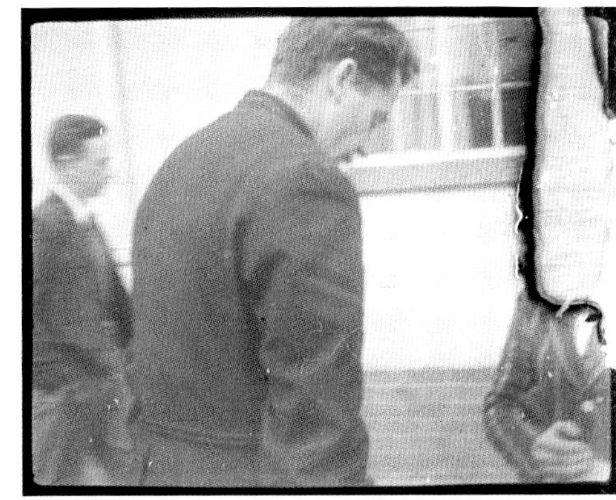
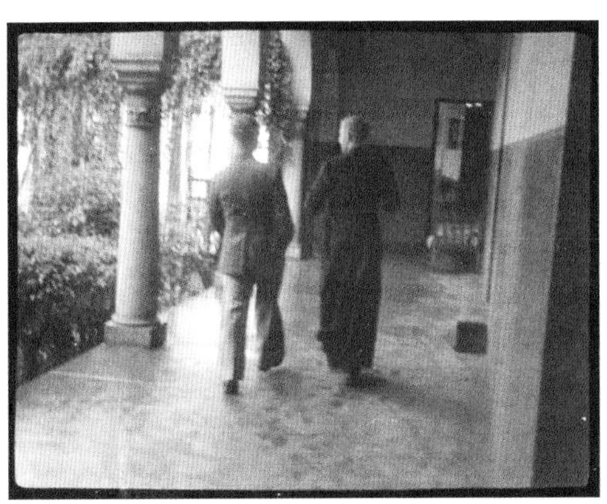
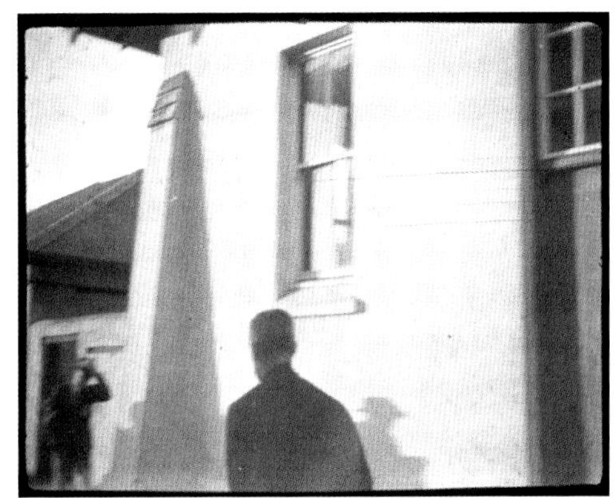
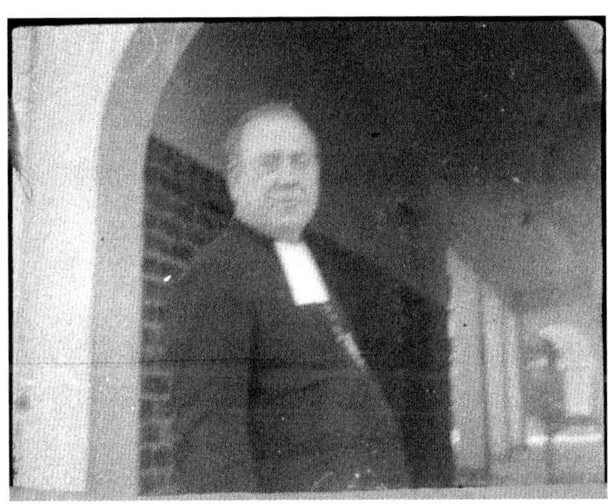
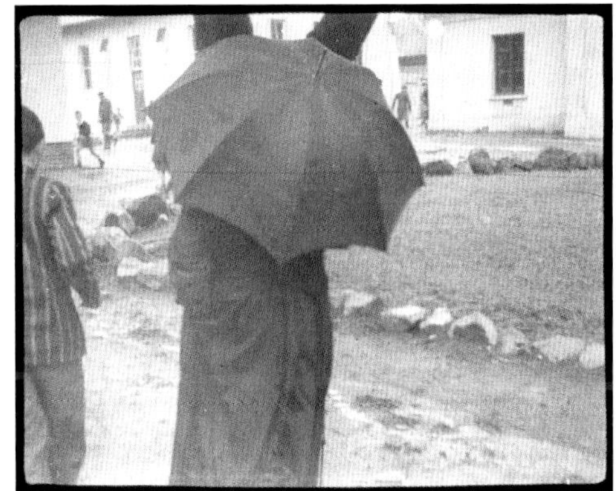

Various scenes from St Joseph's Marist College, taken by the spy camera.

on the dining room table (p. 8). We may speculate that this was perhaps the last photograph taken with the spy camera, soon to be discarded for the superior optics of the Wega. Whereas the amateur snapshots of the spy camera had the character of schoolboy pranks, the new camera allowed Coetzee to pursue his hobby in a more ambitious and technically accomplished manner.

The Wega, which Coetzee still owns today, would become the primary camera with which he developed his craft, learning to manipulate parameters such as shutter speed, aperture and focal length. Many of the photographs show his ambitions to master the new medium: capturing motion with high shutter speeds, shooting in low light conditions, experimenting with flash, and controlling chemical processes and exposure in the darkroom. Several photographs show an experimentalism and a pushing of technical boundaries, for example images shot deliberately into the light (for example p. 33). A considerable number of images show his fascination with movement and speed, using high shutter speed settings to capture fast motion during sports events, or, at home, where a sequence of images shows him attempt to capture his brother David in mid-air, as he jumps down from a ladder in the back yard (pp 142-143).

Coetzee soon developed the habits of a photographer, having the camera to hand at all times and ready to take pictures whenever an interesting subject presented itself, whether he was at home, walking on the streets, or at school. As he became more confident and assured as a photographer, the teachers at school appear to have condoned his activities. When the school photographer came to St Joseph's to

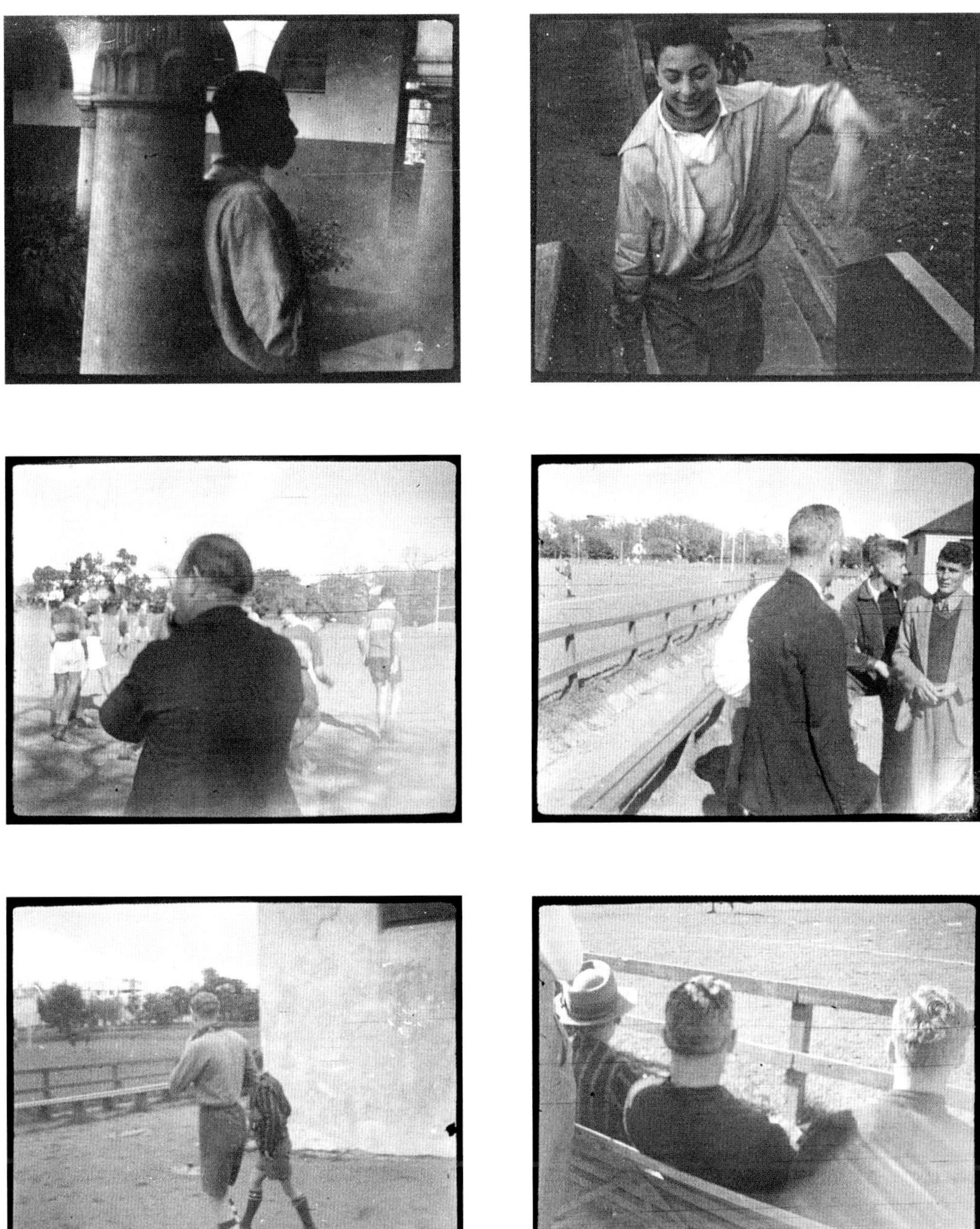

At St Joseph's Marist College, Coetzee mostly took pictures of teachers and class mates. But one photograph also shows that he noticed the black workers who were employed at the school.

take the official class pictures, the boy emulated him by taking similar pictures at the same time, thereby slipping into the role of a professional photographer. Some of these staged group images show the class of boys posing formally for the camera, but he also caught the more informal before and after moments (left). Coetzee no longer needed to take pictures in secret, and could even approach the intimidating Mr Scully to take his photograph (p. 127).

Many of the pictures taken with the Wega continued to show the earlier influence of the spy camera. Several images are blurry or have tilting horizons, possibly snapped by a camera held discreetly in the hand, rather than in front of the eye. He still shot pictures secretly at school, but at home he also took many improvised and unposed images where the subject seemed unaware of the camera. This can be seen in several candid pictures of his mother, as well as in a rare photograph of his father which catches the moment in which he is being admonished by a finger-wagging Aunt Annie (p. 67). The angle and the tilting horizon suggests that this photograph was not carefully composed with the eyes behind the rangefinder, but was quickly shot on the spur of the moment. We may speculate that the boy was drawn to the rising voices of the altercation, and caught the moment by unobtrusively pointing the hand-held camera through the open door. In other photographs, his roaming eye was drawn to scenes on the streets, or to passing views from the car or train. Coetzee's approach was influenced by the documentary photojournalism that he would have seen in magazines and newspapers at the time. He remembers reading books about photography and notes that he "imitated as best I could the kind of

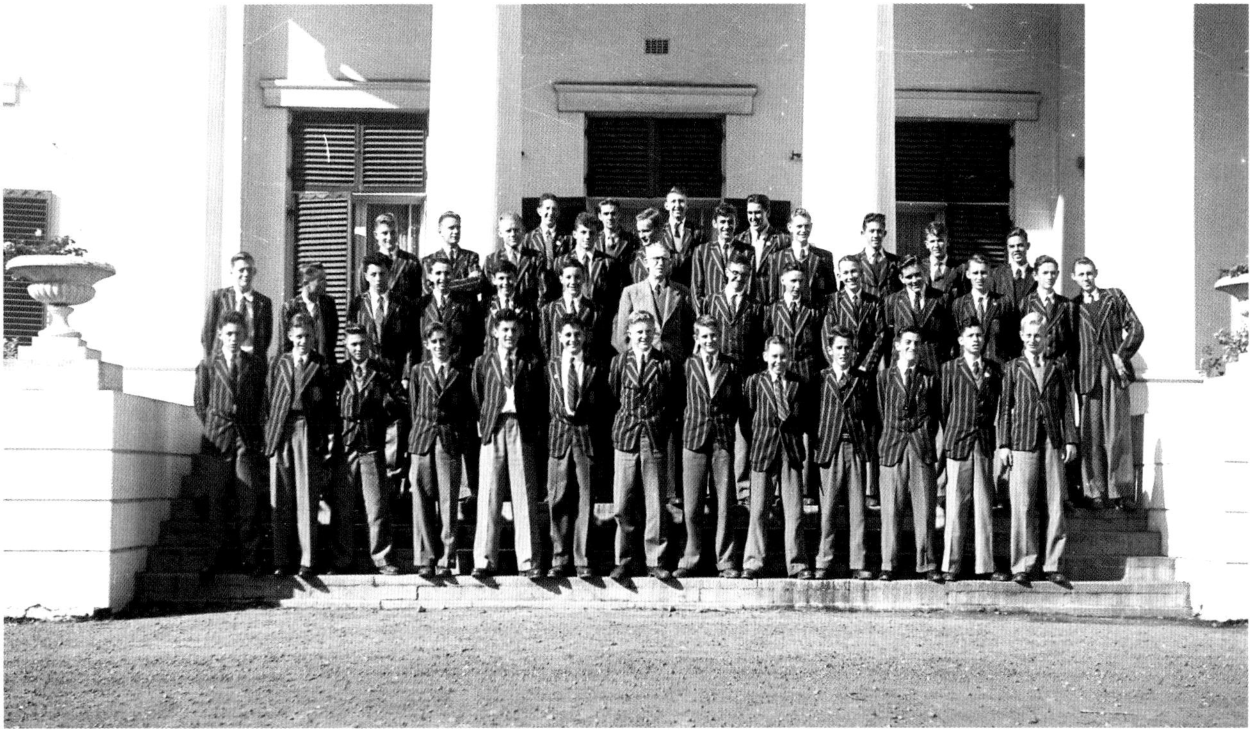

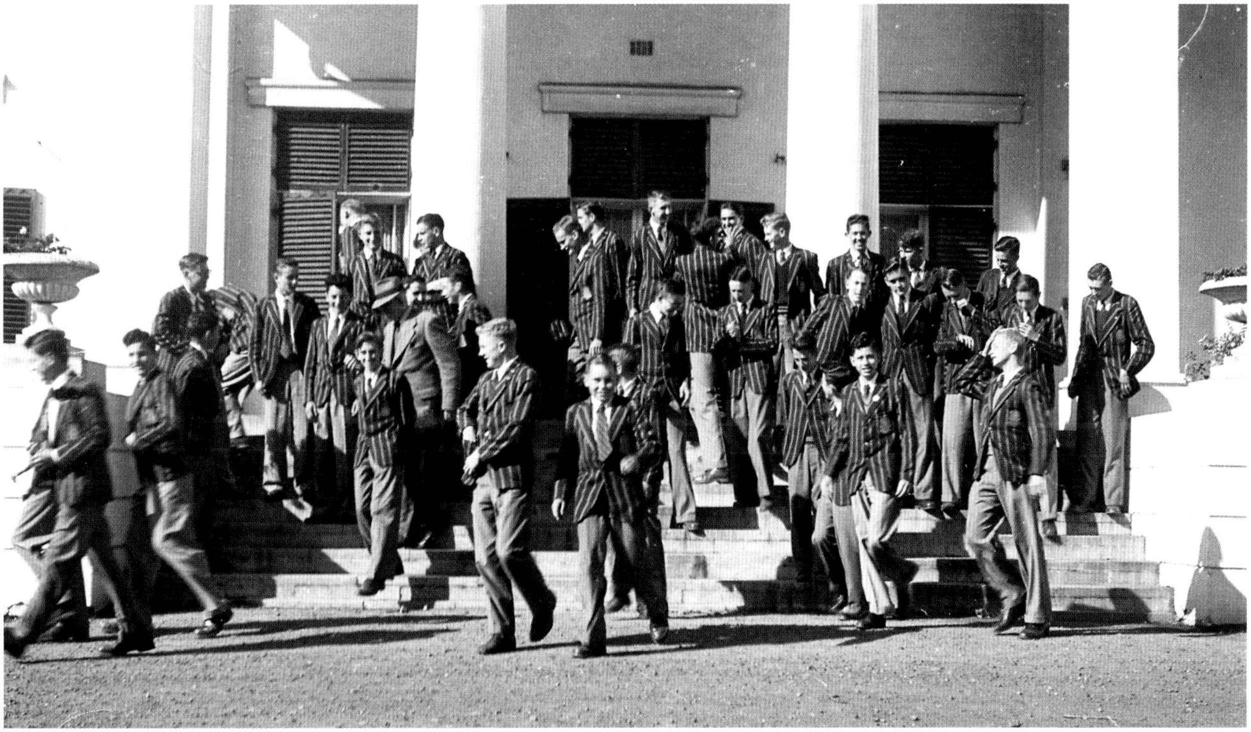

photographs I saw in *Life* and other magazines."[7] Although Coetzee's initial need to take pictures clandestinely may have shaped his documentary, improvised mode of photography, this was also a style that he found exemplified in the work of the celebrated French photographer Henri Cartier-Bresson. Coetzee's belief in the ability of the camera to capture an elusive "moment when truth revealed itself, a moment which one half discovered but also half created"[8] was drawn directly from the practice of photographers like Cartier-Bresson.

The earnestness with which Coetzee approached his new interest is apparent in a photographic society which he and his friends established at school. He remembers that he was "the driving force behind the photographic club at St Joseph's" and that the boys "had the use of a notice board to pin up our photographs."[9] Some of the larger format photographs, which would have been entered in these competitions, still show the holes in the corners made by pins that would have attached the prints to the display boards. A scoring sheet in Coetzee's own hand has survived, and it records him getting second and third prizes in a competition of some 20 other entrants, mostly Grade IX boys. The competition was adjucated by his teachers, and the "marks" show that Coetzee scored well for 'composition' and 'enlarging technique', but was below average in the categories 'depth and detail' and 'neatness'. On the reverse side of one of these competition photographs, an image of the famous equestrian statue at Cape Town's Rhodes Memorial, the young Coetzee had carefully recorded the technical specifications and processes:

No.	Entrant	25. Composition	25 Enlarging Technique	25 Depth and Detail	25 Neatness and General Work	Total
1	P. Wynne (IX)	20	12	15	14	[cut off]
2.	J. Coetzee (IX)	20	20	12	8	[cut off]
3.	J. Coetzee (IX)	10	24	20	4	[cut off]
4.	K. Kenny (IX)	15	15	15	12	[cut off]
5a	J. Everett (IX)	18	15	20	2	[cut off]
5b	J. Coetzee (IX)	5	20	15	15	[cut off]
7	P. Wynne (IX)	10	24	15	5	[cut off]
8	A. Lykiardopulos (IX)	15	18	15	5	[cut off]
9	N. Stathakis (IX)	18	15	18	10	[cut off]
10a	J. Rabie (X)	15	15	15	5	[cut off]
10b	P. Wynne (IX)	10	10	20	10	[cut off]
10c	A. Lykiardopulos (IX)	20	15	10	5	[cut off]
13	A. Lykiardopulos (IX)	15	12	12	10	[cut off]
14.	A. Lykiardopulos (IX)	12	15	15	5	[cut off]
15a	P. Wynne (IX)	15	15	10	5	[cut off]
15b	C. Thompson (IX)	20	10	5	10	[cut off]
17	E. Buchanan (IX)	15	12	12	5	[cut off]
18a	P. Wolff (X)	20	35	15	3	[cut off]
18b	M. Colussi (VIII)	15	15	10	3	[cut off]
20a	J. Rabie	15	10	5	10	[cut off]
20b	A. Lykiardopulos (IX)	5	10	15	15 10	[cut off]
22	D. Herron (IX)	12	10	10	5	3[cut off]
23	G. Colussi (X)	12	8	8	5	8[cut off]

The scoring sheet of the St Joseph's Photographic Society.

This is a photograph of the Statue of Energy by Watts in front of the Cecil John Rhodes Memorial on the slopes of Table Mountain.

It was taken on Ilford Pan F film with and exposure of 1/20th sec, at f/12.5. The camera was a Wega 35mm. f 3.5 shutter to 1/1000th coupled rangefinder.

Developer: N B Promicrol

Fixer: Johnson Acid Fixer

Paper: Ilford Multigrade glossy

Paper Developer: I.D. -20.

An interest in documenting the technology of image making is perhaps not unusual for an aspiring photographer, but a number of photographs also reveal a self-reflexive, conscious fascination with the medium itself. In the case of the carefully composed Rhodes Memorial photograph, Coetzee did not only meticulously record the way he shot, developed and printed the image, but also took a photograph of this photograph in his darkroom, where we can see it newly developed and still wet from its immersion in the chemical bath (right). He photographed not only photographs, but also his own camera, his enlarger and his darkroom. In one fascinating blurry image, he pointed the camera at himself in the mirror (p. 5).

Some of the self-reflexive and metafictional literary strategies that would later become the hallmark of the novels are perhaps rehearsed in these early images. Coetzee's curious and self-conscious engagement with the photographic medium prefigured the way he would subsequently write novels that often concerned themselves with the

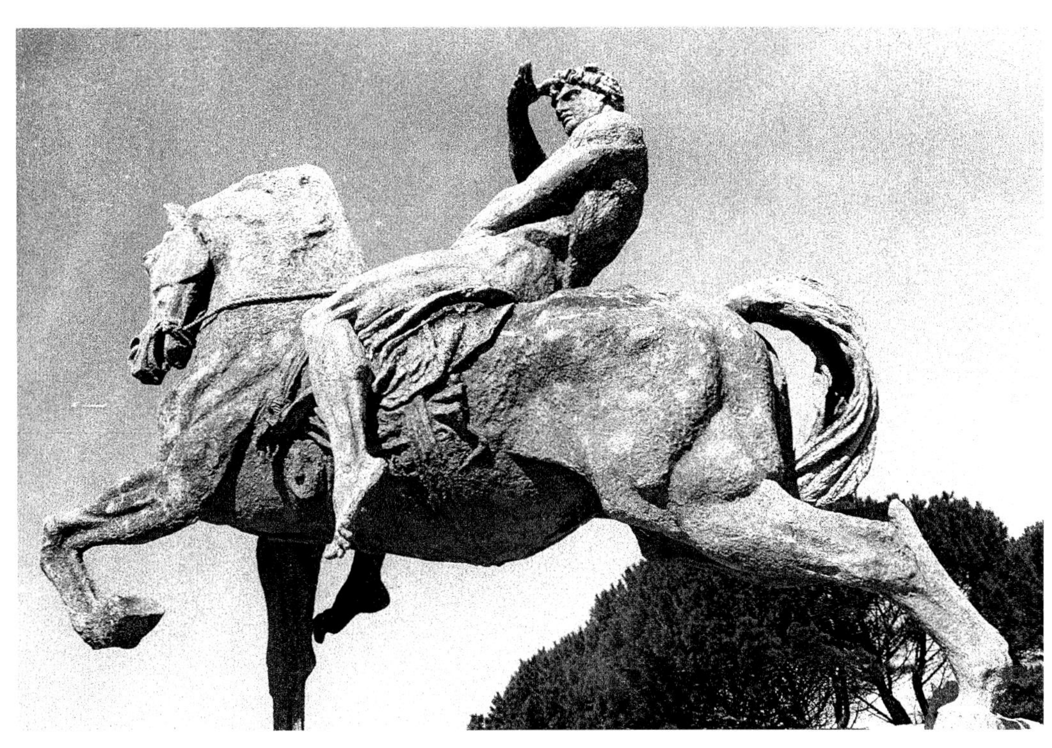

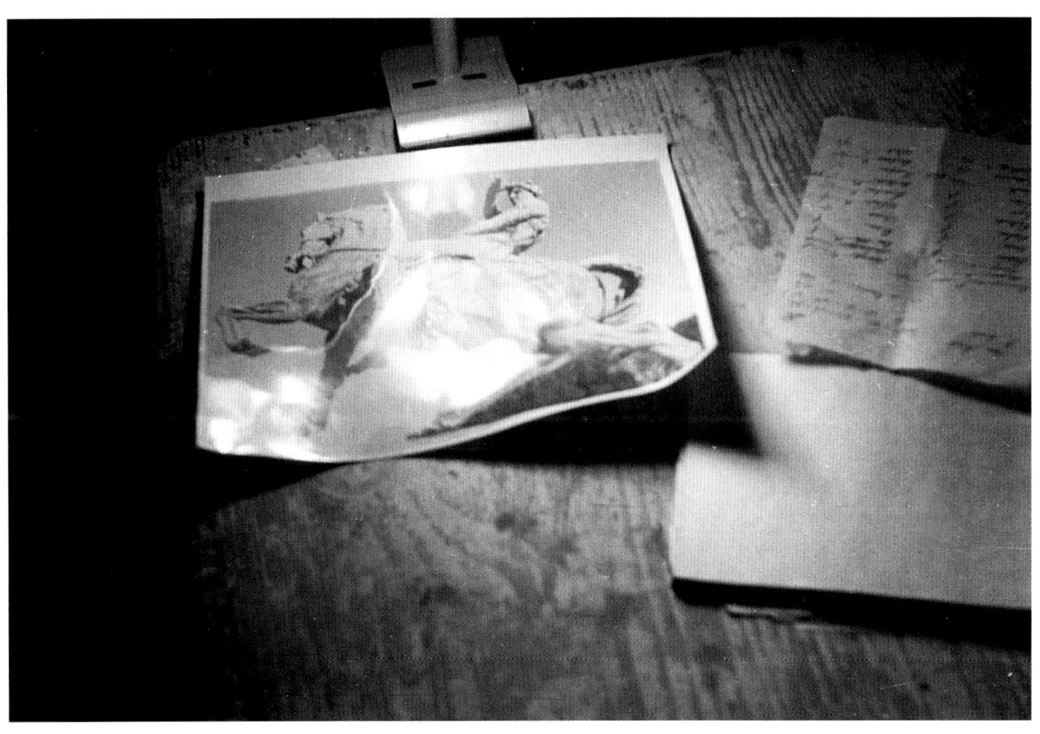

process of writing itself. Given what we know of Coetzee's literary career, it is perhaps not surprising to see that some of the early photographs reveal a fascination with scenes of writing. There are photographs showing his typewriter, and he trained the lens on newspapers, magazines, poetry and sheet music, and most remarkably, the bookshelf of his first library (p. 179). A particularly striking image shows his writing desk with an open book, together with notepaper, pens and pencils (right). The image is shot audaciously into the blinding light of the reading lamp, creating dramatic shadows and chiaroscuro effects. It is perhaps not coincidental that Coetzee's early photographs often depict books and writing, and conversely, that the novels he would later write frequently reference photographs.

How do these photographs then relate to the published fiction? Most obviously, the photographs are a visual chronicle of adolescent life and invite comparisons with *Boyhood*, the first volume of the autobiographical trilogy. The relationship between the pictures that were snapped by a teenage boy, and the words written by an almost 60-year-old man looking back in time, is both complex and fascinating, especially if we consider that these photographs were evidently not used as an *aide-mémoire* when *Boyhood* was written. The photographs and *Boyhood* share a common world, and there are several moments of direct correspondence, with some images appearing to authenticate events and scenes in the memoir. One example of such congruence occurs in the beginning of the memoir, where we read about John's interest in all things Russian, and like many boys of his age, his obsession with World War II warfare. "Again and again," we read in *Boyhood*, "he came back

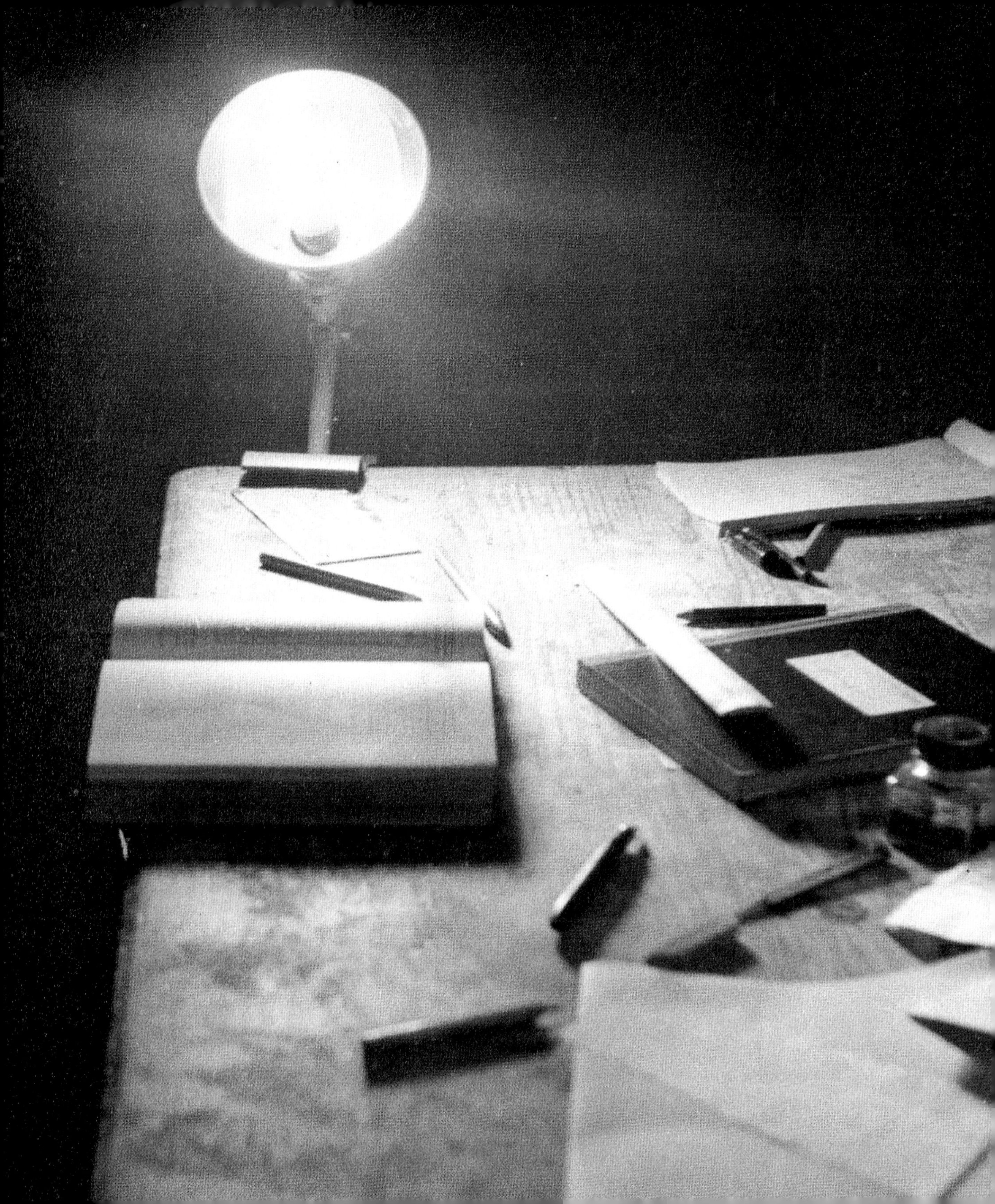

to a painting of a Russian dive-bomber over a burning and devastated German tank column."[10] What we do not, though, read in the memoir was that the boy was so fascinated by this particular illustration that he photographed it (right), enlarged and printed it, and signed it with his name. Pin holes in the corners suggest that the photograph may have been entered for a photographic club competition at school, but it might also have been pinned up in his bedroom in Plumstead, where the Coetzees lived.

There are several other instances where the photographs and the memoir reinforce each other. In another instance of a direct correspondence, we read in the description of a boring school lesson that Theo, his class mate, "sits squashed against him in his desk, underneath the picture of Jesus opening his chest to reveal a glowing ruby heart."[11] In several of the St Joseph's photographs this particular Jesus portrait is clearly visible (p. 113). Similarly, there is a photograph which appears to illustrate the memoir's description of Aunt Annie's flat with its decaying heaps of books, newspapers and magazines (p. 85). The description of the beloved Karoo farm is also corroborated by several photographs, for example, one image (p. 93) which shows the "labyrinth of stone-walled kraals that belong to the old days when the sheep in their thousands had to be brought from the veld to be counted or shorn or dipped."[12]

But we also need to remember that the memoir, as all autobio-graphical writing, is partly fictionalised. In *Summertime*, the last of the trilogy, there is an explicit cautionary note, as articulated by the text's invented biographer: "What Coetzee writes there cannot be trusted, not as a factual record – not because he was a liar, but because he was a

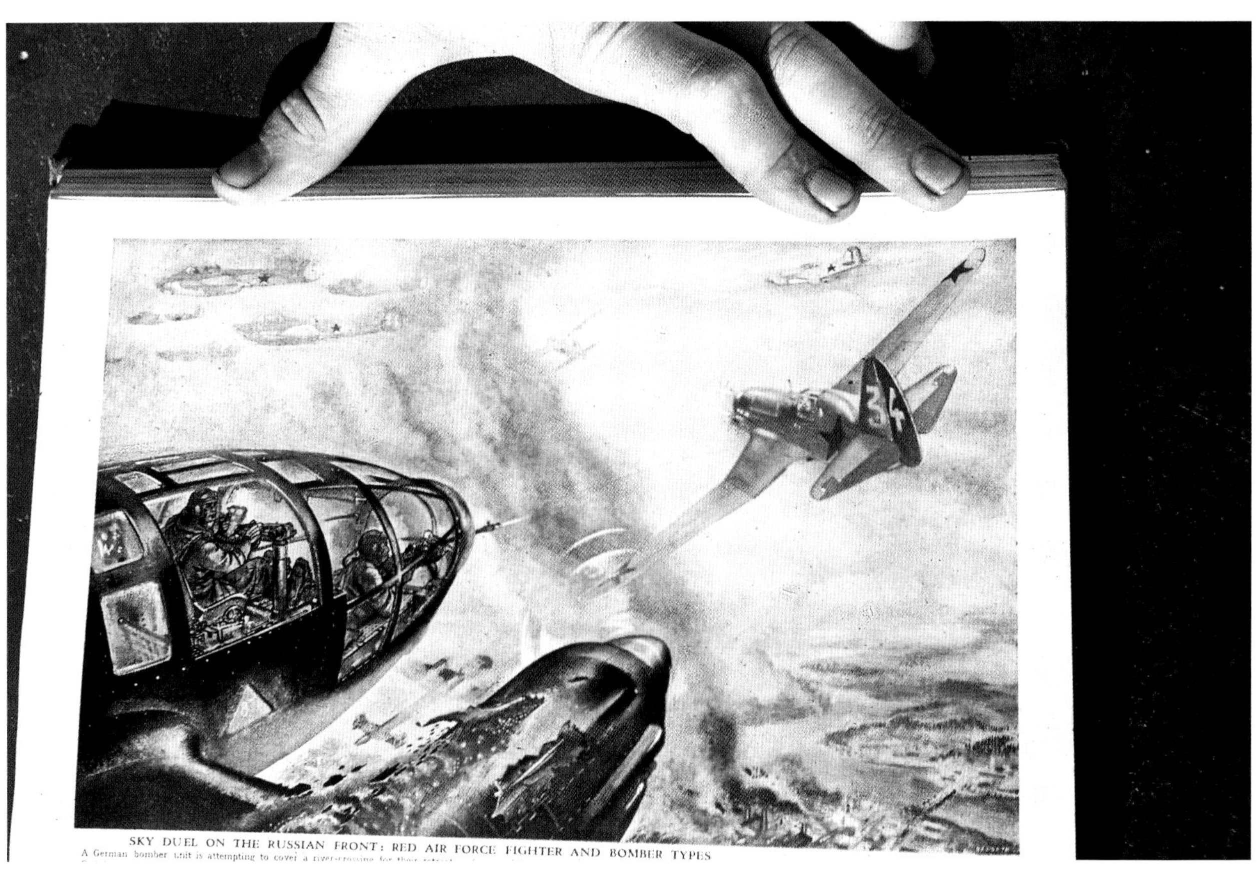

As a boy, Coetzee was fascinated by this particular World War II illustration, which is referred to in *Boyhood*. The negative shows Coetzee's hand keeping the book's page flat but for the enlarged print he cropped the negative so that his fingers were not visible.

fictioneer."[13] Neither autobiographical writing nor photography can offer unmediated, truthful accounts of what once was, but through the optics of Coetzee's camera, fleeting moments of a past time have become fixed in the emulsions of the negatives. Some of these images complicate Coetzee's "fictioneering" as they appear to record what actually once happened – at least for a split second in actual time before the lens of the camera. In another context, Coetzee asserted that the "photograph is read, and justifiably so, as a record of something that really happened" and that the "story in which the moment is embedded may be a fiction, but the event was a real one, it belongs to history."[14]

Coetzee also commented on autobiographical writing in *Doubling the Point* that it is "a kind of storytelling in which you select material from a lived past and fashion it into a narrative."[15] The key term here is the word "select", and one of the interesting aspects of these photographs is that they show us what was not selected and written about, inviting speculation about what may have been omitted and forgotten, perhaps deliberately so. Some of the images depict events that did not find their way into the memoirs, and they can perhaps be regarded as "deleted scenes". One such scene is an enigmatic series of photographs of the two farm workers, Ros and Freek, on Strandfontein beach. In *Boyhood* the two men are described as being rooted to the farm in the remote, rural Karoo, and their presence on a beach in urban Cape Town is surprising. What circumstances would have brought them down to the Cape, where they would have seen the sea for the very first time? As the photographs show, Coetzee was clearly fascinated by the occasion, snapping a number of unobtrusive documentary shots of the two men, walking on the wind-

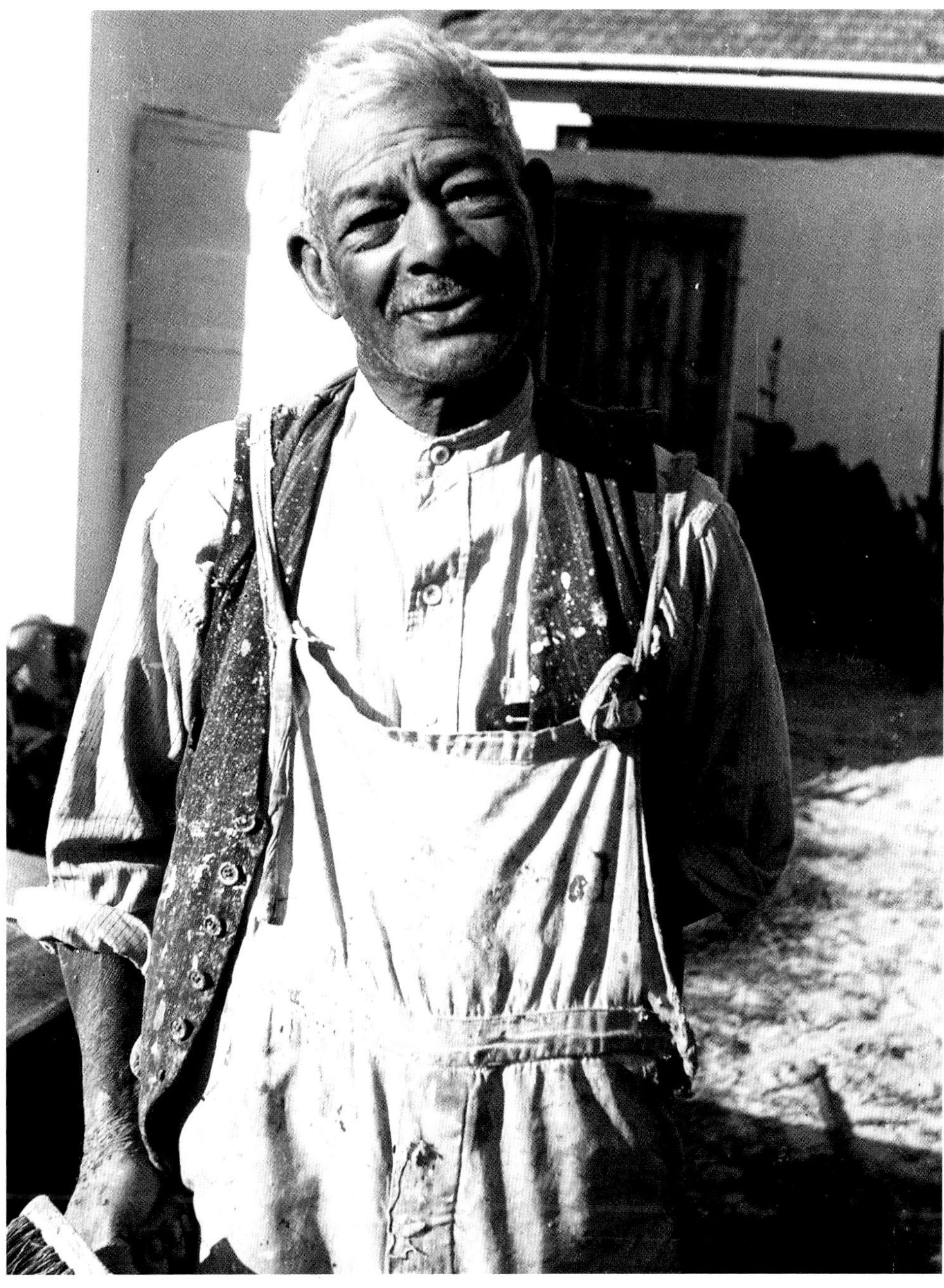

A painter who worked on the house next door. Most of Coetzee's photographs were shot in an unobtrusive, documentary manner; this image is remarkable for the open and trusting way that a stranger posed for his camera.

blown sand in their best Sunday suits. There is no reference in *Boyhood* to this event, and Coetzee's own recently composed caption leaves the matter open: "What they thought of it I will never know."

Indeed, in the farm chapters of the memoir, the young John is persistently curious about the men's inner thoughts and private lives. While he revels in the time he spends with Ros and Freek pursuing various farm activities such as hunting and sheep shearing, he is also conscious of the social distance between a white boy and coloured farm workers. He is discouraged from visiting their houses but desires to know more: "He burns with curiosity about the lives they live. Do they wear vests and underpants like white people? Do they each have a bed? Do they sleep naked or in their work clothes or do they have pyjamas? Do they eat proper meals, sitting at table with knives and forks?"[16] He was particularly drawn to the "gentle and soft-spoken" Freek, who cycled to far-off Fraserburg Road on Sundays, and in the evenings "sits outside his room and plays guitar to himself, smiling a rather remote smile." One of John's secrets is that he "would hero-worship Freek if it were permitted."[17]

As the young boy well knew, friendship and intimacy between black and white people was not permitted in South Africa's racialised social order, but with his unobtrusive, observant camera he would nevertheless try to probe and push against these boundaries. Several of the farm photographs reveal his curiosity to know more about the private lives of the farm labourers, trying to see what they were doing at night, when not at work in the role of servants. These nocturnal photographs, such as that of the vernacular "Tiekiedraai" dance (p. 95), offer glimpses of a

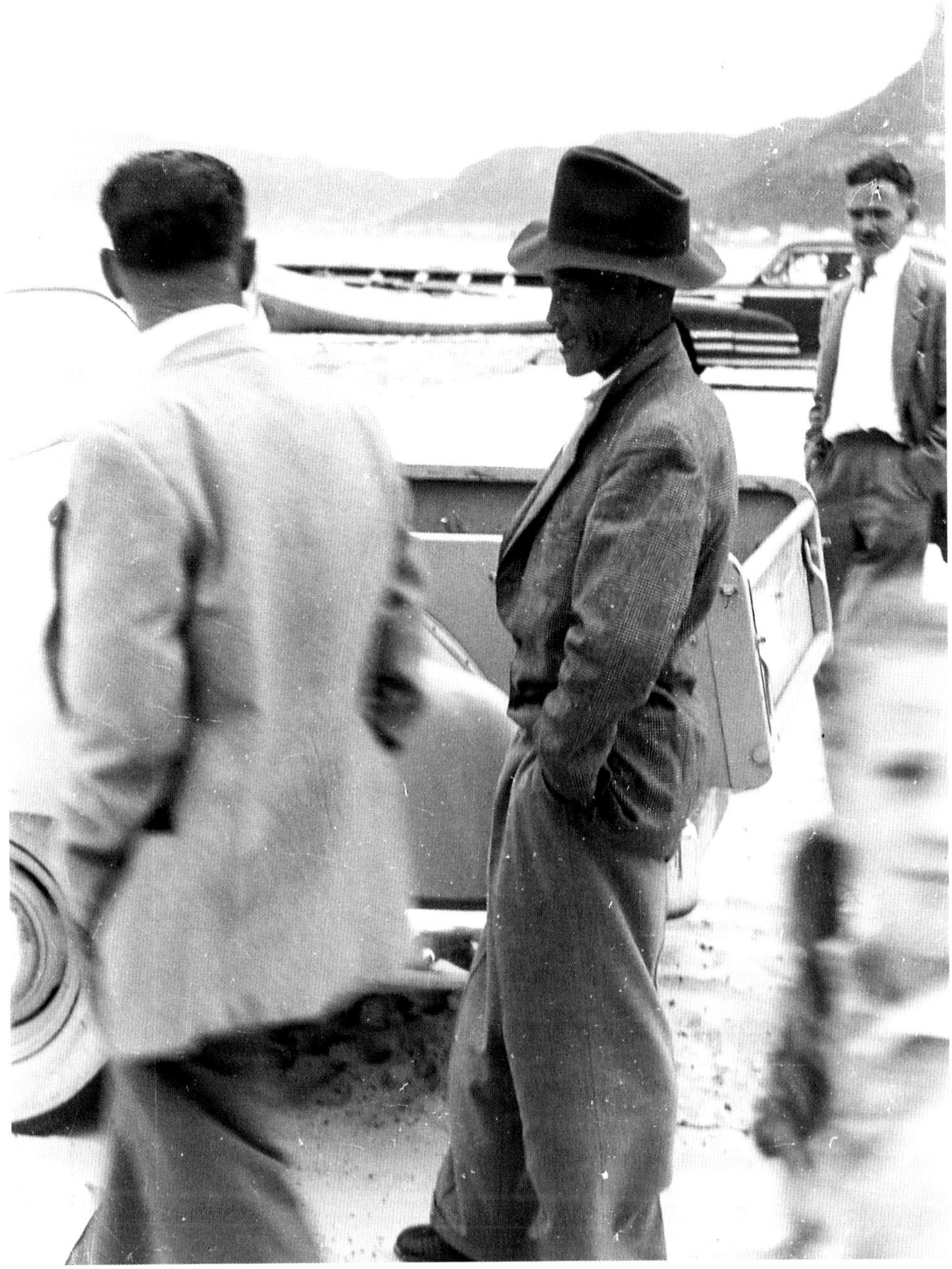

Son Coetzee (left), J.M. Coetzee's uncle, arriving at Strandfontein beach with Freek (centre). In the background is Jack Coetzee, his father. The car in the picture is likely to be Uncle Son's Studebaker, with its "dickey seat" at the back.

different world, where people momentarily attempted to live lives outside of the master and servant hierarchies that governed social relations in South Africa. In one of these photographs (see left), we see a group of men, woman and children sitting outside, facing an open area, perhaps a makeshift dance floor. Some empty plates are on the ground, signs of a shared meal. Freek's bicycle leans against a wall in the background. They are dressed in their best clothes, and one of the men wears a battered three-piece suit. The photograph suggests an intimate, easily shared conviviality among the farm workers, and while they are aware of the youngster with the camera in front of them, he is not part of their circle. As in other photographs shot in the dark, Coetzee struggled to get the flash to synchronise with the shutter and half of the image remained unlit, a perhaps apt sign for the way that his knowledge of other lives remained incomplete.

Using his camera to peer outside of the privileged white world he was brought up in was not limited to the farm. Also in Cape Town, Coetzee took pictures of black subjects in his neighbourhood. One such image offers a telling insight into the emerging apartheid order in South Africa in the 1950s. It was taken on Paradise Road, Newlands, close to Avenue Road, where his family had moved to from Plumstead. The photograph (p.43) depicts a squad car patrolling the street, and in the background we see two black people on the pavement. They are in a public space and not at work, though the woman wears an apron and headscarf, the standard uniform of a domestic worker. Coming under the watchful eye of the white police officer, the stance and body language of the woman and man is wary and defensive. The photograph would have been taken

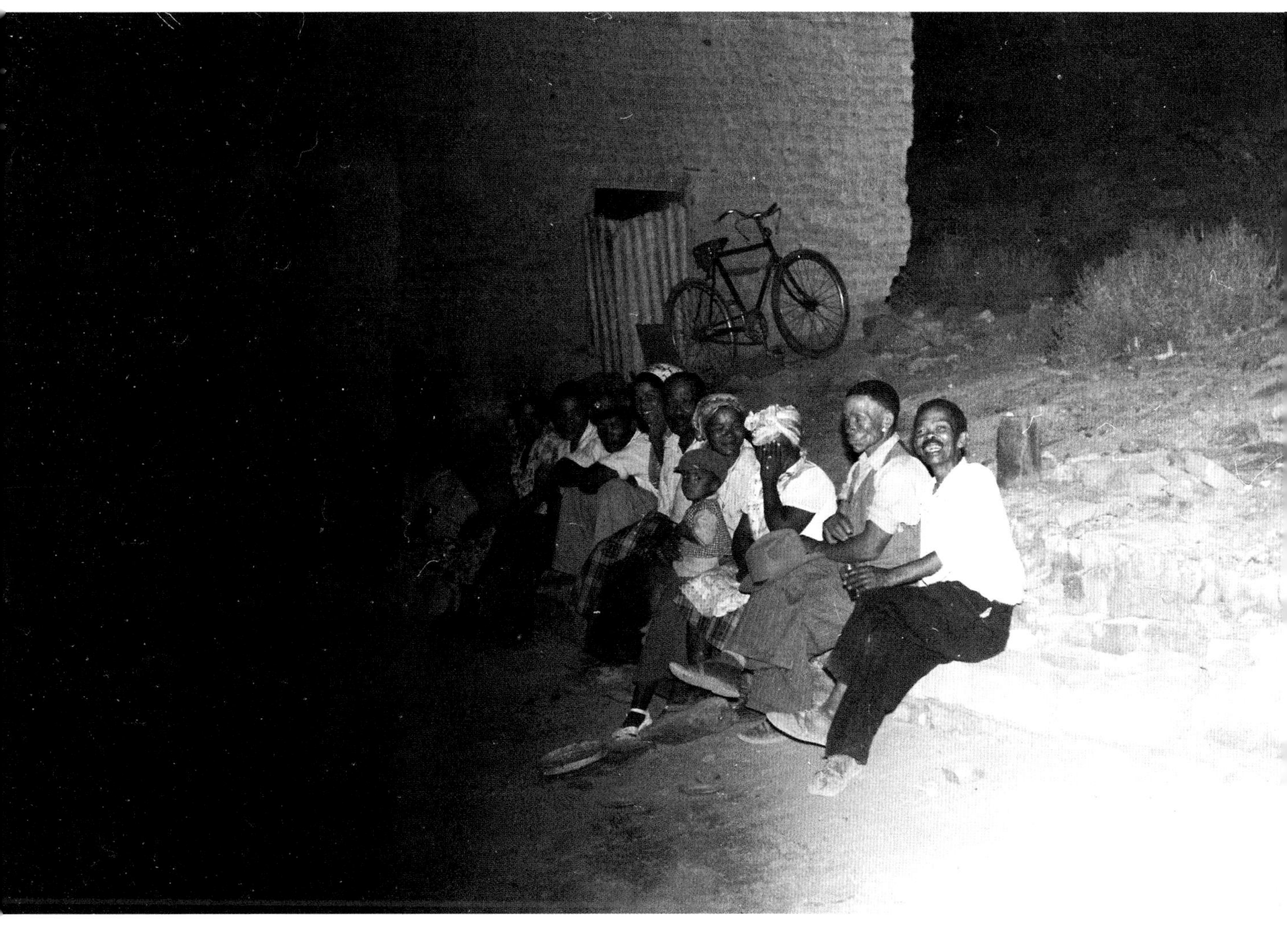

a few years after the notorious Group Areas Act of 1950 had established
a legal framework for racially segregated cities, where white residential
suburbs were out of bounds for blacks, except on a temporary basis
when coming in to work. Police were charged to patrol these strict
apartheid boundaries, and black South Africans were regularly arrested
for trespassing into white areas if they did not have the required papers.
The photograph conveys the daily drama of racial segregation and
surveillance that occurred in South Africa at the time.

Seen in the context of this hardening apartheid order, the photographs
of Ros and Freek on the beach appear even more remarkable. The
Separate Amenities Act, which came into operation after 1953,
introduced racially based separation of all public buildings and
recreational spaces, and Strandfontein would in time be proclaimed as
a "coloured beach". Shooting his photographs in the liminal zone of
the shore, as yet unmarked by the racial segregation that had begun to
divide public space in South Africa, Coetzee's camera recorded a rapidly
vanishing time when it was still possible for white and black people to go
to the seaside together.

*

Although photographs feature in many of Coetzee's fictions and essays,
there appears to be only one direct reference to these particular images.
In *Summertime*, John's semi-fictionalised girlfriend secretly rummages
through his possessions:

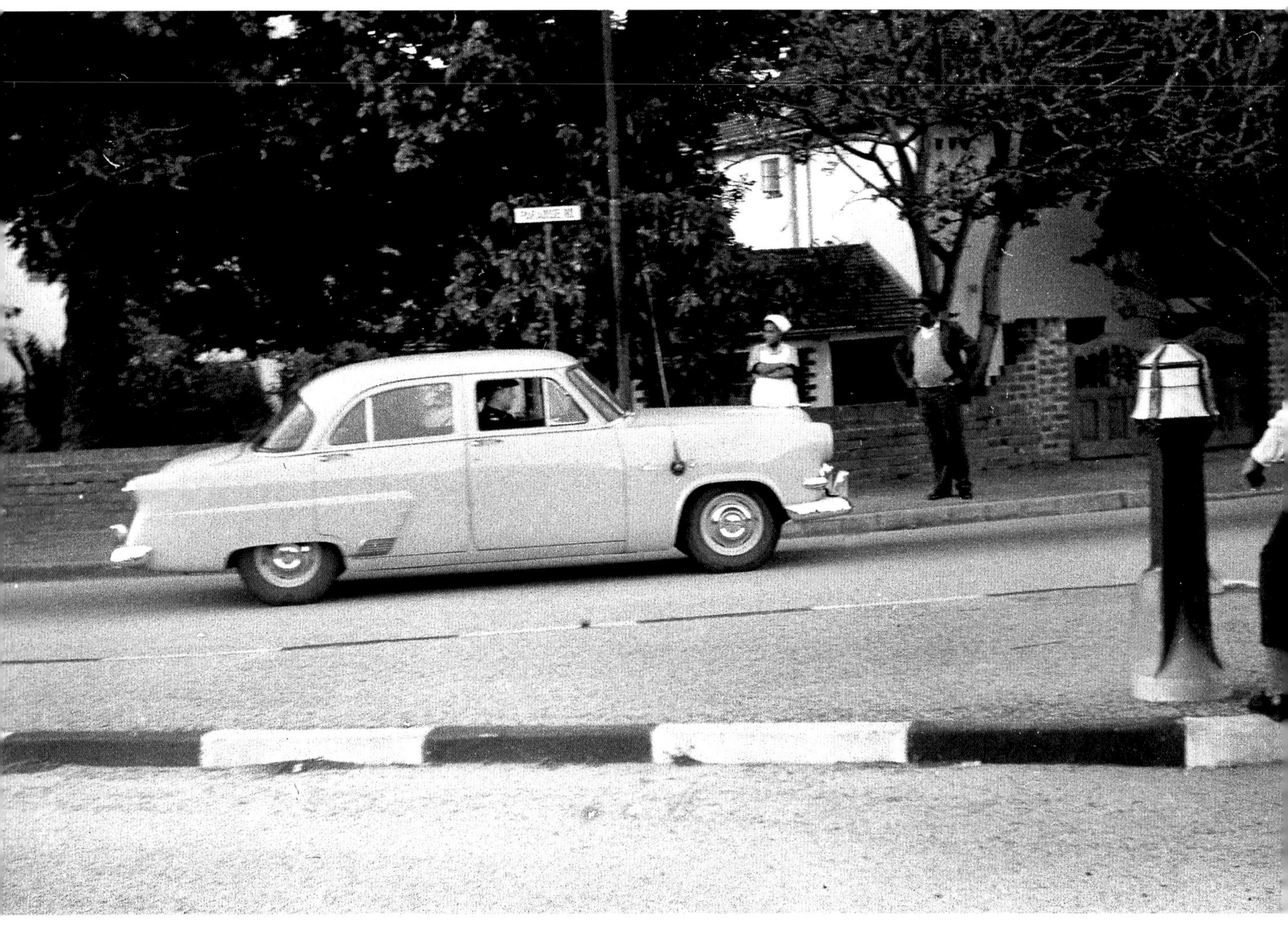

John's room, where I had slept, was larger and better lit. A bookshelf: dictionaries, phrasebooks, teach yourself this, teach yourself that. Beckett. Kafka. On the table, a mess of papers. A filing cabinet. Idly I searched through the drawers. In the bottom drawer, a box of photographs, which I burrowed amongst. What was I looking for? I didn't know. For something I would recognize only when I found it. But it was not there. Most of the photographs were from his school years: sports teams, class portraits.[18]

44

The box of photographs does not yield its secrets, but the encounter nevertheless reveals a fascination with images and a sense of their latent power to tell a truth. In a revealing biographical note on the dust jacket of the debut novel *Dusklands* (1974), Coetzee lists among his interests "images, particularly photographs, and their power over the human heart." The idea that photographs have an emotive force is discernible in many of the fictions, from *Dusklands* right up to the recent novel, *The Schooldays of Jesus* (2016). The narrative of *Dusklands*'s "Vietnam Project" is structured around a set of disturbing war photographs, and the protagonist acknowledges the affective force of images when he says, "I respond to pictures as I do not to print."[19] In *Schooldays of Jesus*, Dmitri's collection of secret photographs reflects his erotic obsessions, and after the murder, he turns himself in to the police after seeing a photograph of Ana Magdalena on the front page of a newspaper. Photographs are present in seminal moments in most of Coetzee's fictions, and in *Slow Man*, a professional photographer would be the novel's protagonist. Images play a central role in Coetzee's writing, not

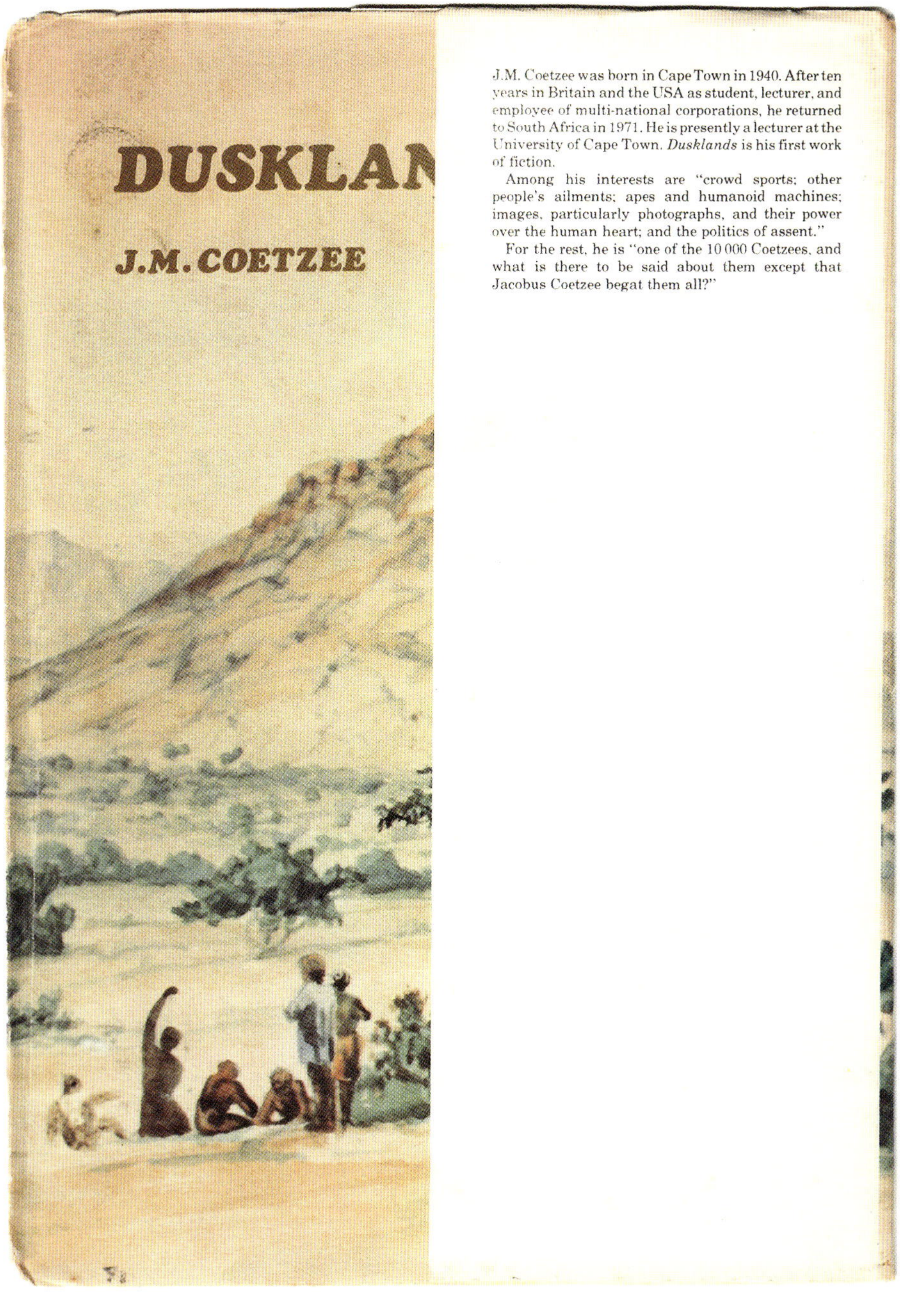

DUSKLAN

J.M. COETZEE

45

The biographical note on original jacket cover of *Dusklands* (folded out).
Coetzee had not authorised this eccentric authorial self-stylisation;
his publisher had lifted the text from correspondence with the author.

only as explicit motifs and source materials, but they also pervade the narrative style which is influenced by the camera's framing, scene-setting and point of view. Lighting, the most vital element in every photograph, is frequently present in the way Coetzee sets up and describes a scene.[20]

It is not surprising then to find a responsiveness to photography emerge early in life. If we can trust the semi-fictionalised memoir *Boyhood*, the young John is repeatedly fascinated by photographs and pictures. We read early on that he "loves to page through his mother's albums. No matter how indistinct the images, he can always pick her out from the group: the one in whose shy, defensive look he recognizes himself."[21] Referring to one of the books he owns, a children's encyclopaedia, he dislikes the prose, but "pores over the pictures."[22] And of his other book, *Scott of the Antarctic*, he writes: "He often looks at the photographs, but he does not get far with reading the book: it is boring, it is not a story."[23] Early in life, images appear to have taken precedence over words: they have the power to tell stories and stimulate the imagination. The stories he imagines wanting to write as a schoolboy in *Boyhood* have a highly visual, cinematic quality: his writing would be "something darker, something that, once it began to flow from his pen, would spread across the page like spilt ink. Like spilt ink, like shadows racing across the face of still water, like lightning crackling across the sky."[24] The word "photography" literally means "writing with light", and the photographs Coetzee would take as a teenager, first with the spy camera and then with the Wega, can be read as early attempts to tell his own story with the light that he captured through the lens of his camera.

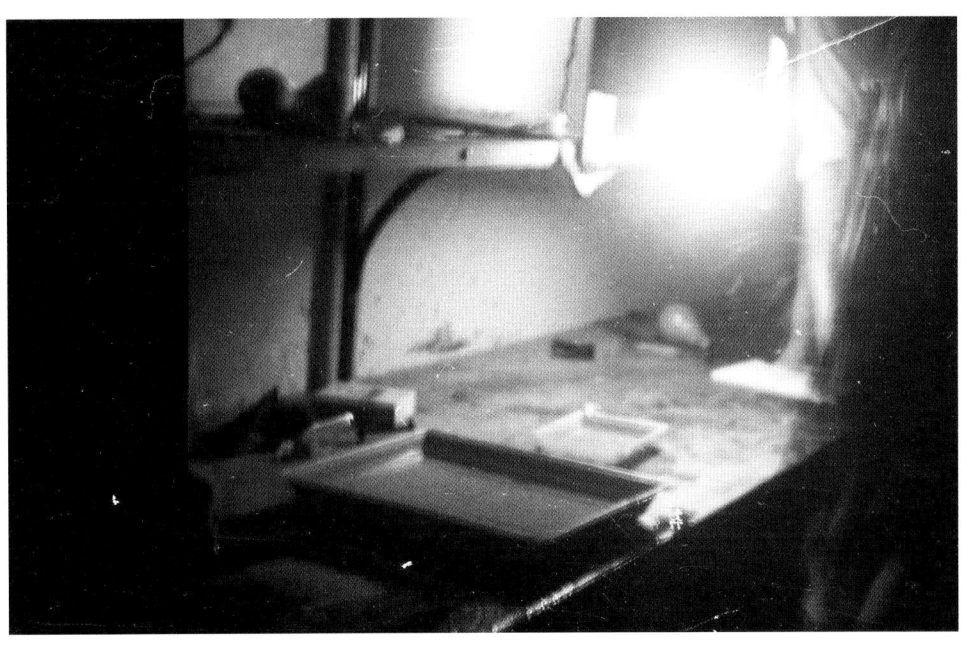

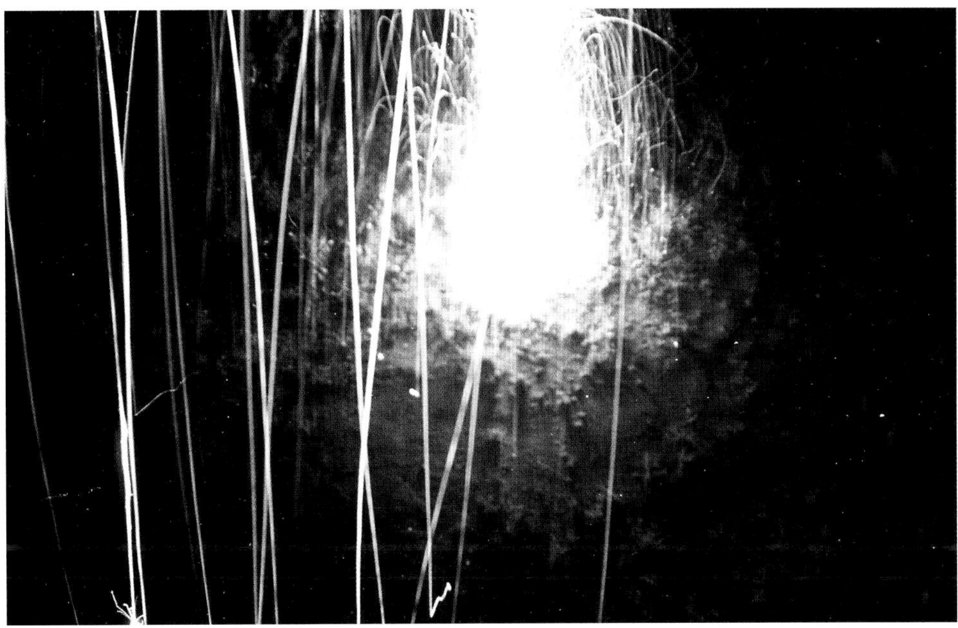

Top: Coetzee's darkroom, in the house in Milford Street, Plumstead, circa 1955.

Bottom: Capturing fireworks.

Coetzee continued practicing photography in his 20s, including the period he was working and studying in London. One of his friends at the time recalled that he "was interested in p'graphs then" and remembered Coetzee's playfulness, for example seeing "him jumping out from behind trees on walks in Virginia Water, sometimes taking photographs."[25] But as we can see in the photograph albums now kept at the Ransom Center, the early inventiveness and experimentalism of the boyhood photographs gave way to more conventional pictures of children growing up, birthdays, family events and holiday snapshots. Coetzee's early creativity with the camera in a sense became transferred into his fictions. "But I was never – how shall I put it? – an artist of the camera. I was always more of a technician,"[26] the photographer-protagonist of *Slow Man* acknowledges, perhaps reflecting some of Coetzee's own critical self-assessment that he "didn't have the eye of an artist-photographer."[27] Unlike the novel's Paul Rayment, Coetzee did not become a professional photographer, but instcad directed his creative energies towards writing, and by the time *Dusklands* appeared in 1974, he had become single-mindedly focused on establishing himself as an author. The early absorption and interest in photography is however discernible in this book and in most subsequent novels. "The marks of photography," Coetzee remarks in an interview, "are all over my work, from the beginning."[28]

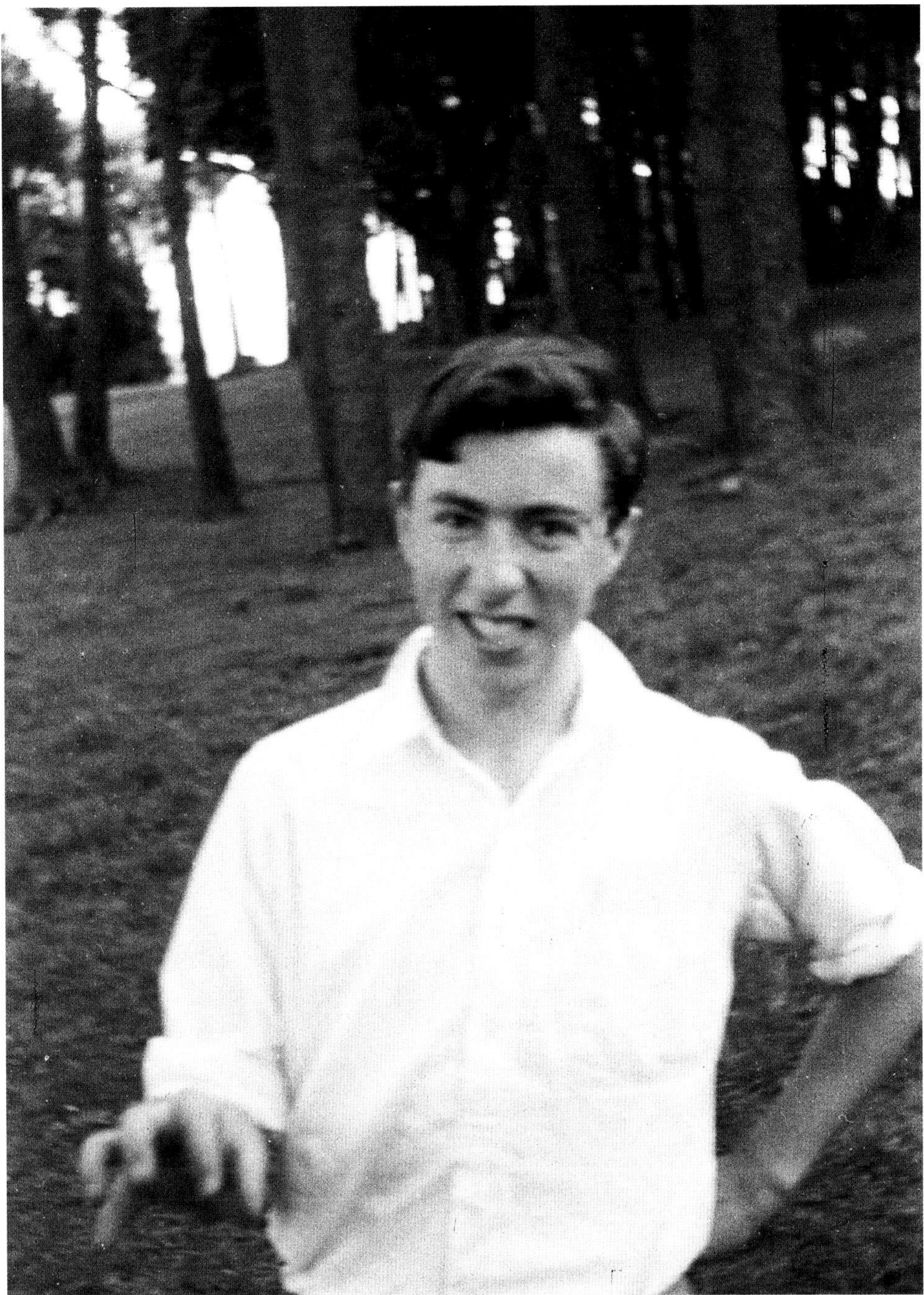

Portrait, taken in the Rhodes Memorial area, probably on the occasion when the photograph of the equestrian statue was taken.

3

Photographs from Boyhood

Photographs and text by J.M. Coetzee,

unless otherwise indicated.

Family and Home

52   My mother, Vera Coetzee, in front of the house in Milford Road, Plumstead.

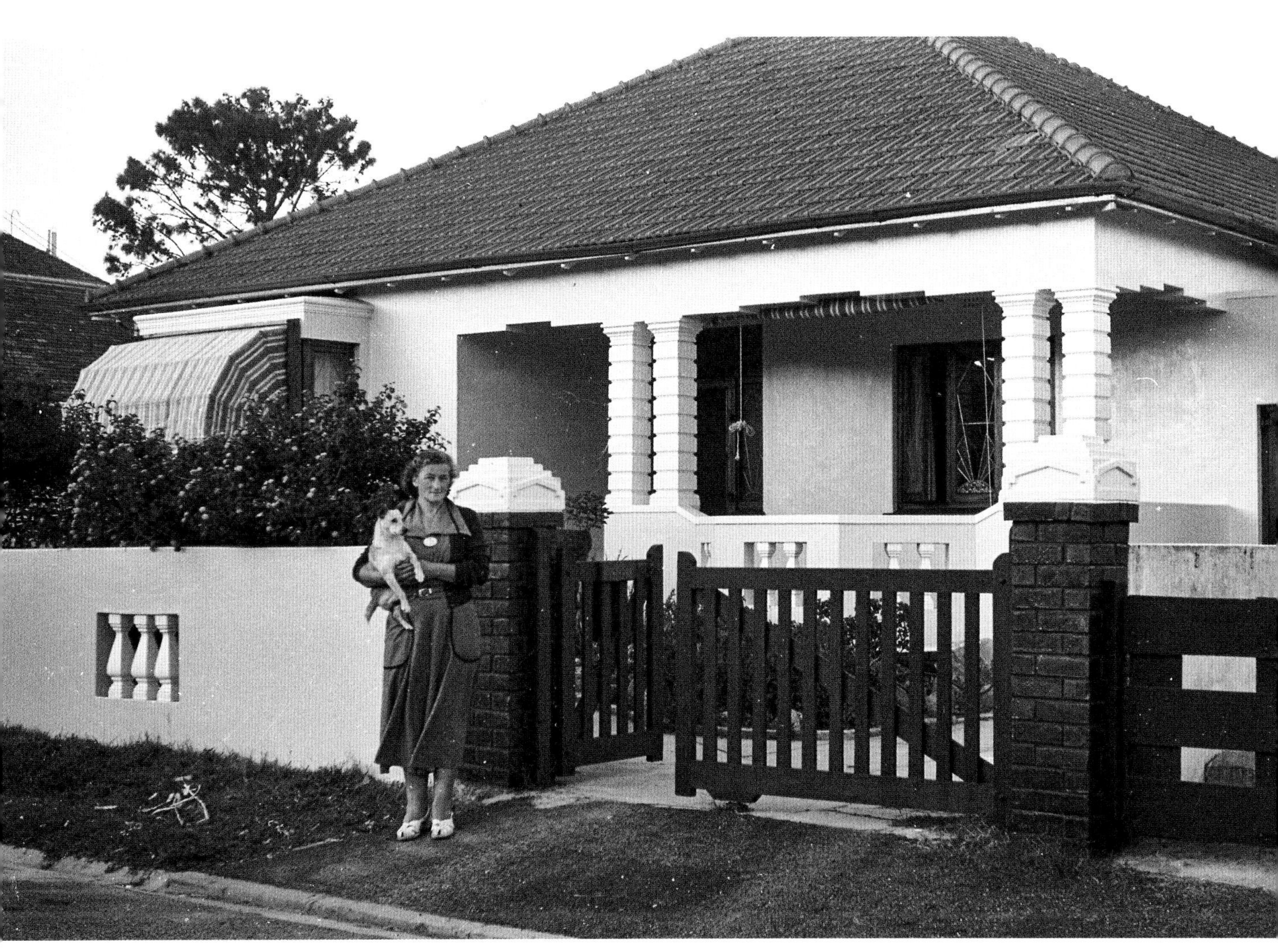

54 Vera outside Winnie & Charles Sale's Shop, Andringa Street, Stellenbosch.
At Sale's you could buy canned goods, sugar, cigarettes, fly-swatters, paraffin
by the bottle (bring your own bottle) pumped from a ten-gallon can. In the dim
storeroom at the back, sacks of flour and dried beans.

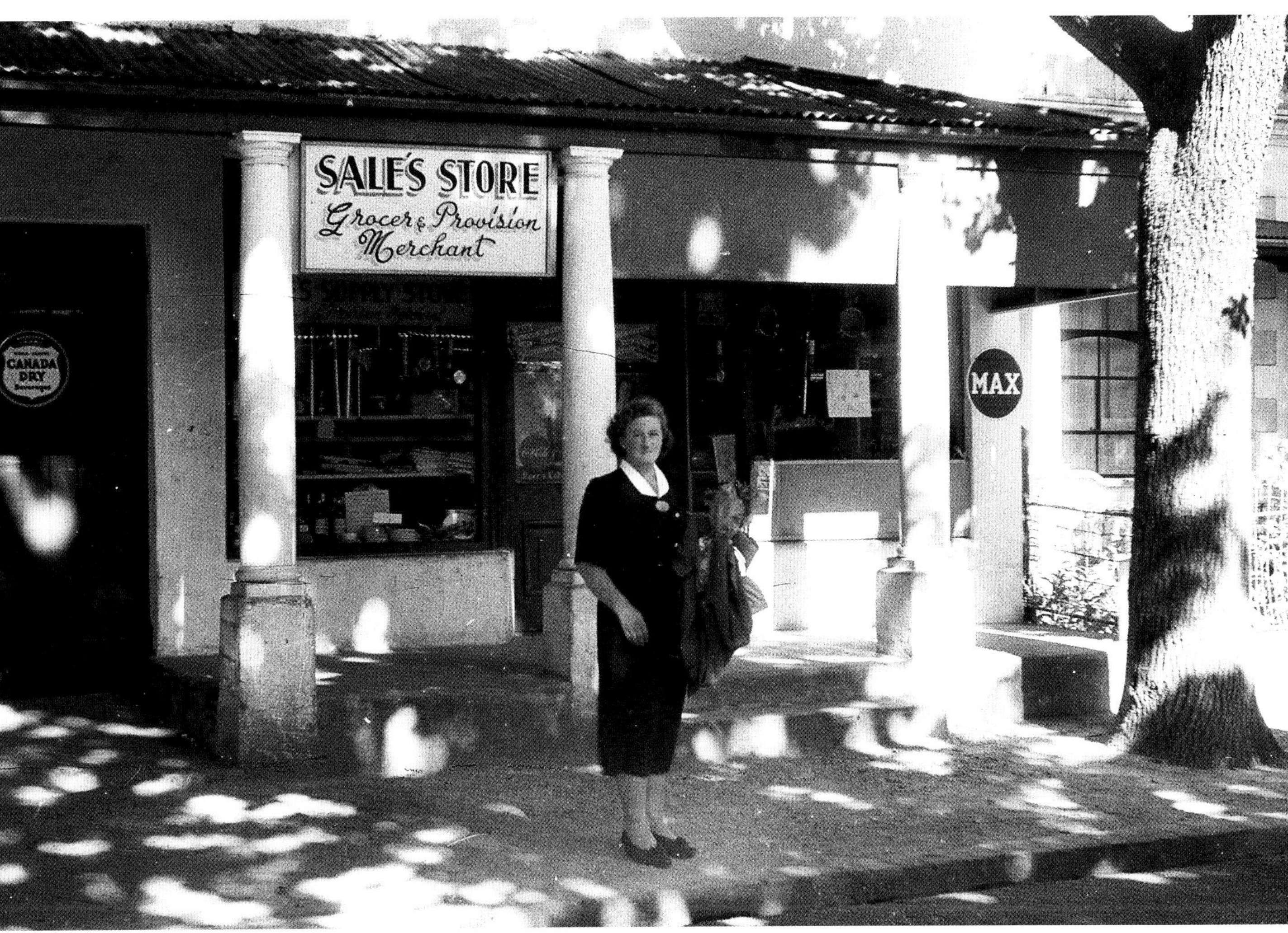
SALE'S STORE
Grocer & Provision
Merchant
CANADA DRY
Beverages
MAX

56   "His mother's name is Vera: Vera, with its icy capital V, an arrow plunging

downwards." (*Boyhood*, p.27)

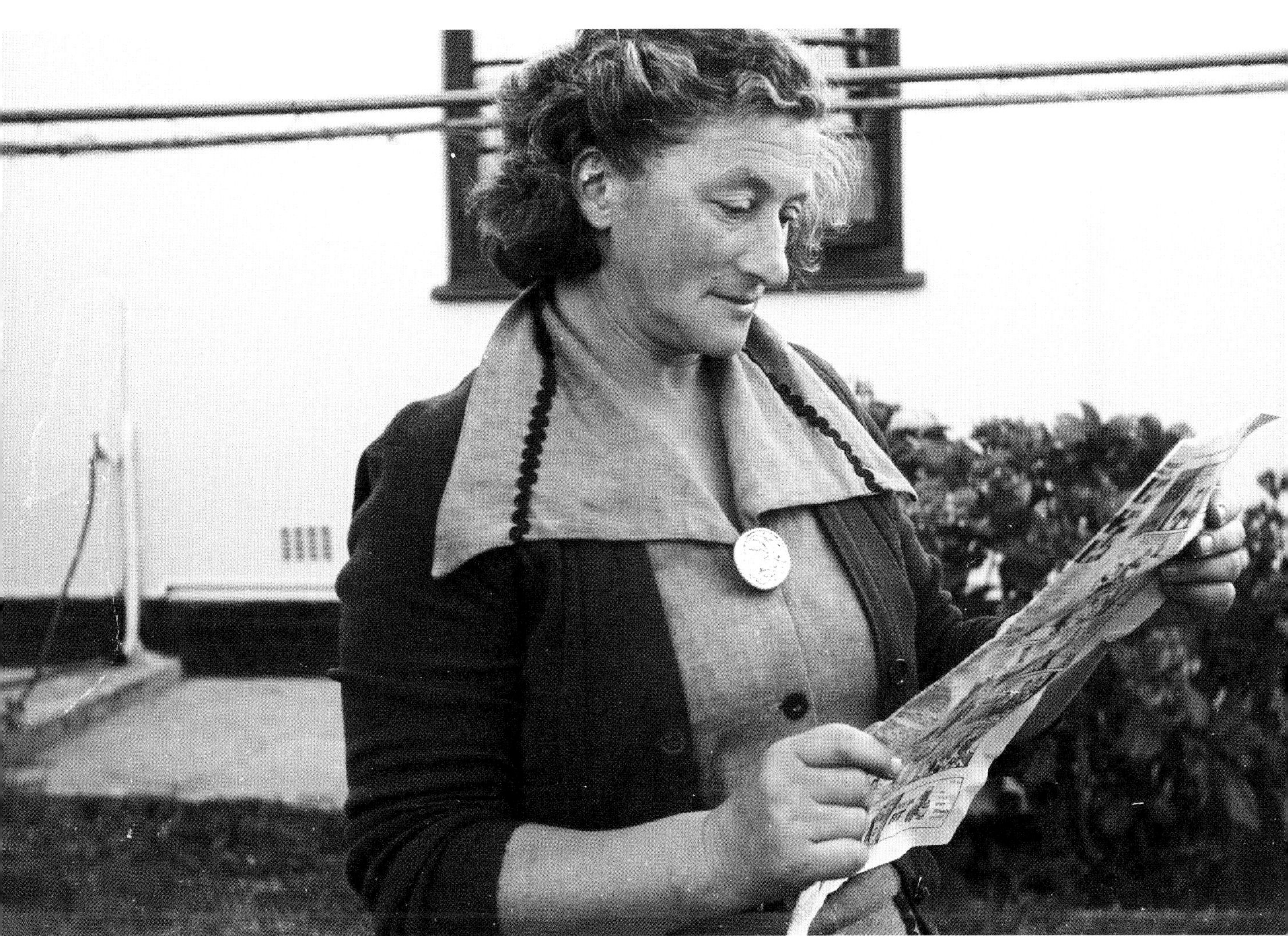

"He is always trying to make sense of his mother." (*Boyhood*, p. 37)

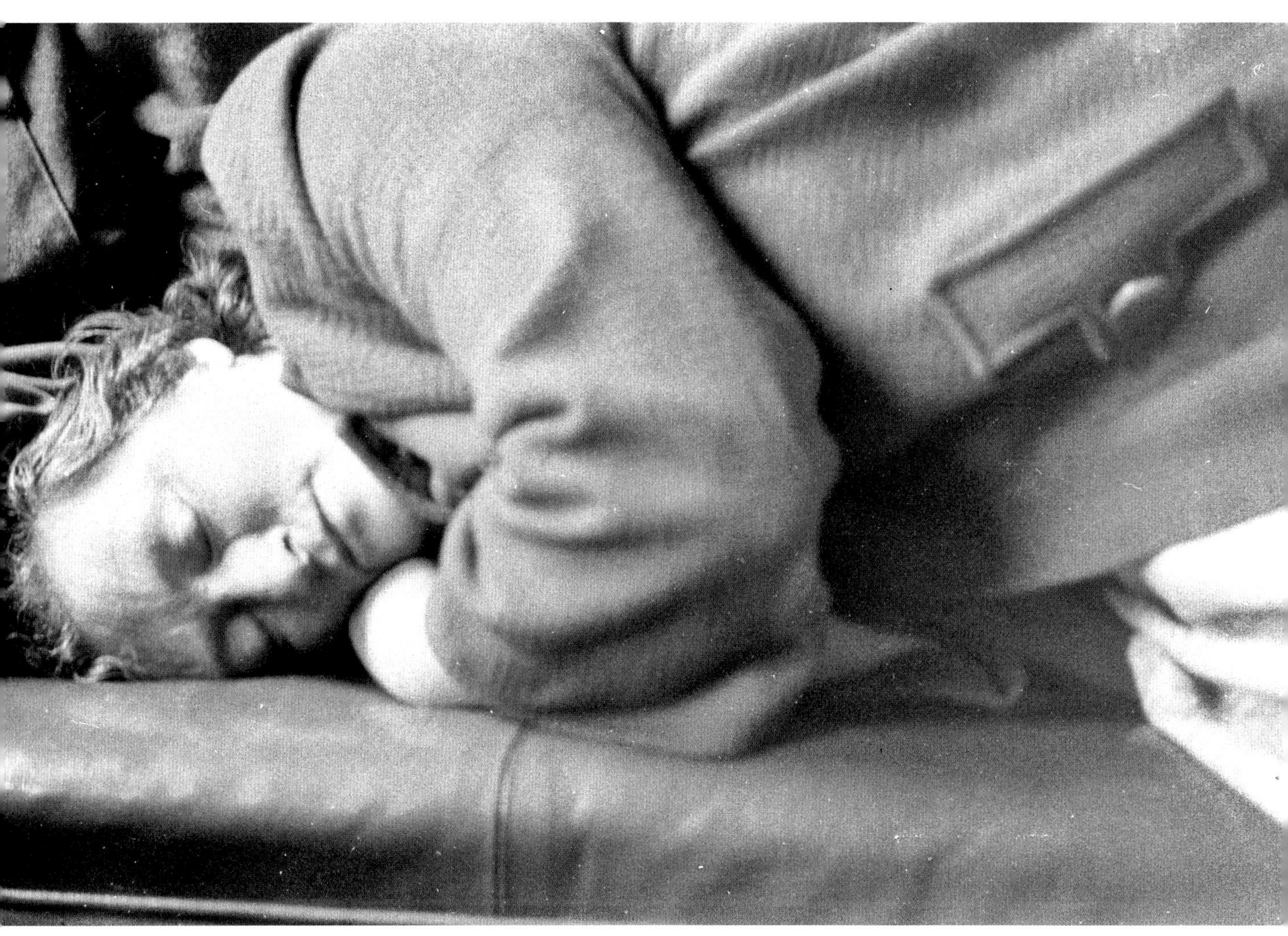

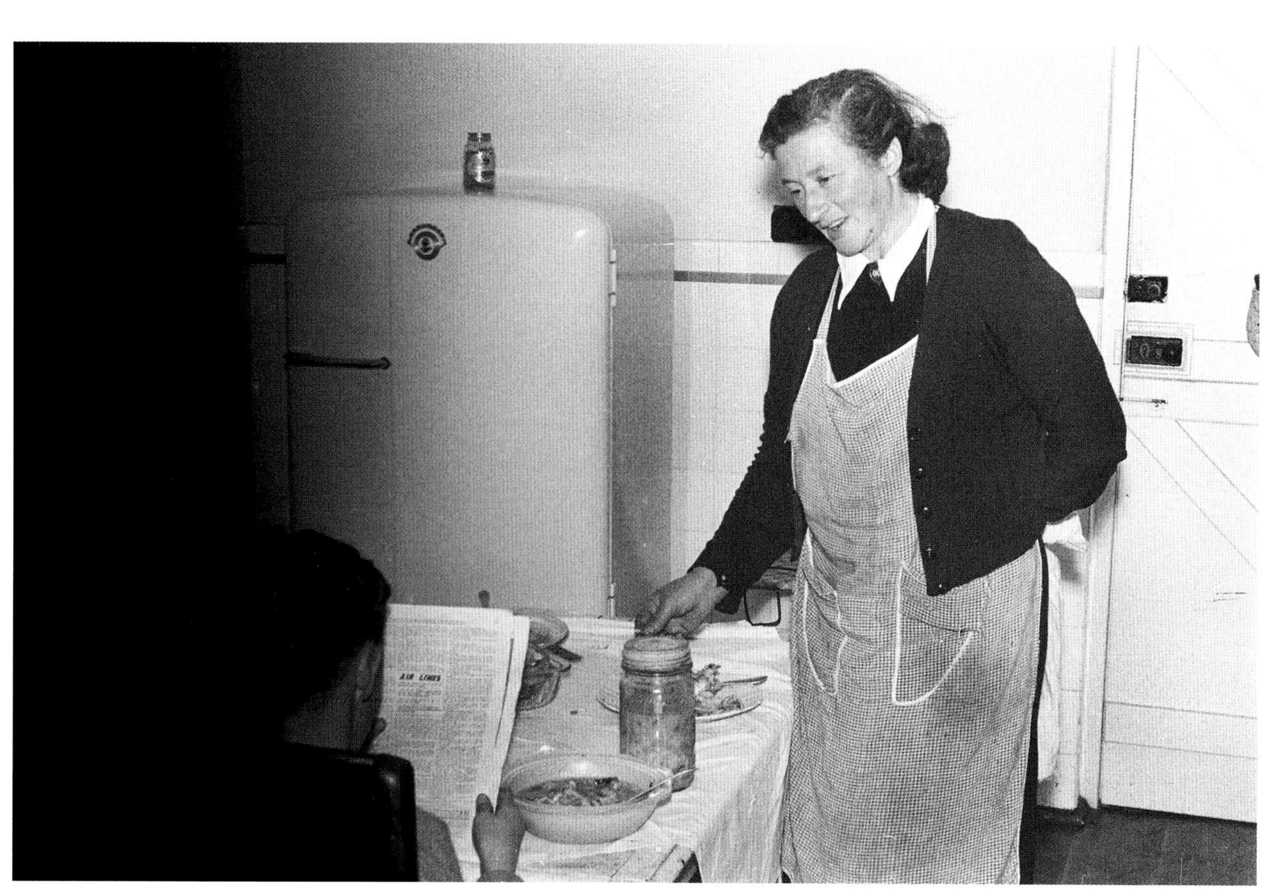

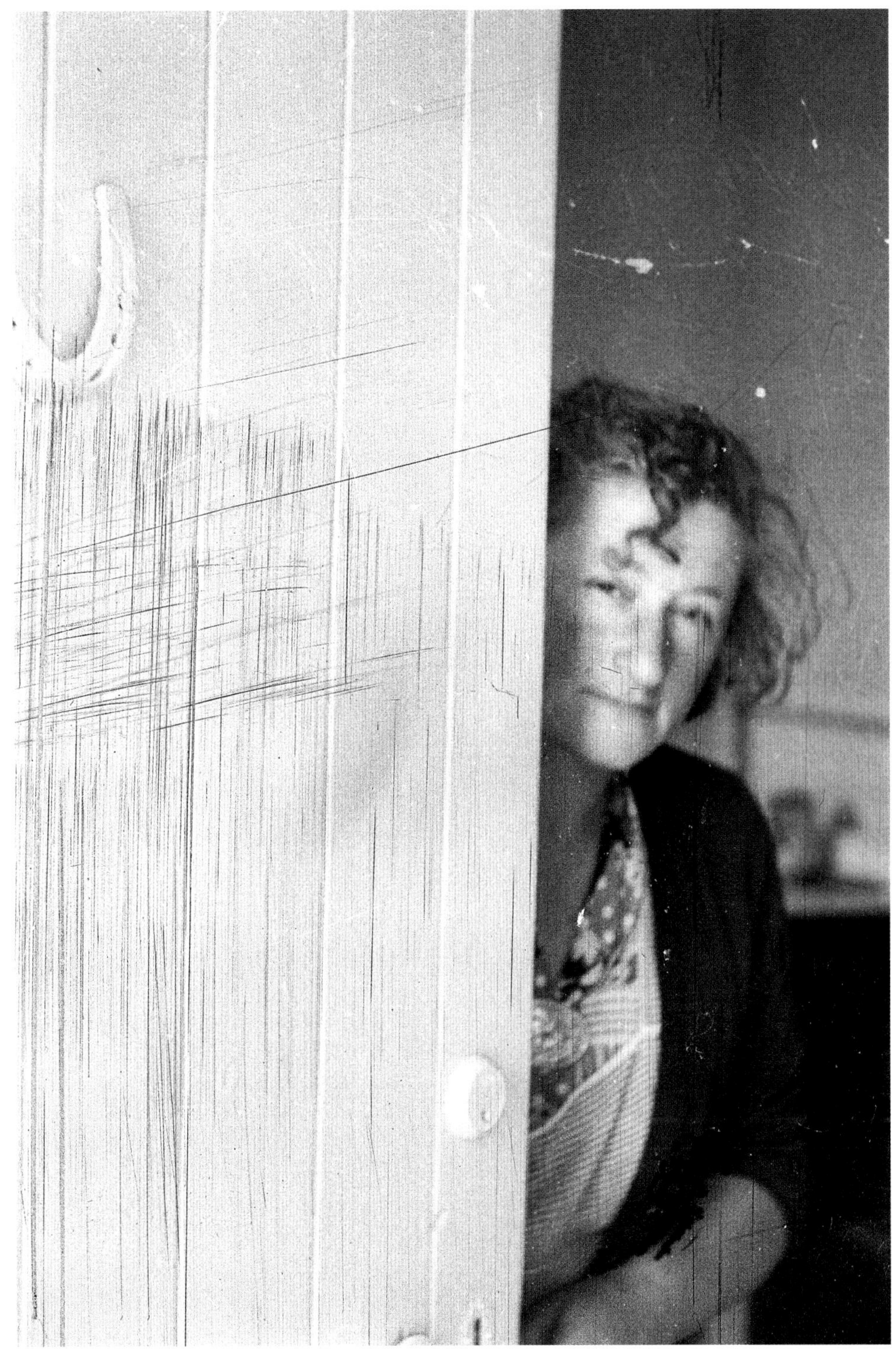

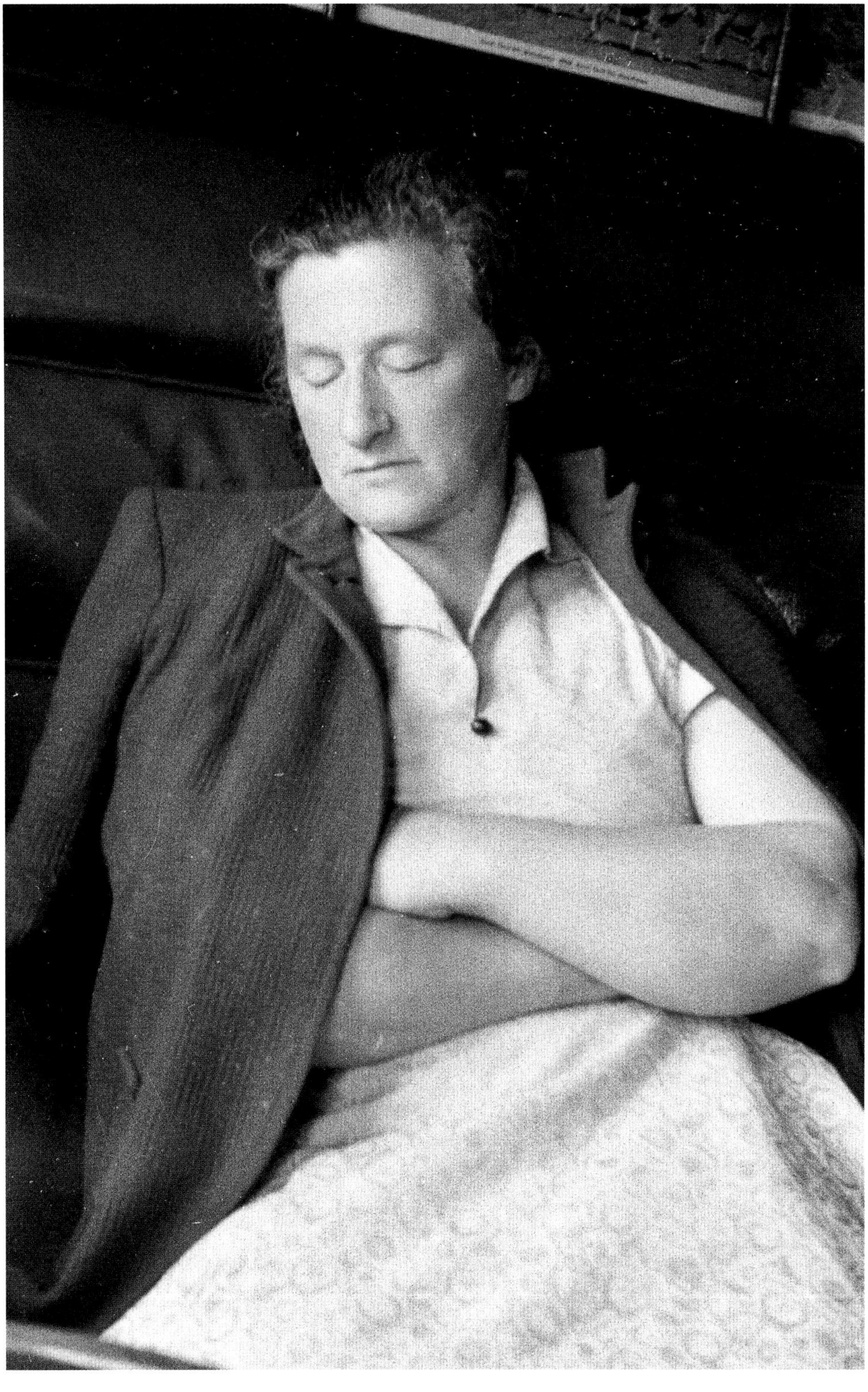

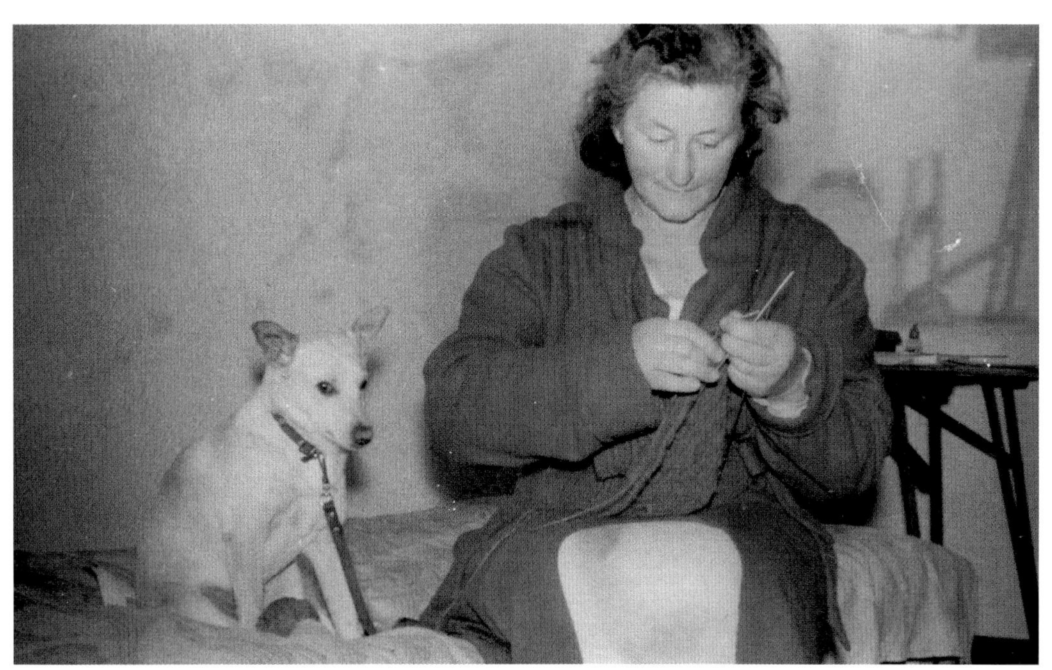

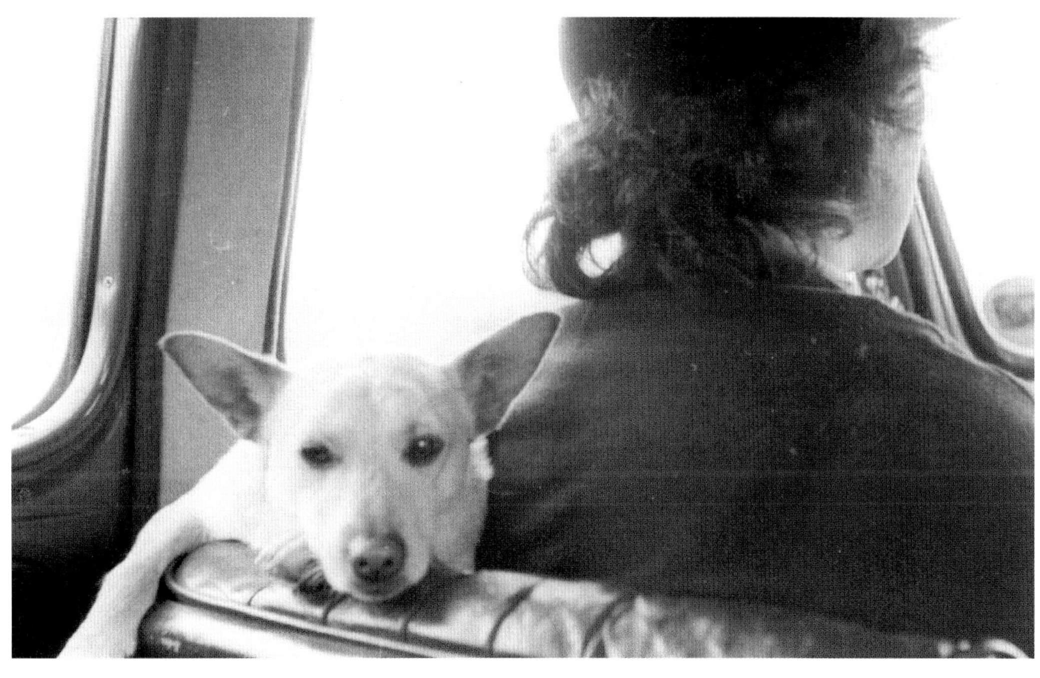

64   David and Vera Coetzee.

"He keeps driving her into corners, demanding that she admit whom she loves most, him or his brother. Always she slips the trap. 'I love you both the same,' she maintains, smiling." (*Boyhood*, p.13)

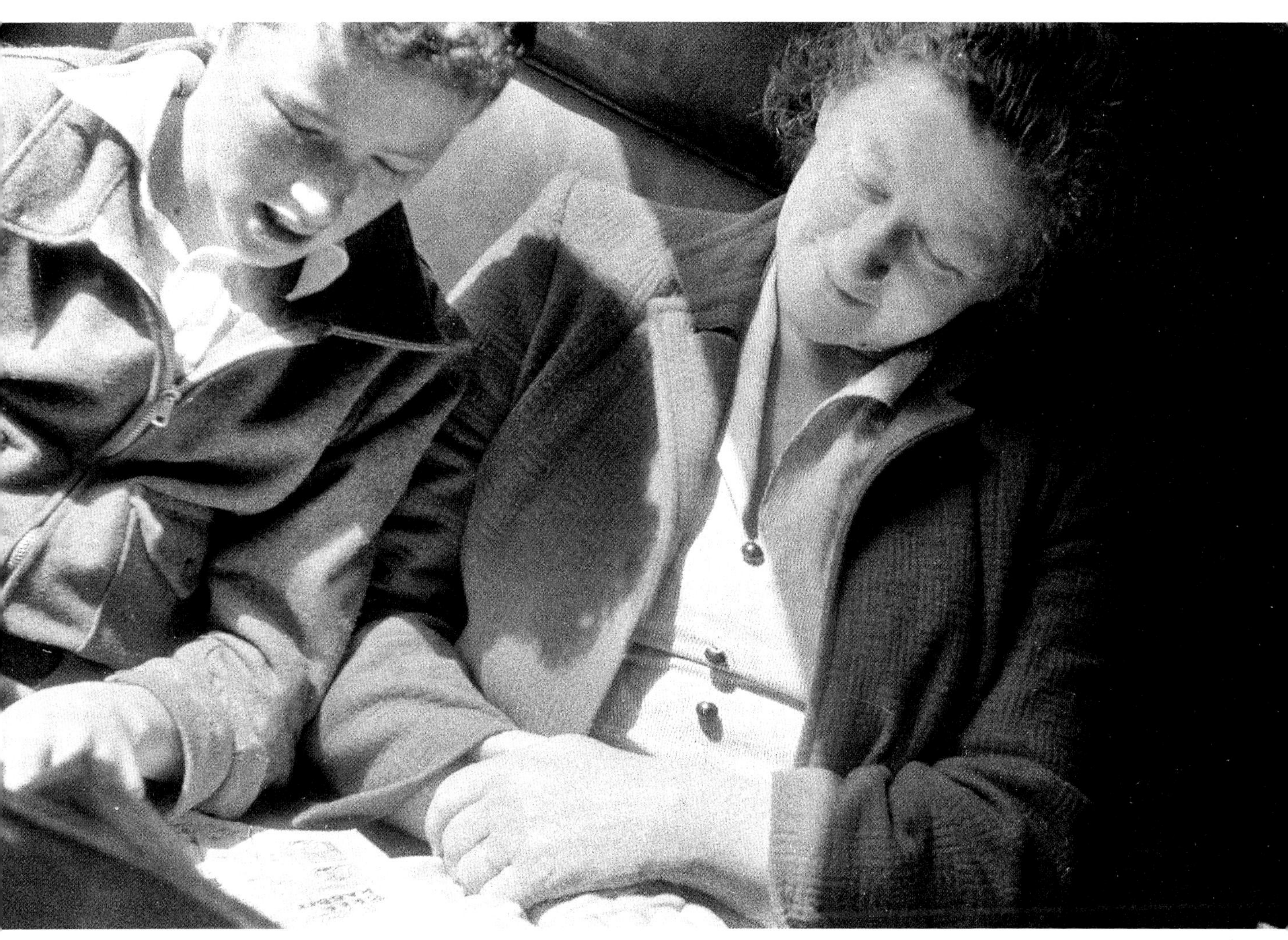

66   My father Jack (Zac) Coetzee with Aunt Annie. *Undependable, errant, wayward*:
words that my mother's side of the family attached to my father.

"He has never worked out the position of his father in the household. In fact, it
is not obvious to him by what right his father is there at all." (*Boyhood*, p.12)

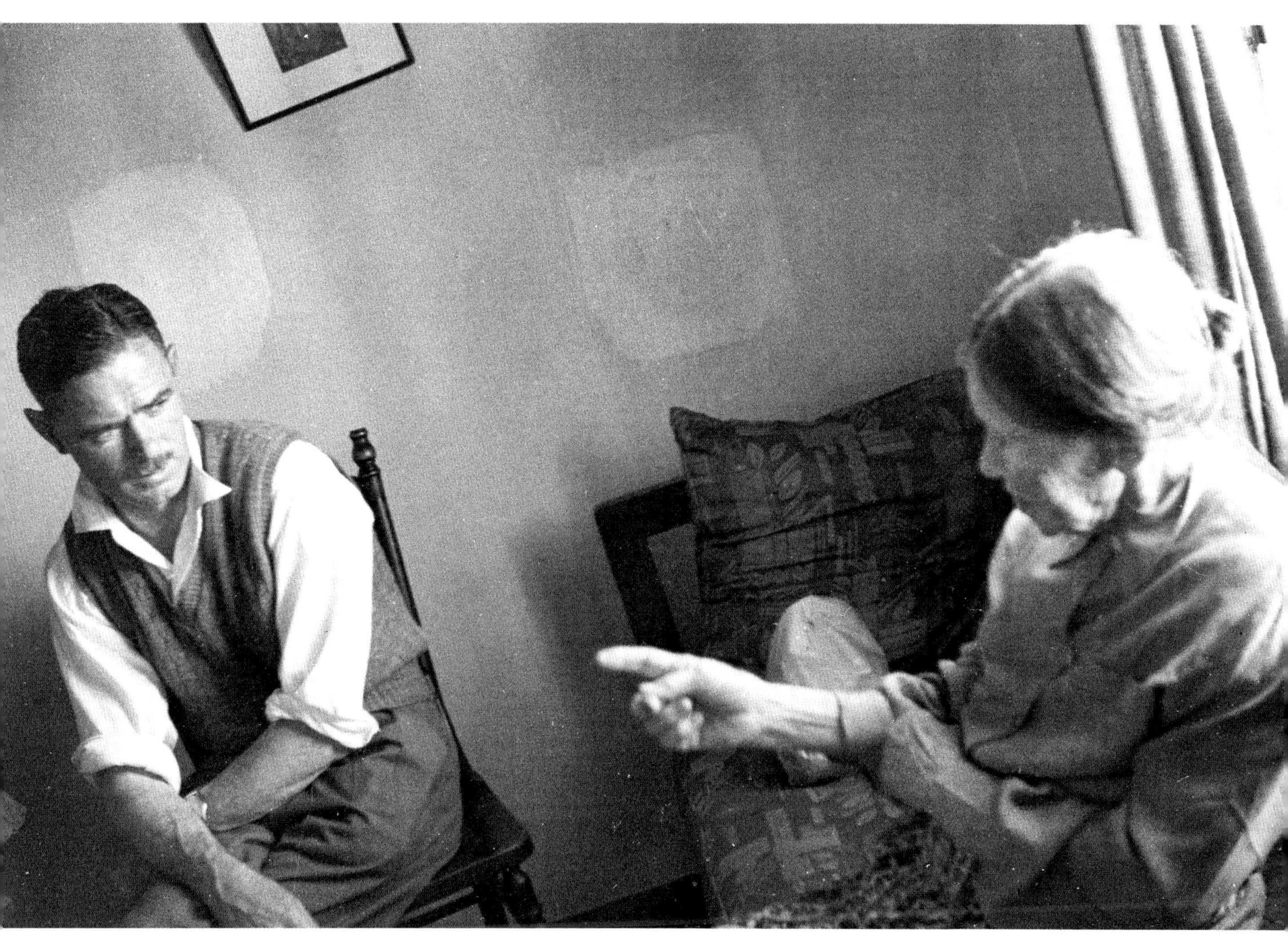

68   Christmas in Milford Road, Plumstead. Around the table are my uncle Norman Wehmeyer, my uncle Lance Wehmeyer, my mother with her dog Tuppy, my father, my grandmother Lenie (my father's mother), and my brother David. Norman seems to be in the dark because I could not get the flash to synchronize with the shutter.

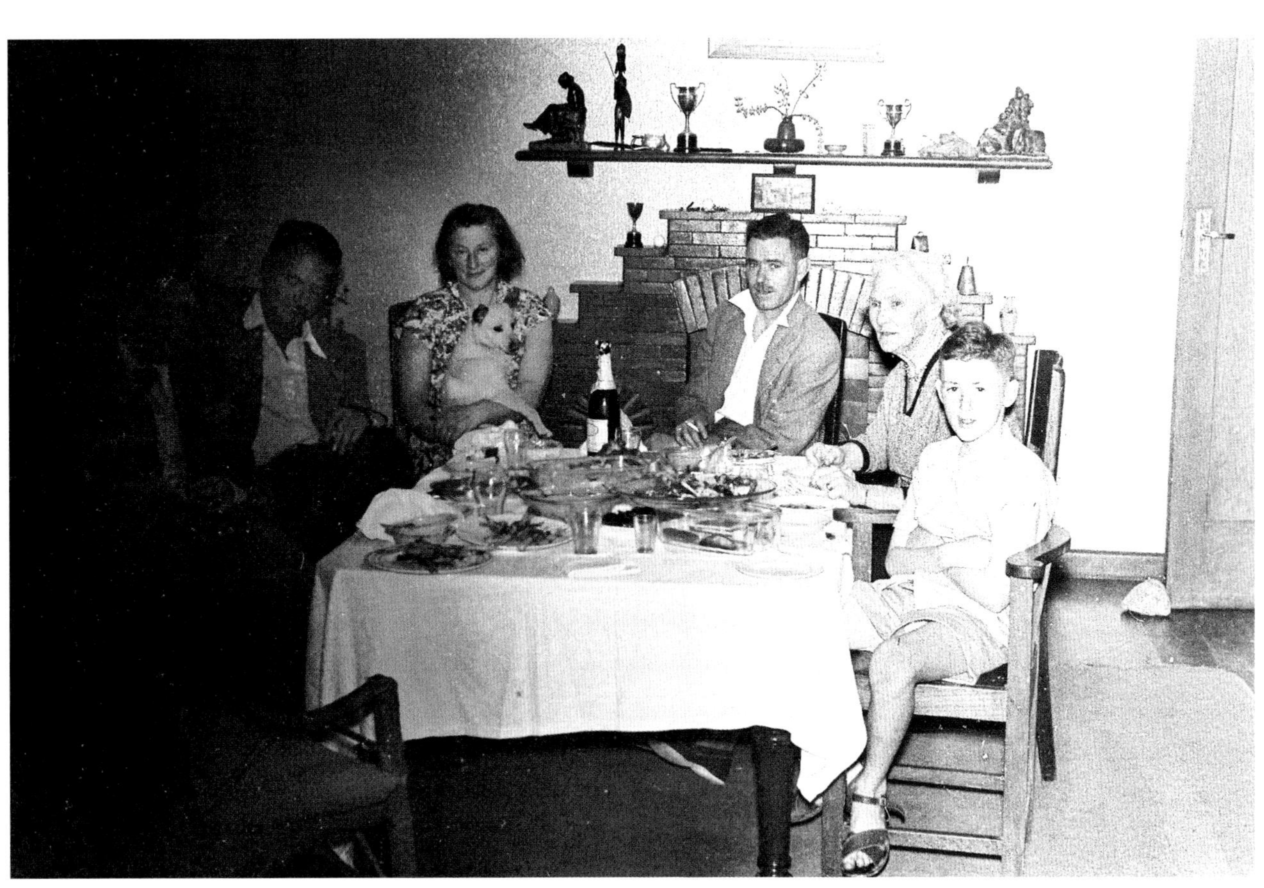

Who is this person? First steps toward surprising and uncovering his soul.

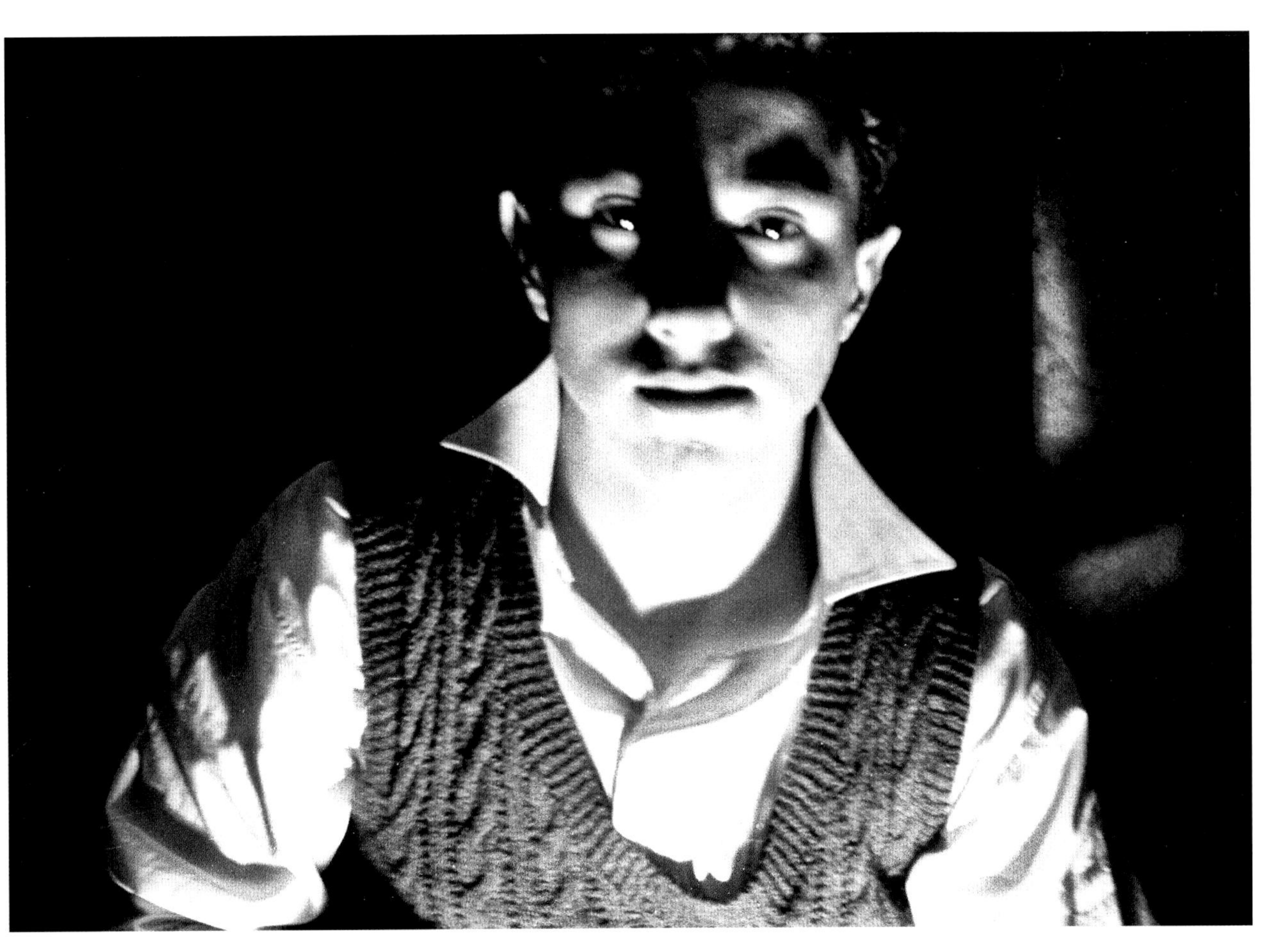

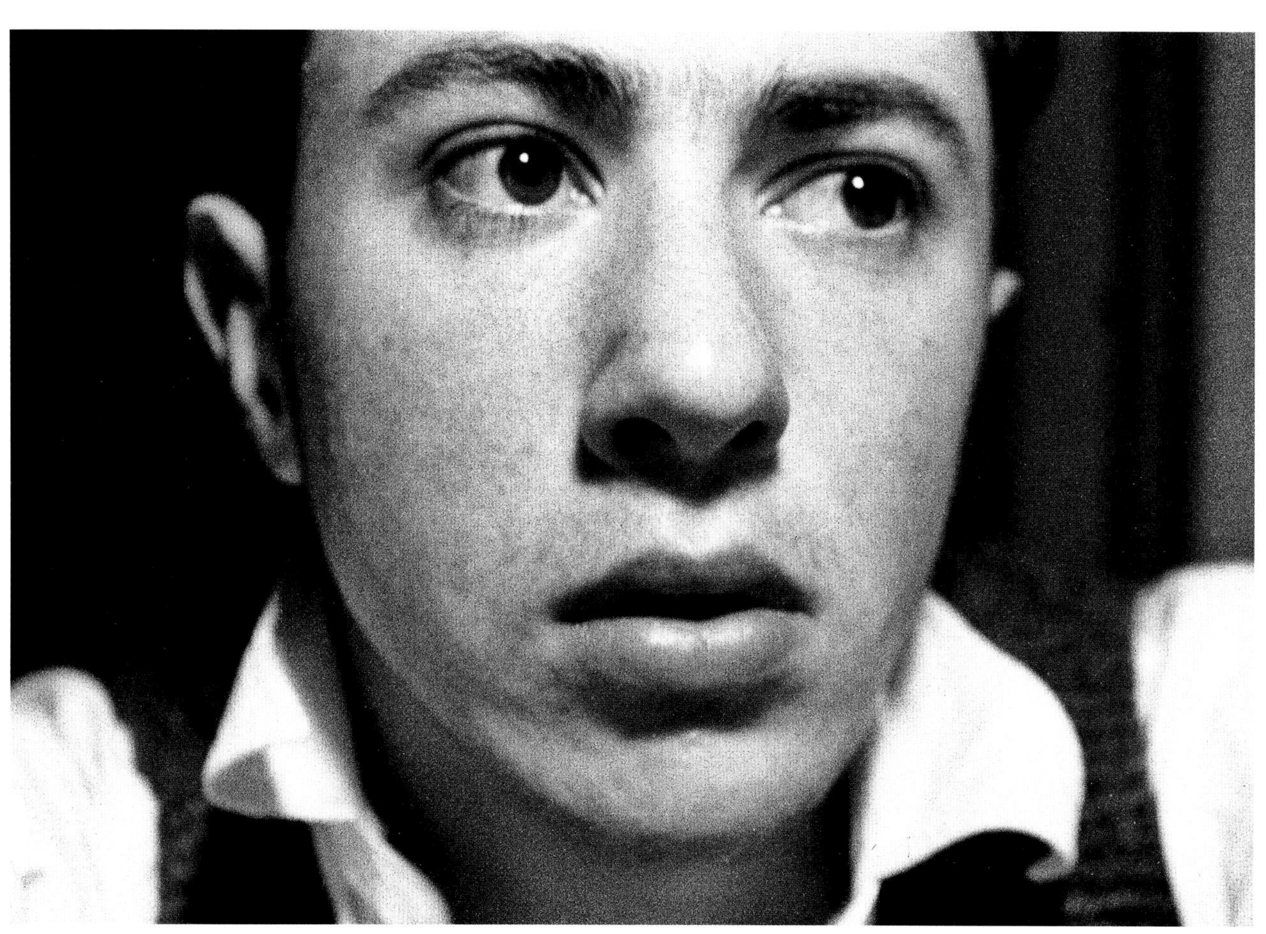

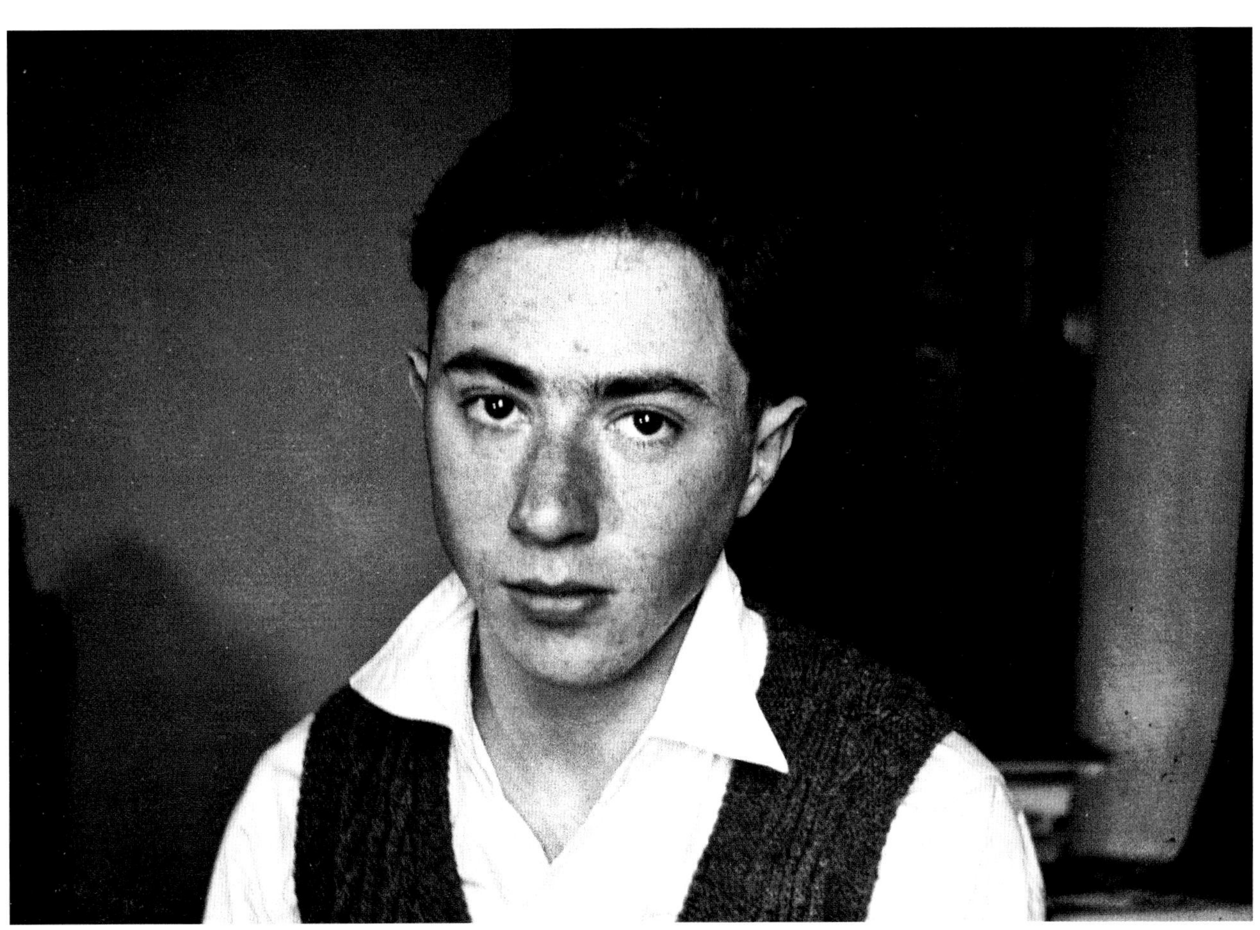

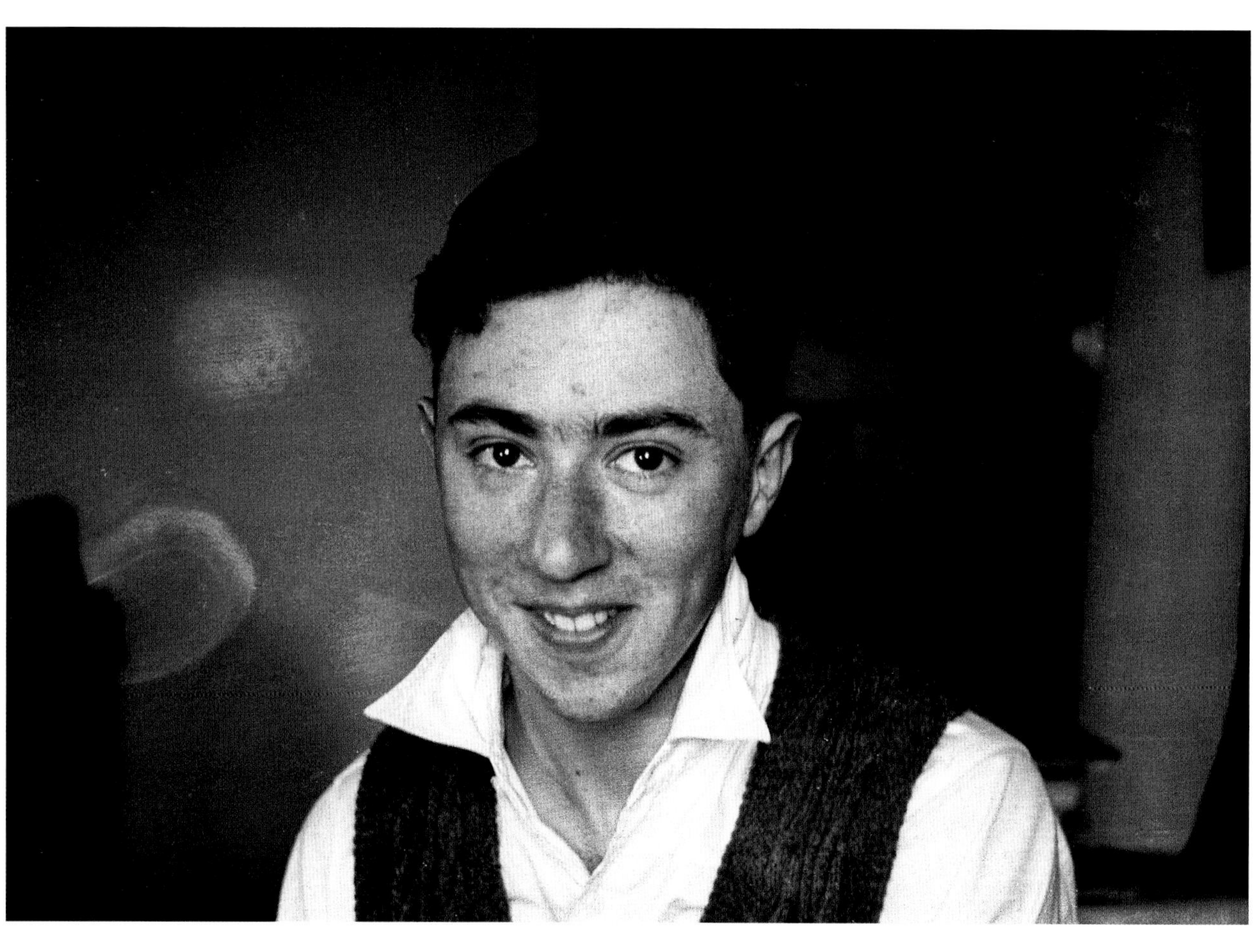

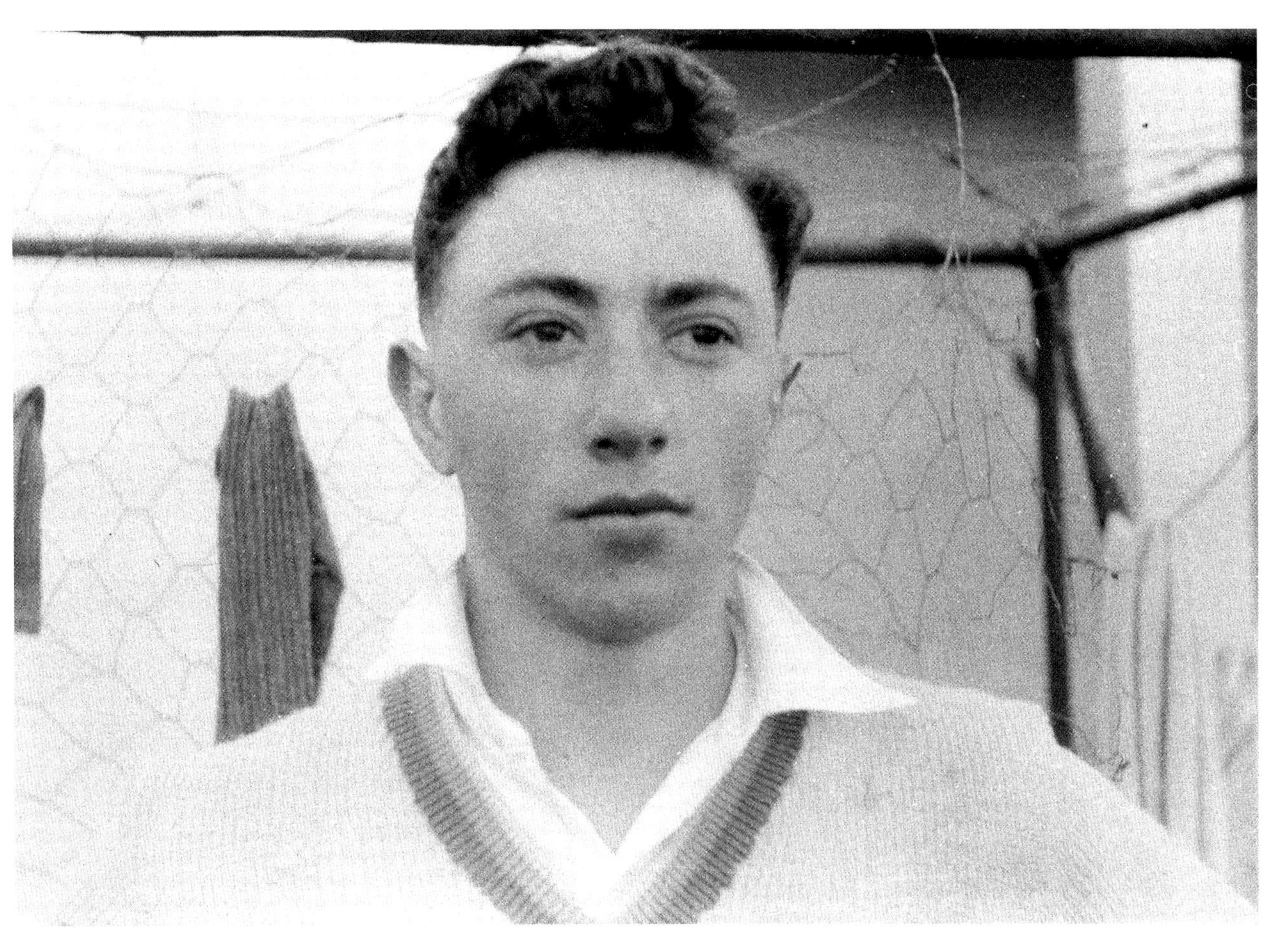

76   "He sees himself in his white shirt with rolled-up sleeves and the grey trousers he is on the point of outgrowing: not a child, not what a passer-by would call a child, too big for that now..." (*Boyhood*, p. 160)

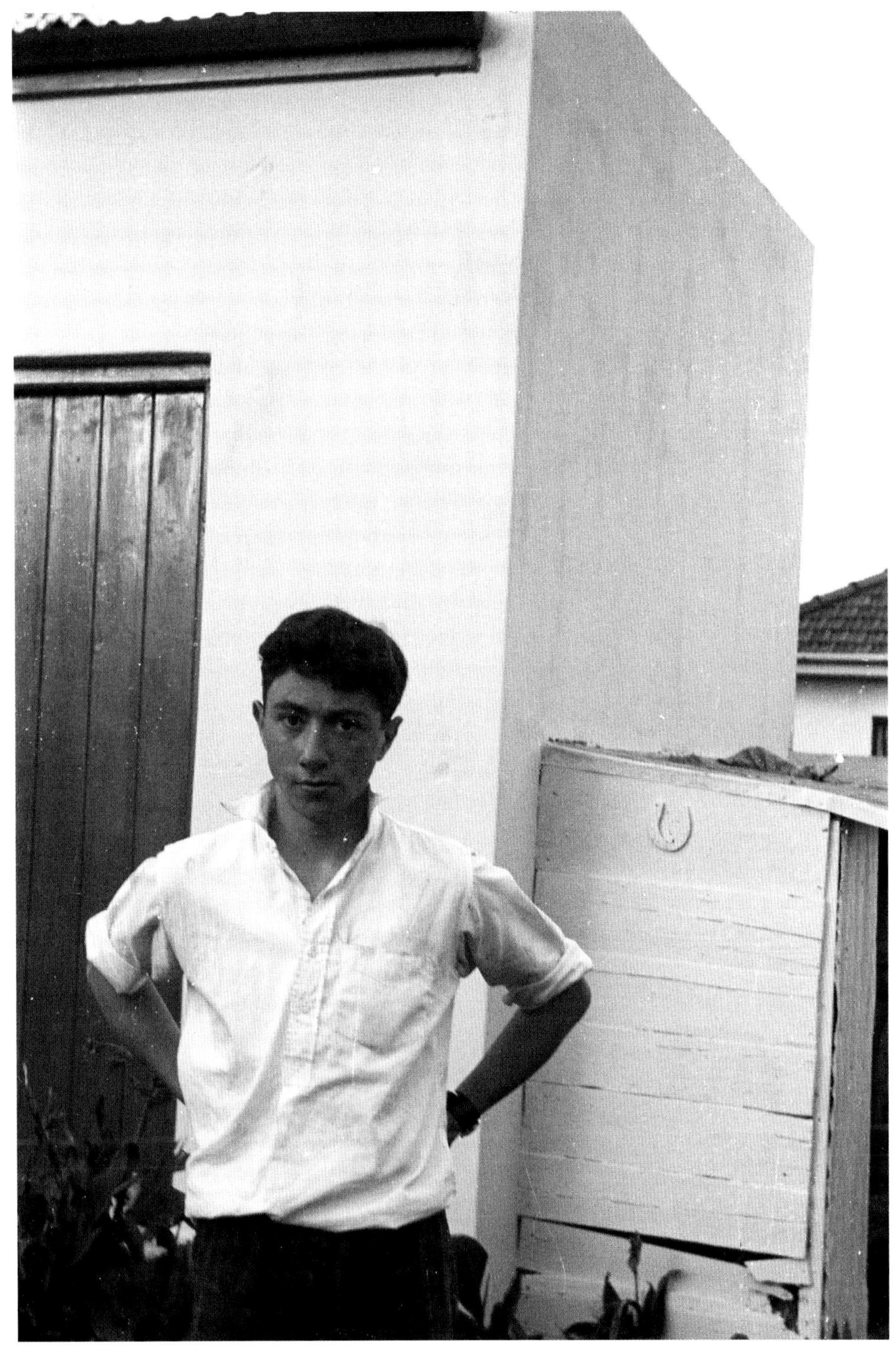

"The only passion that has not abated is his passion for cricket. He knows no one who is consumed with cricket as he is. He plays cricket at school, but that is never enough. The house in Plumstead has a slate-floored stoep. Here he plays by himself, holding the bat in the left hand, throwing the ball against the wall with his right, striking it on the rebound, imagining he is on a field."

(*Boyhood*, p. 144)

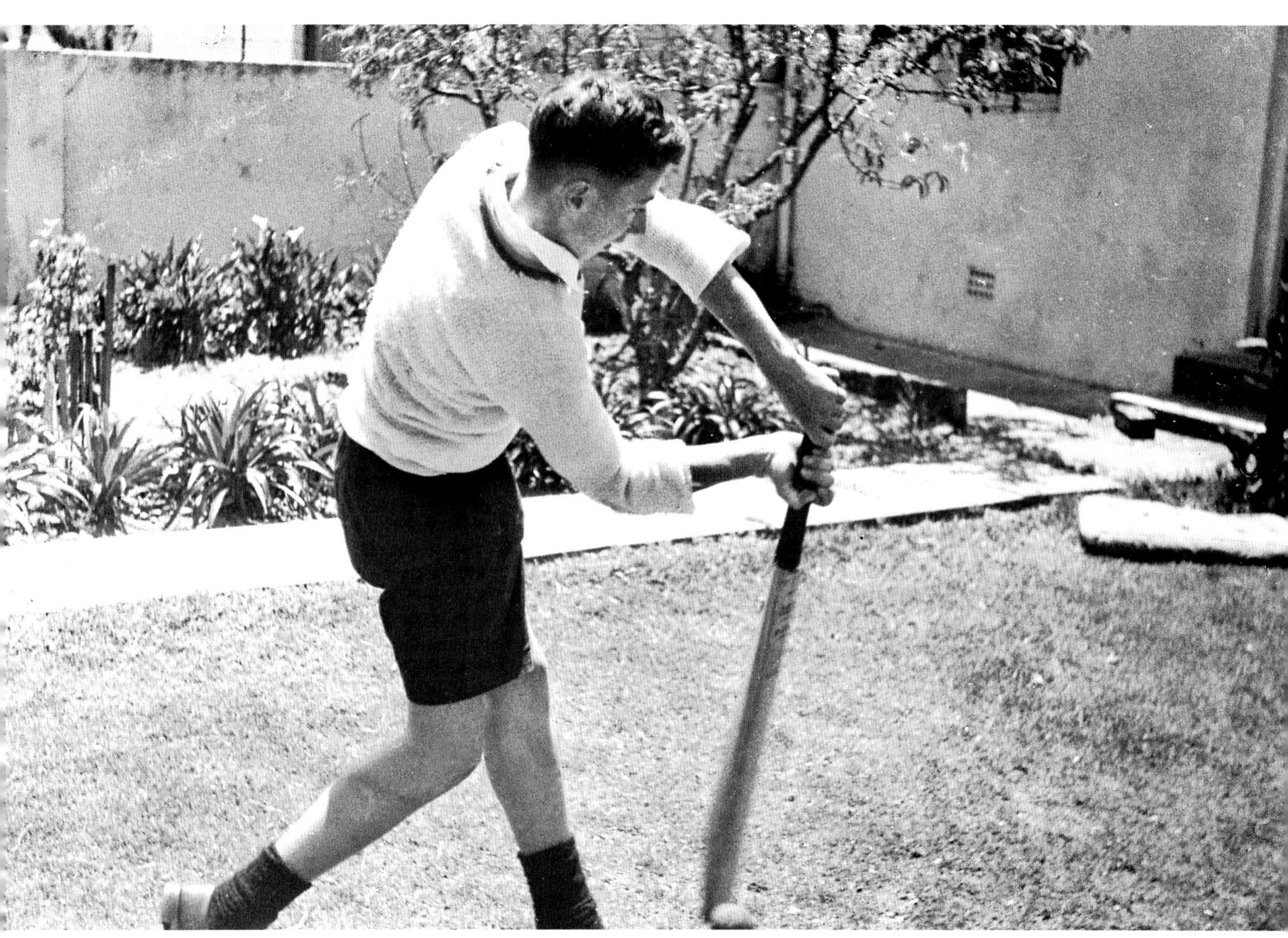

80   My brother David in the back yard of our house in 81 Camp Ground Road,

Rondebosch.

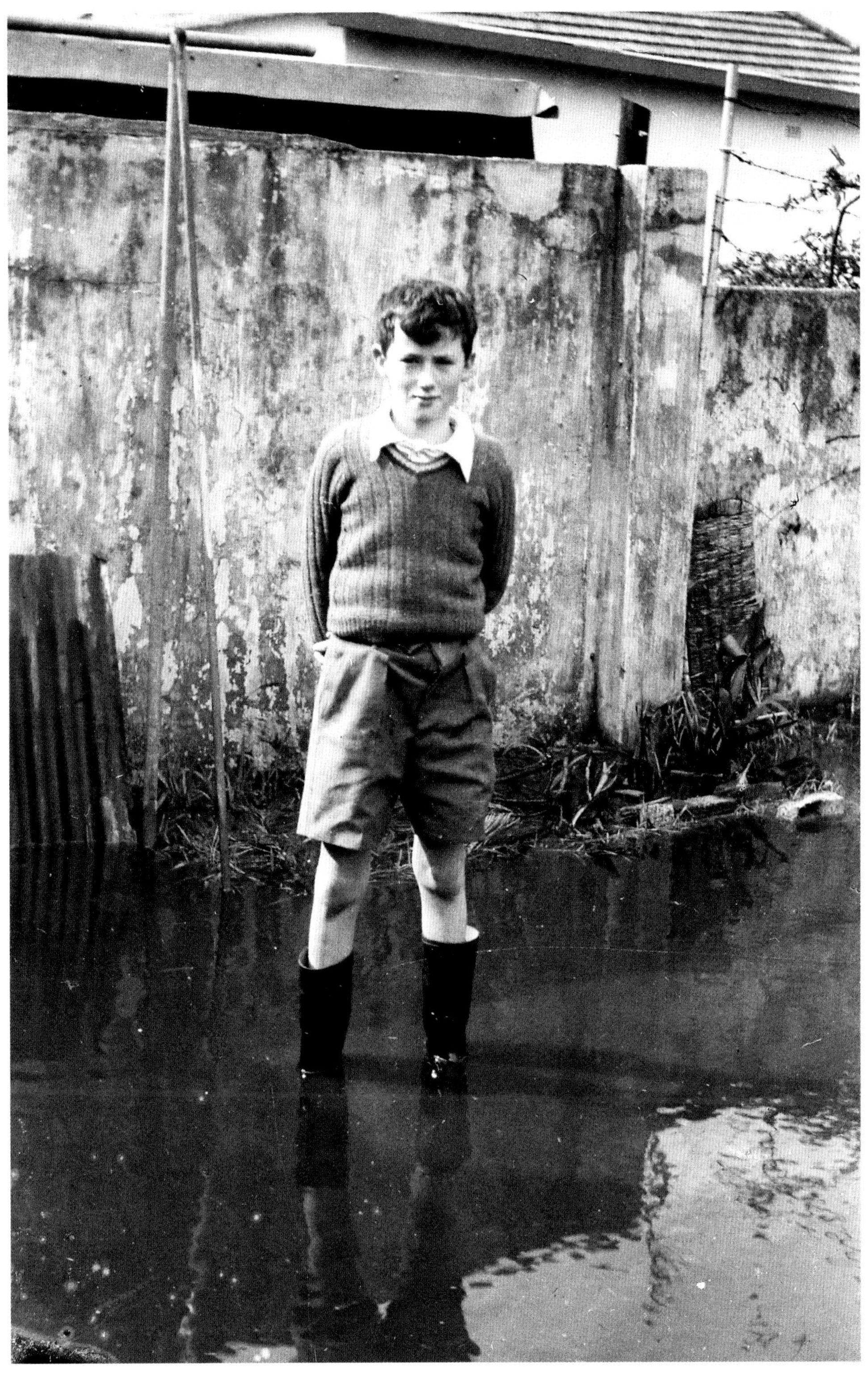

Aunt Annie's flat, Rosebank. Books that came from Germany with my great-grandfather Balthazar du Biel (Balcer Dubyl), in Gothic type that I could not decipher.

"The only room in Aunt Annie's flat that he likes is the storeroom. The storeroom is piled to the ceiling with old newspapers and cartons. There are shelves full of books..." (*Boyhood*, p. 117)

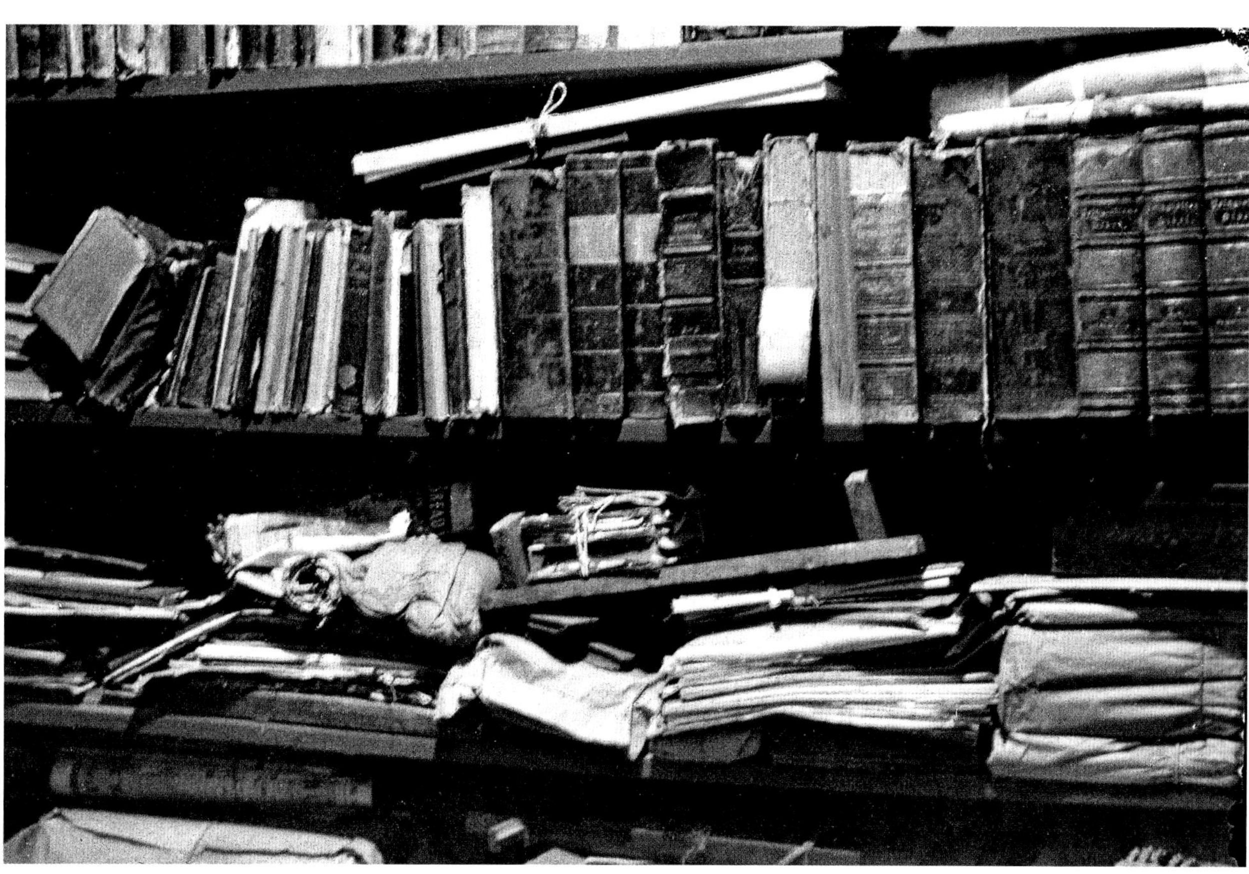

84   The living room in Aunt Annie's flat, Alma Road, Rosebank.

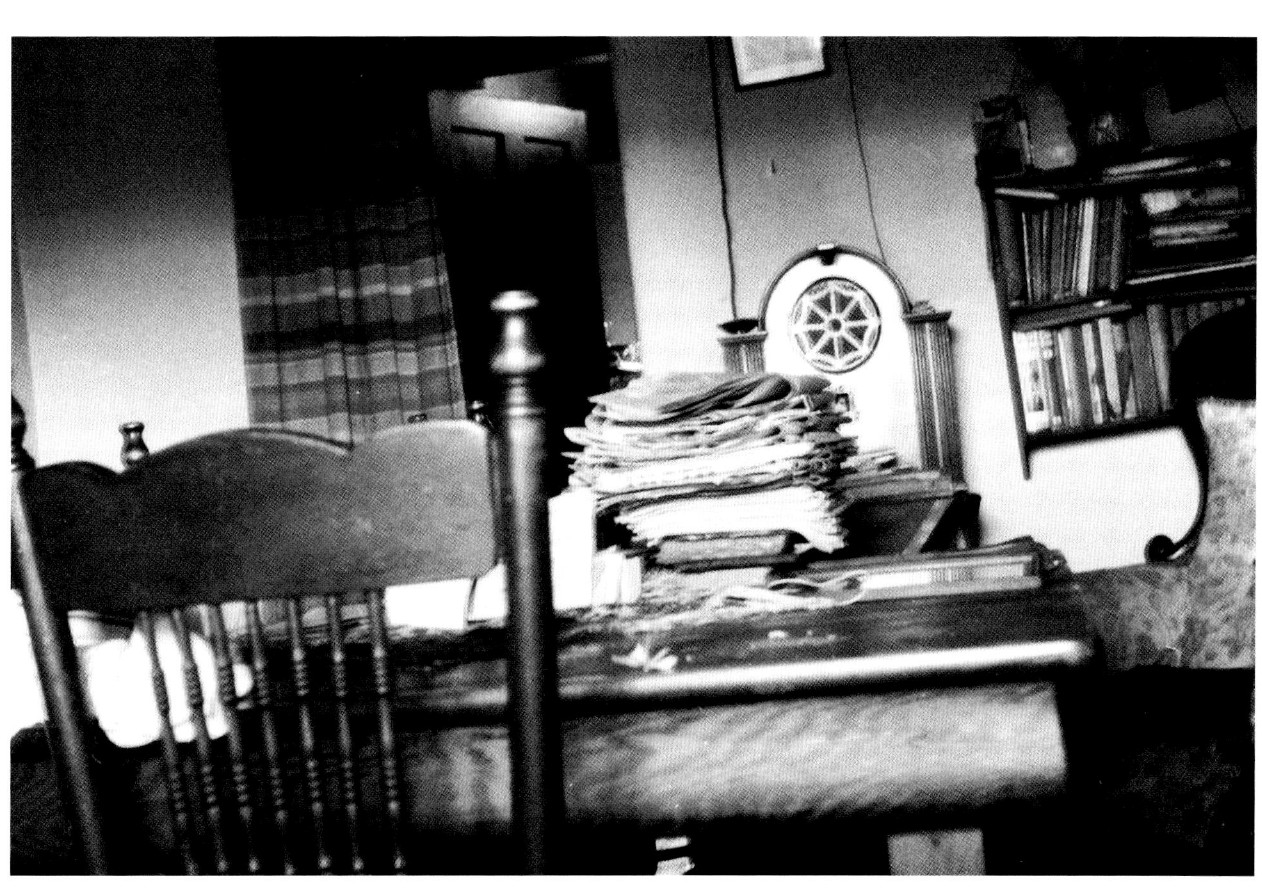

"How he could once have been so infatuated by Keats as to write Keatsian sonnets he cannot comprehend." (*Youth*, p.21)

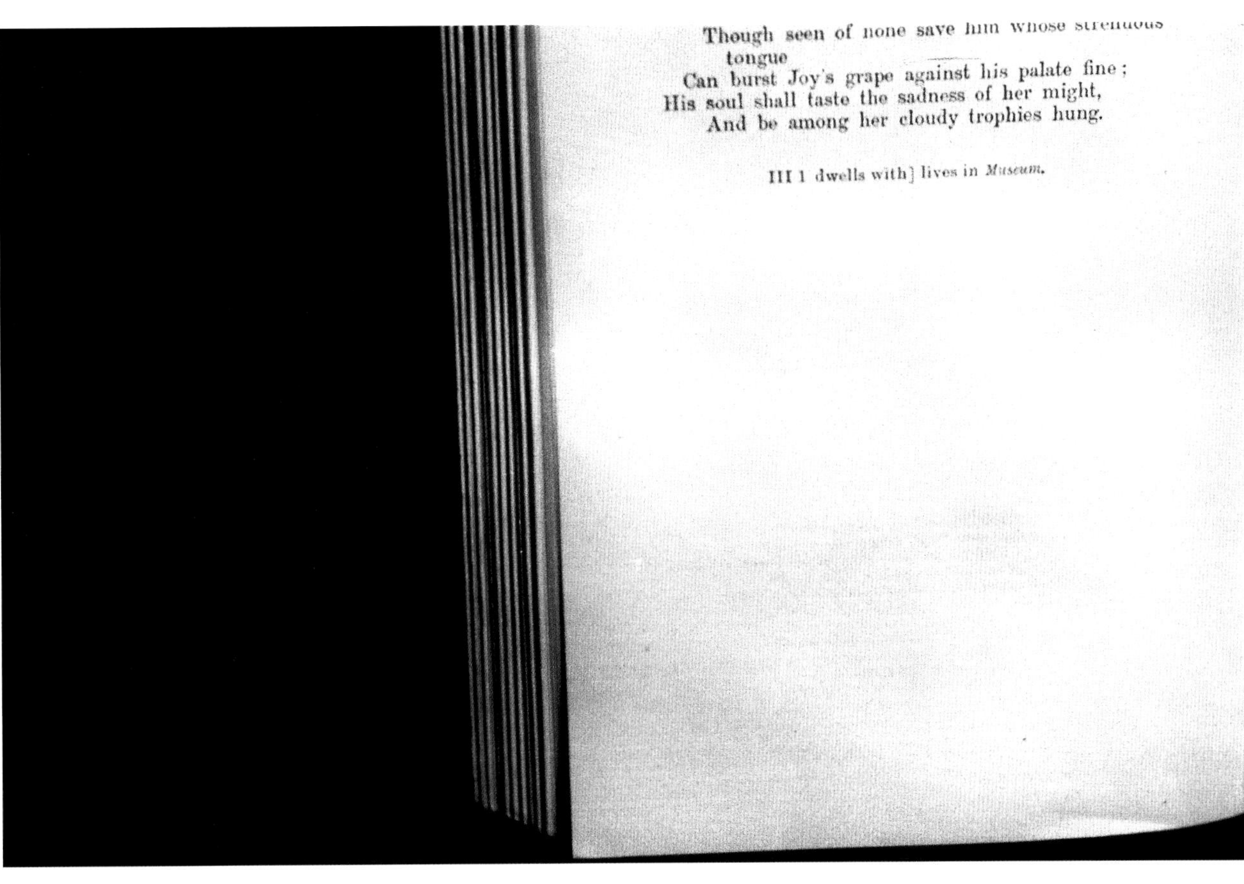

Though seen of none save him whose strenuous tongue
    Can burst Joy's grape against his palate fine;
His soul shall taste the sadness of her might,
    And be among her cloudy trophies hung.

III 1 dwells with] lives in *Museum*.

88   "For Mr Scully he writes essays on The Character of Mark Antony, on The Character of Brutus, on Road Safety, on Sport, on Nature. Most of his essays are dull, mechanical performances; but occasionally he feels a spurt of excitement as he writes, and the pen begins to fly over the page." (*Boyhood*, pp. 138-139)

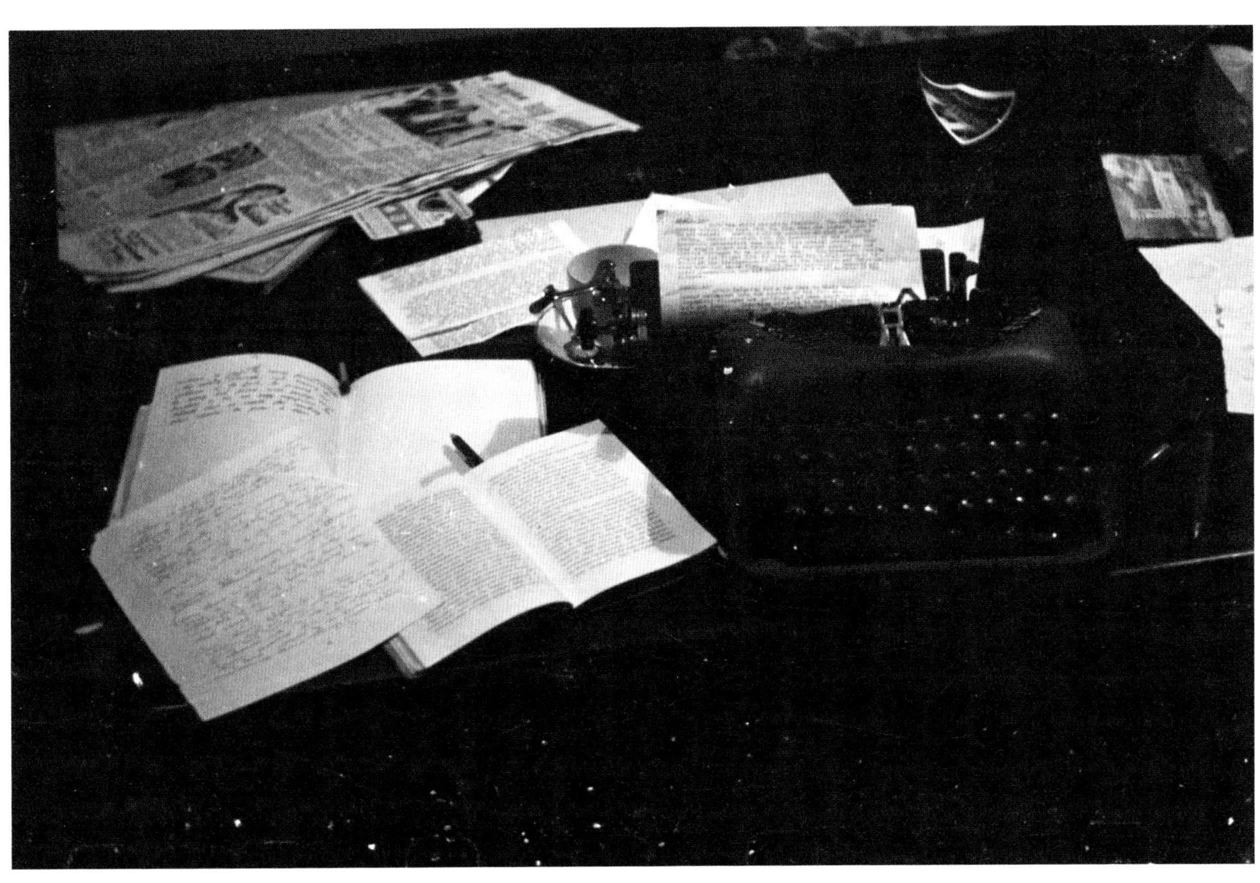

Voëlfontein

  The Coetzee family farm, Prince Albert Road, Karoo.

"The farm is called Voëlfontein; he loves every stone of it, every bush, every blade of grass, loves the birds that give it its name, birds that as dusk falls gather in their thousands in the trees around the fountain, calling to each other, murmuring, ruffling their feathers, settling for the night." (*Boyhood*, p.80)

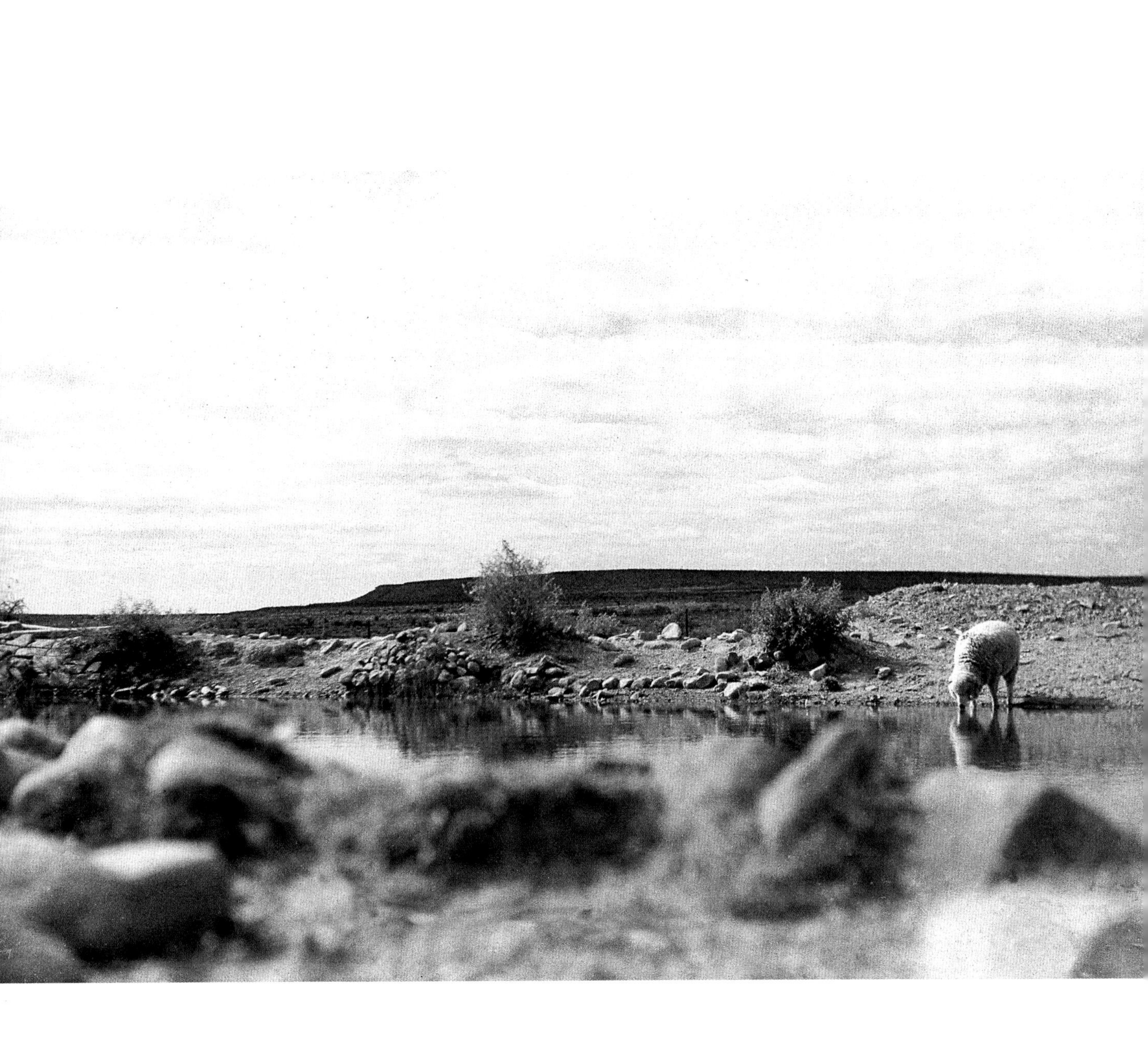

92

"He knows Voëlfontein best in summer, when it lies flattened under an even, blinding light that pours from the sky. Yet Voëlfontein has its mysteries too, mysteries that belong not to the night and shadow but to hot afternoons when mirages dance on the horizon and the very air sings in his ears. Then when everyone is dozing, stunned by the heat, he can tiptoe out of the house and climb the hill to the labyrinth of stone-walled kraals that belong to the old days when the sheep in their thousands had to be brought from the veld to be counted or shorn or dipped." (*Boyhood*, p.91)

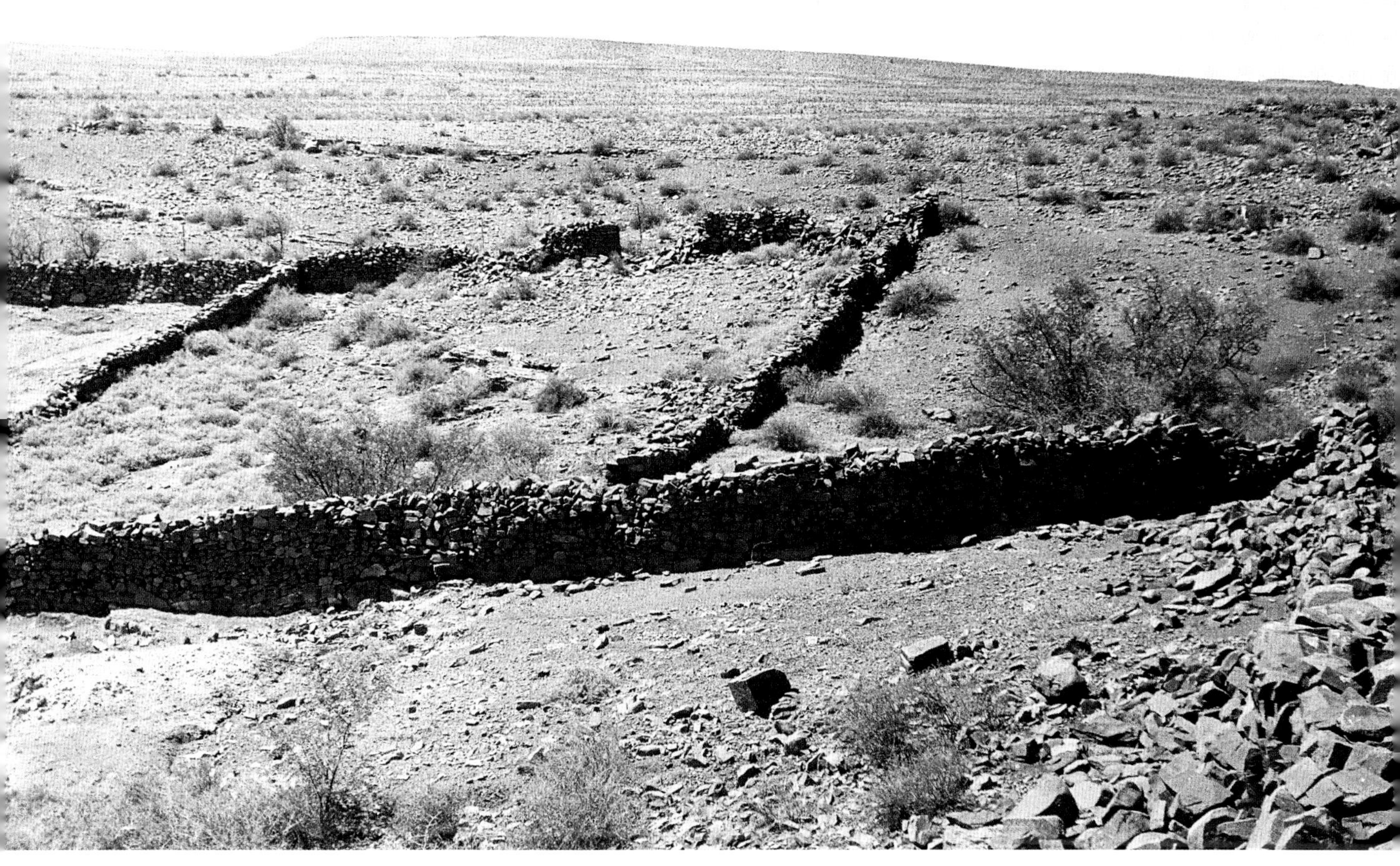

Tiekiedraai on New Year's Eve. I had a flash attachment on the Wega but could never get the flash to synchronize with the shutter.

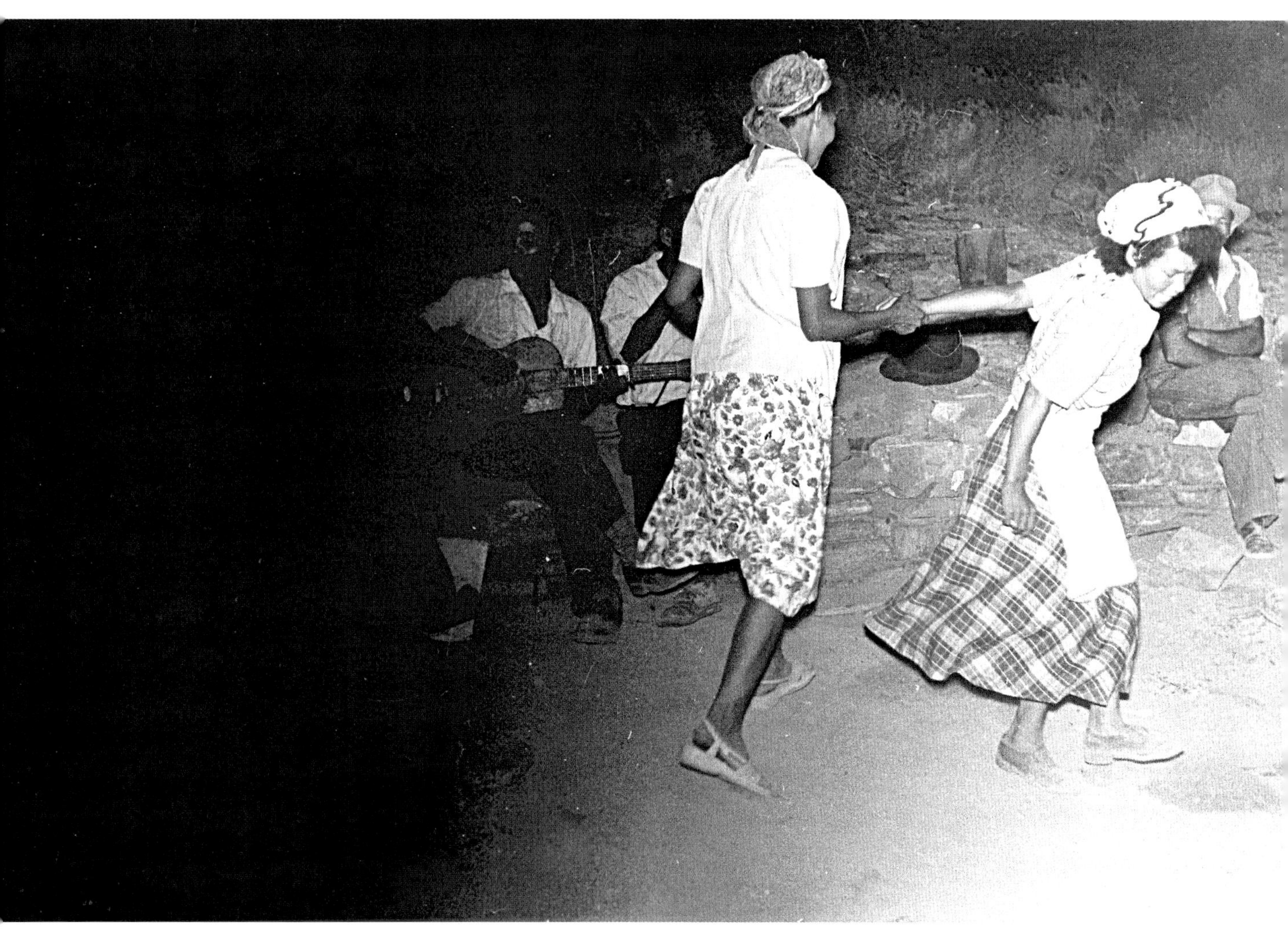

96   Ros (kneeling) and Freek (cleaning offal) with a younger man whose name
I don't remember.

"Ros sharpens the blade every day, spitting on the whetstone, brushing the blade
across it back and forth, lightly, easily.
'You shouldn't be watching that,' says his mother, after one of the Friday
slaughterings." (*Boyhood*, p.99)

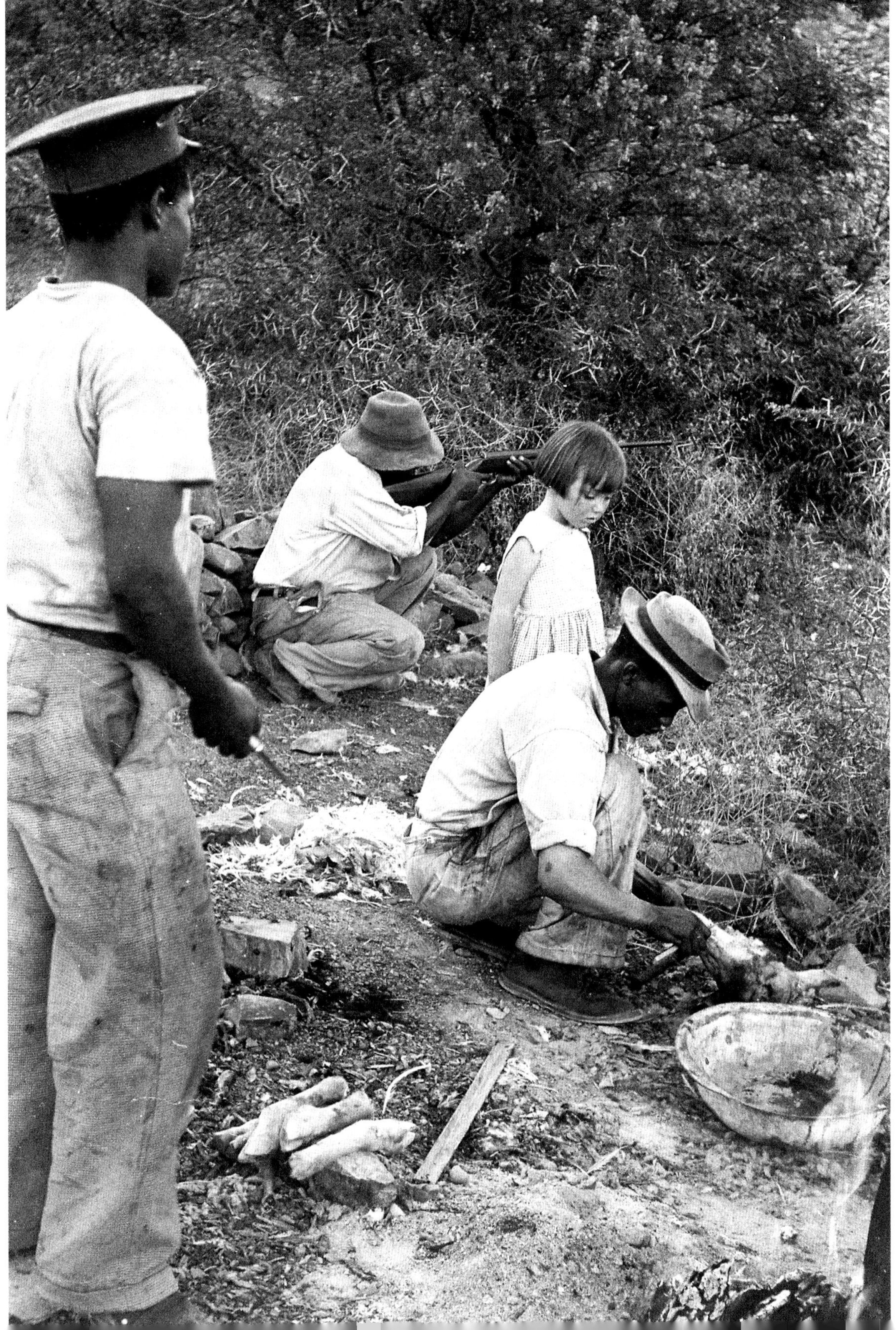

Lance Wehmeyer, my uncle.

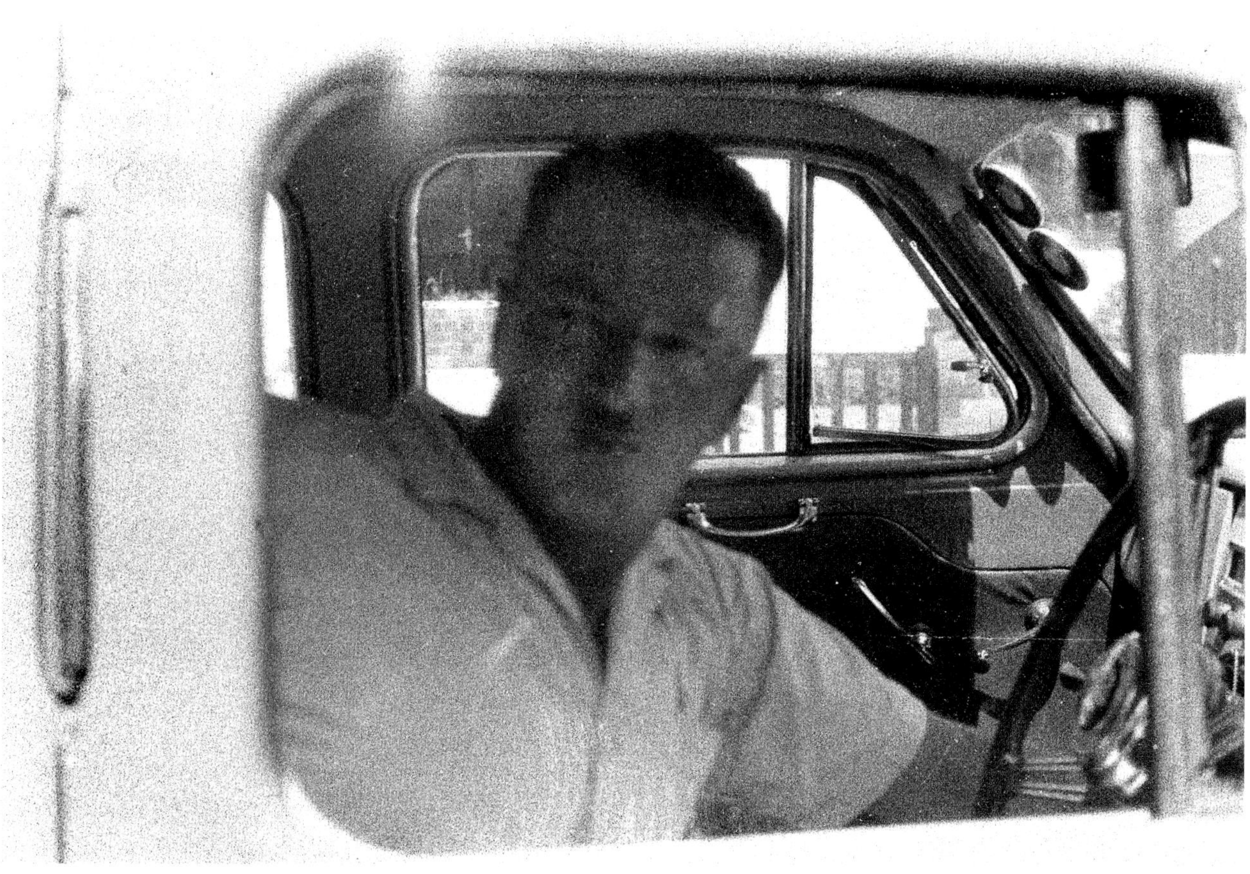

Jan, who was later to lose his larynx to cancer. In his fifties Jan took as wife a girl of fifteen, which caused a minor scandal on the farm.

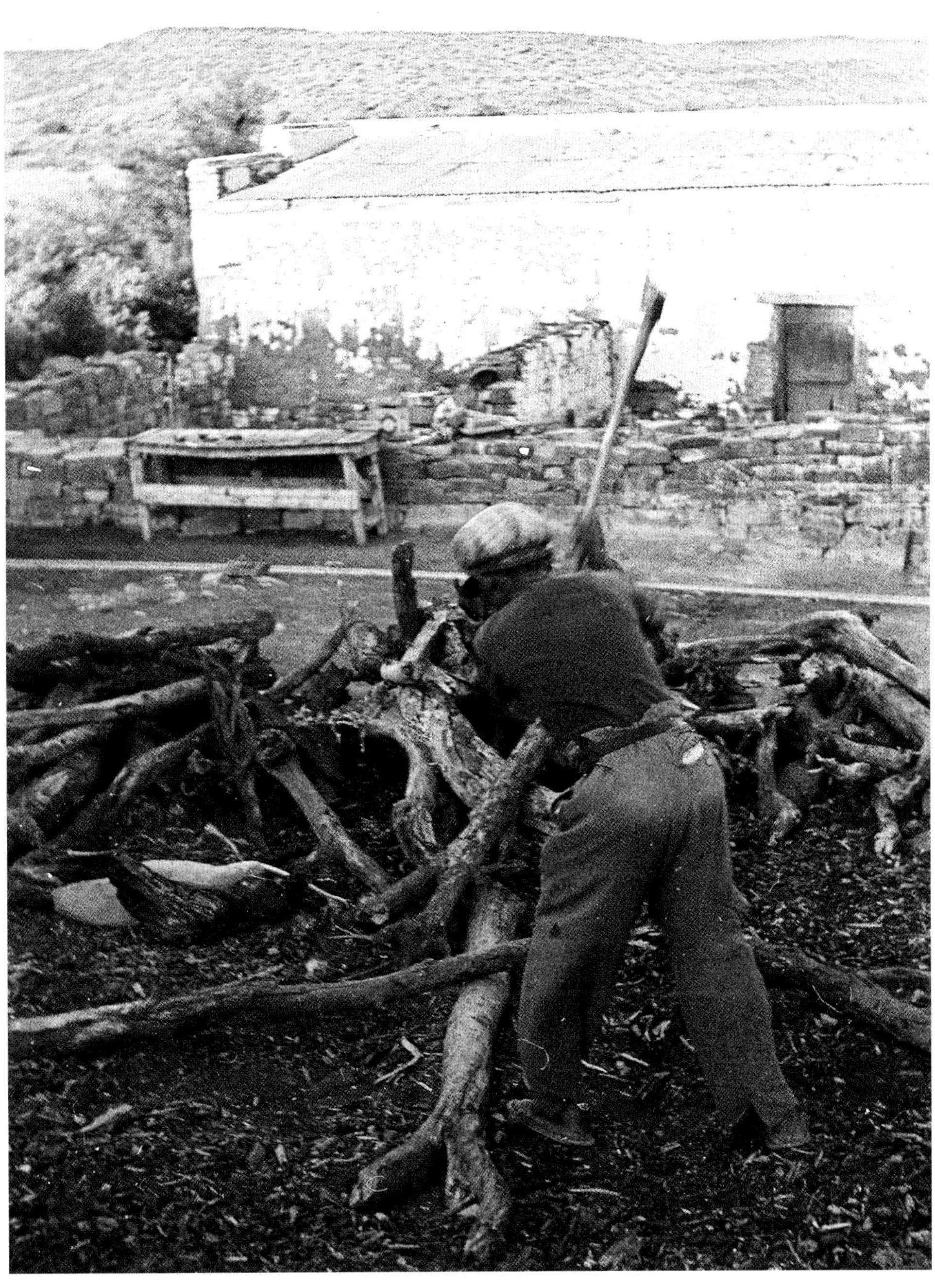

My cousin Valmé Coetzee on the stoep of the Voëlfontein farmhouse, with grandmother Lenie Coetzee and other family members in the background.

"The whole extended family congregates. Beds and mattresses and stretchers are set out in every room, and on the long stoep too: one Christmas he counts twenty-six of them. All day long his aunt and the two maids are busy in the steamy kitchen, cooking, baking, producing meal after meal, one round of tea or coffee and cake after another, while the men sit on the stoep, gazing lazily over the shimmering Karoo, swapping stories about the old days.

Greedily he drinks in the atmosphere, drinks in the happy slapdash mixture of English and Afrikaans that is their common tongue when they get together." (*Boyhood*, p. 81)

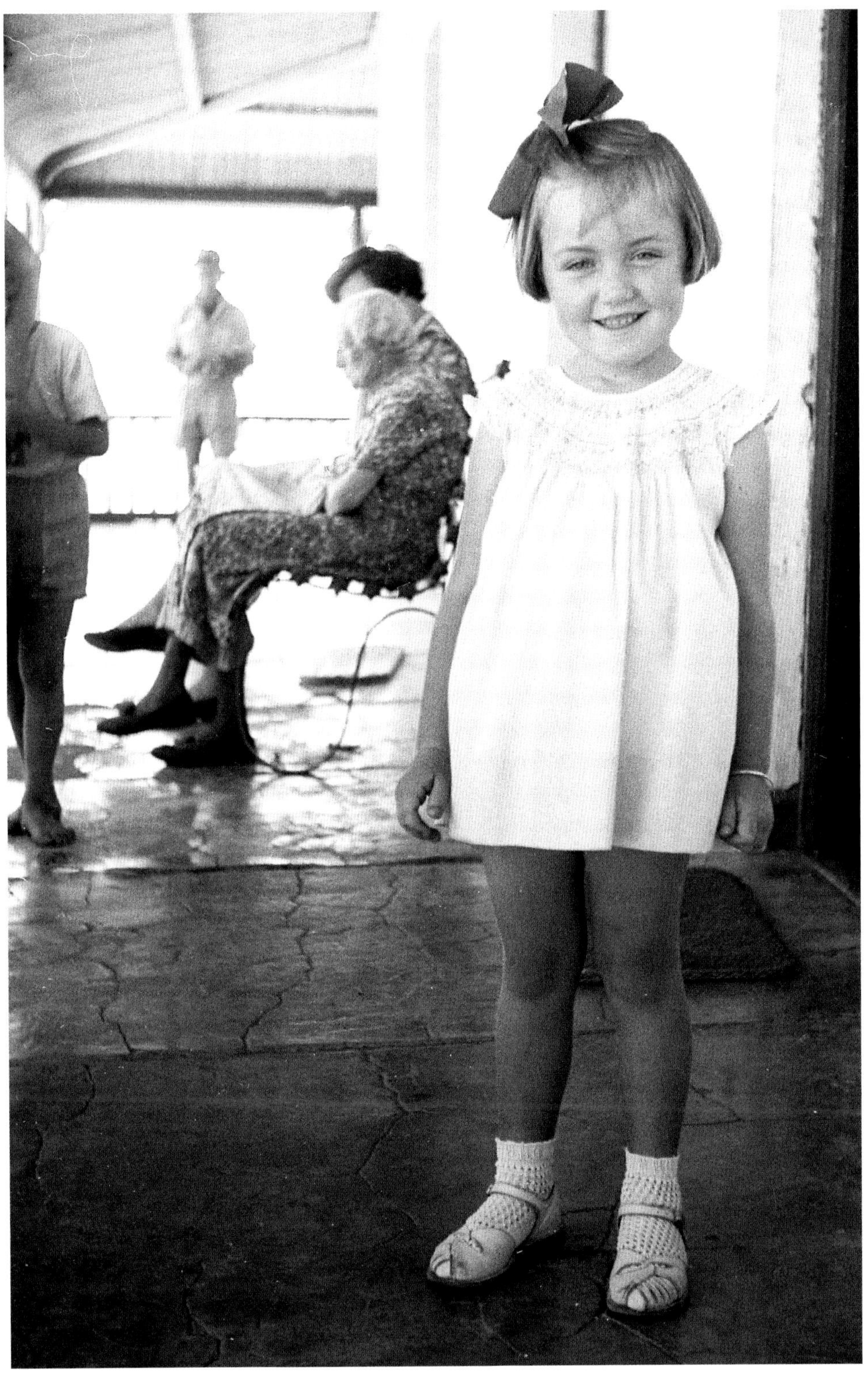

104   Freek, with the air rifle in the garden.

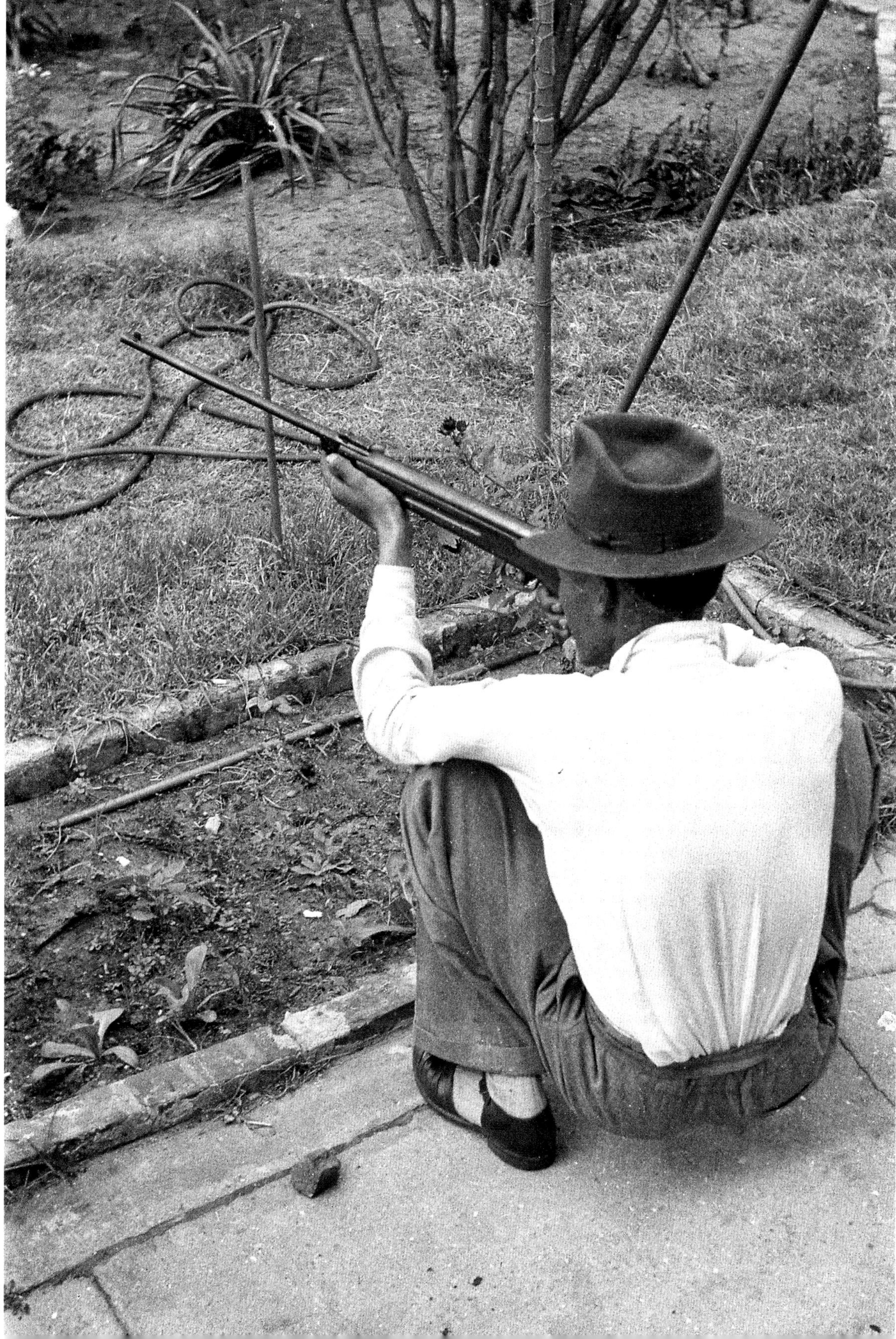

106   David Coetzee, Voëlfontein.

"Just above the farmhouse is a stone-walled dam, twelve feet square, filled by a windpump, which provides water for the house and garden." (*Boyhood*, p. 83)

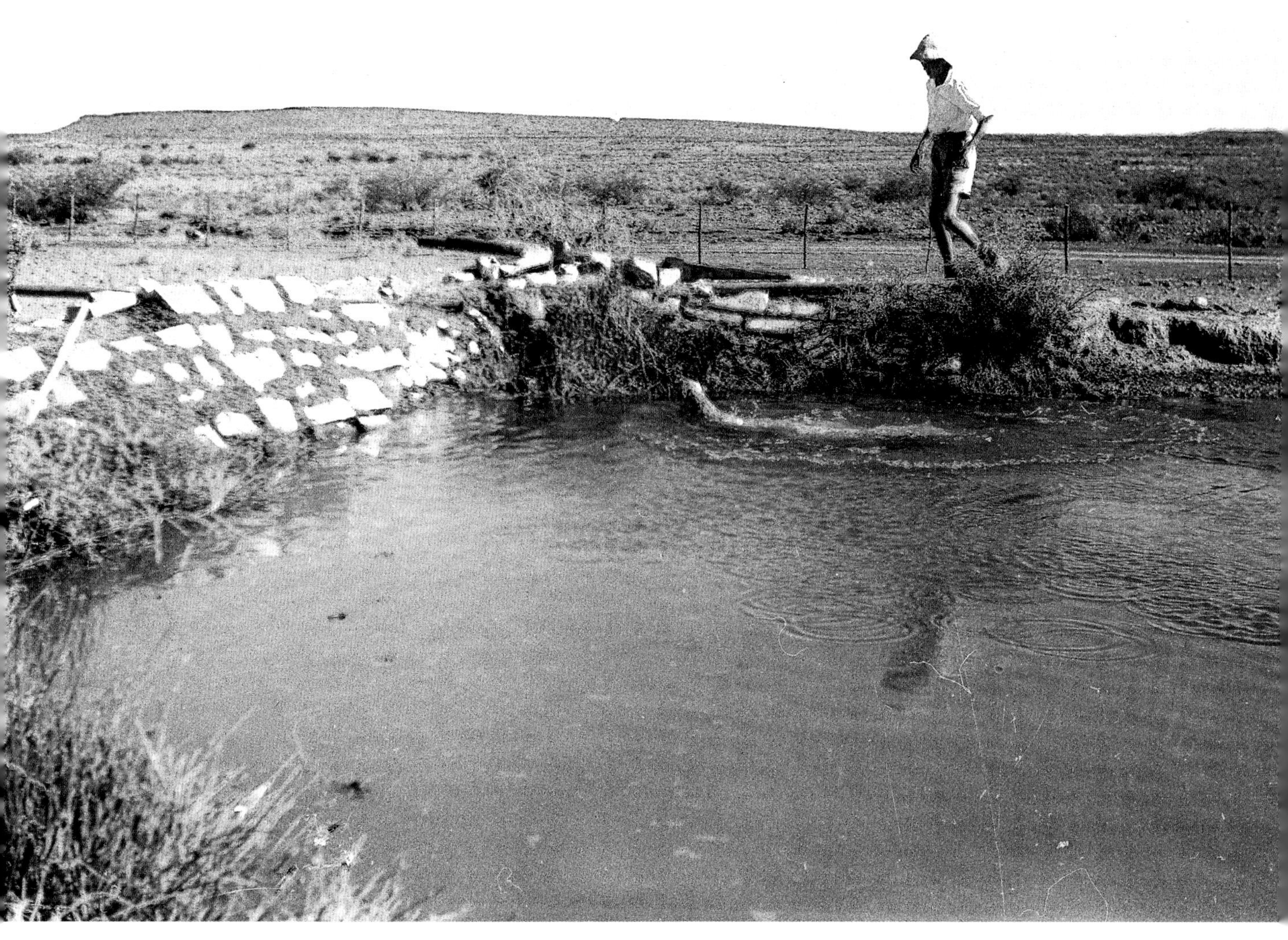

108   Ros and Freek, born in the Karoo, on Strandfontein beach – their first ever sight
       of the sea. What they thought of it I will never know.

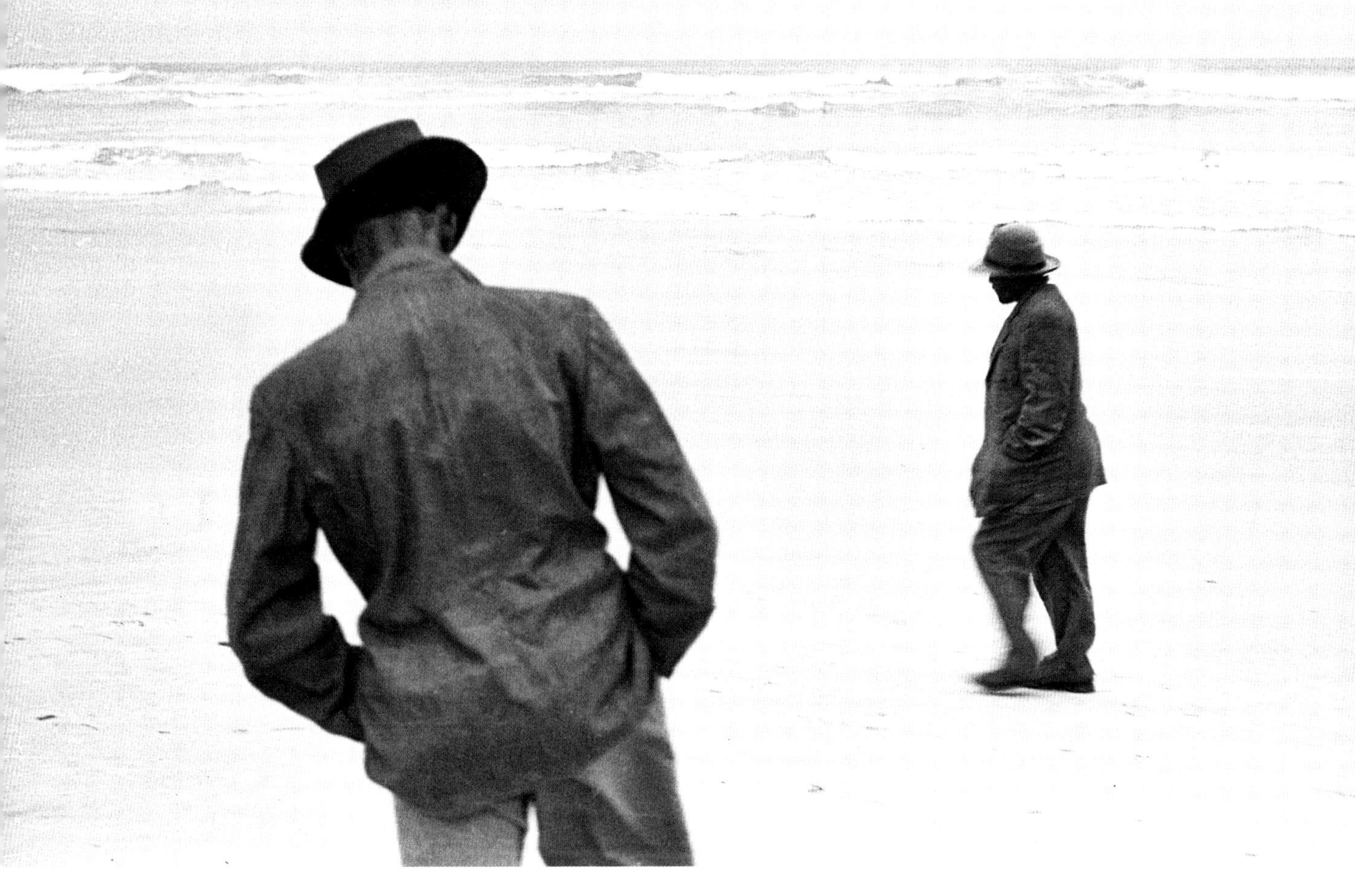

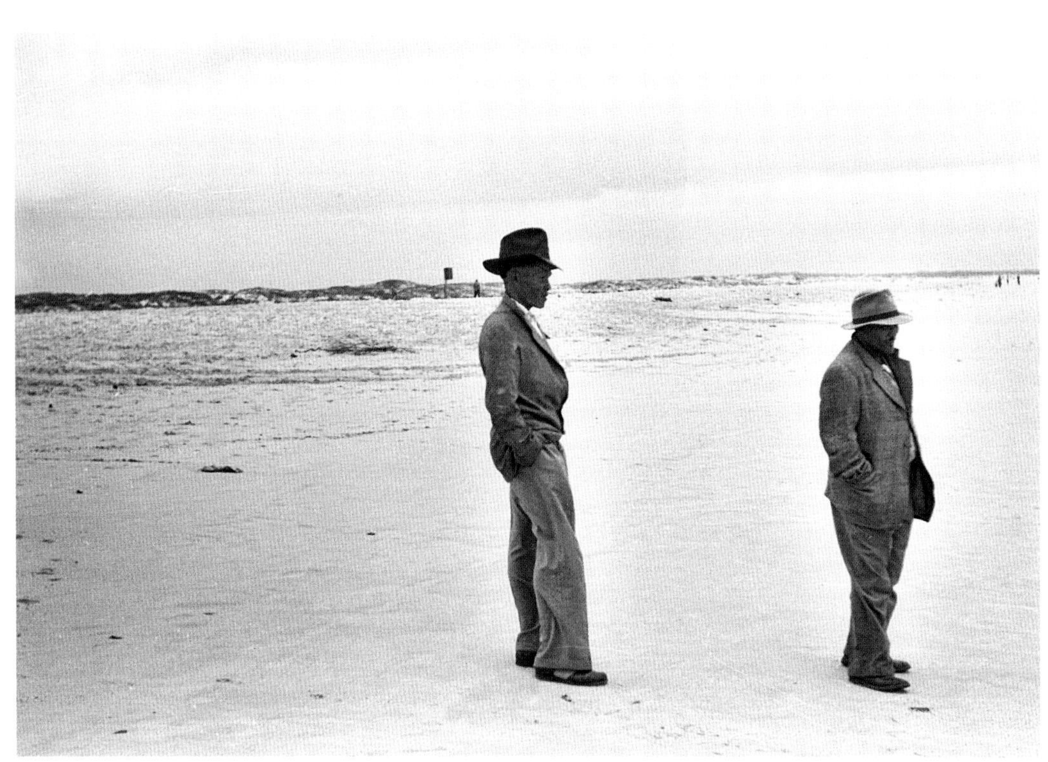

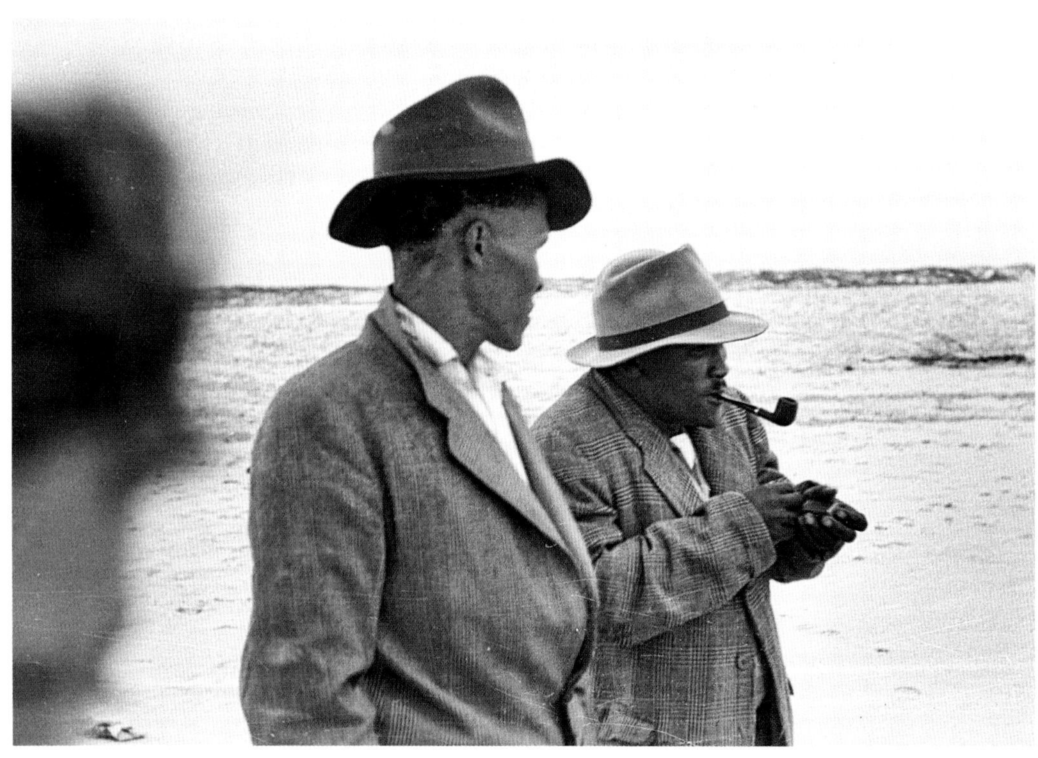

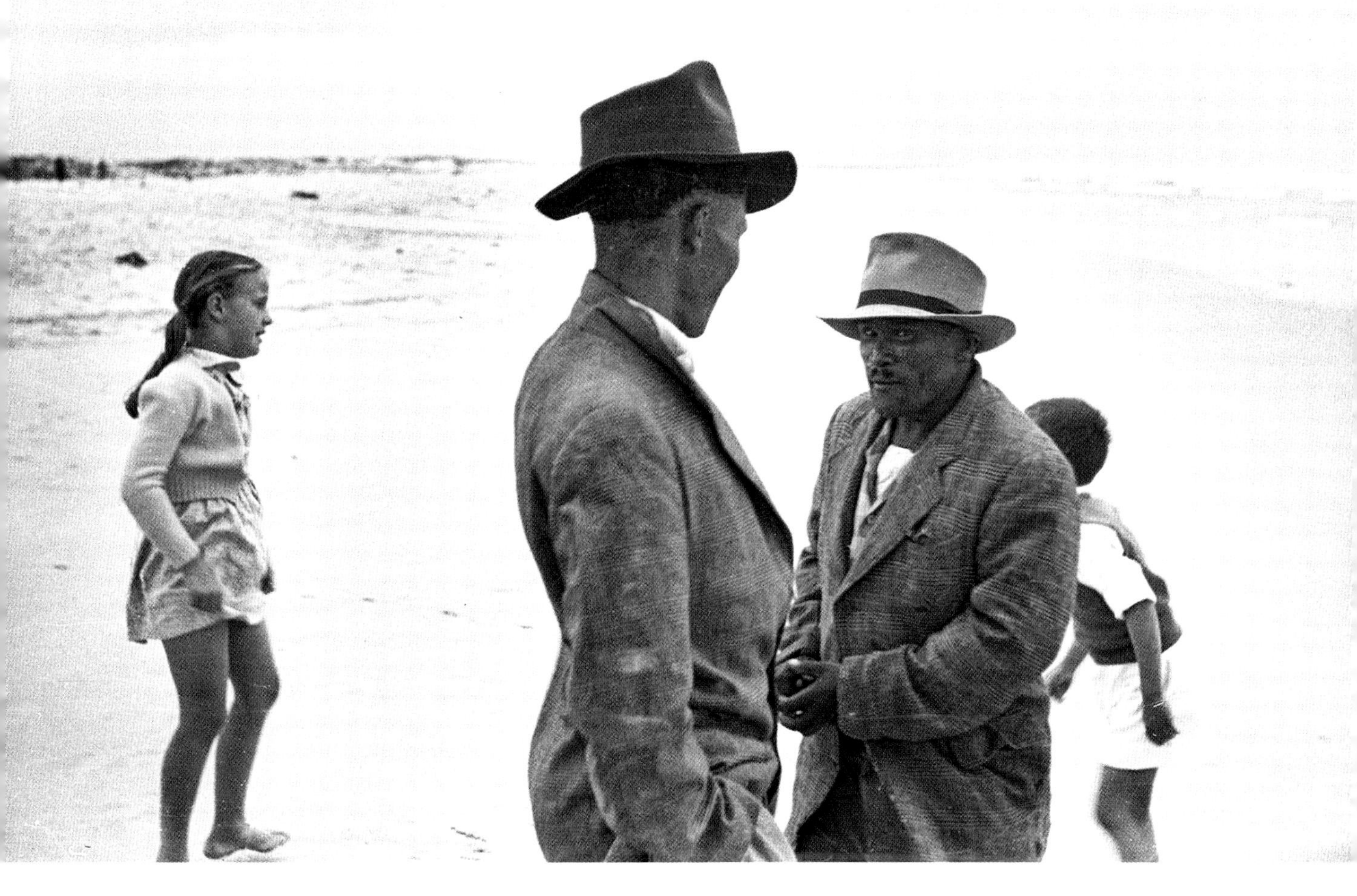

St Joseph's Marist College

Brother Alexis, Std IX classroom. So tedious did he find the role of teacher that Brother Alexis would doze off in class. But when aroused he had a fearsome hand with the cane.

"Theo sits squashed against him in his desk, underneath the picture of Jesus opening his chest to reveal a glowing ruby heart. They are supposed to be revising the history lesson..." (*Boyhood*, p. 149)

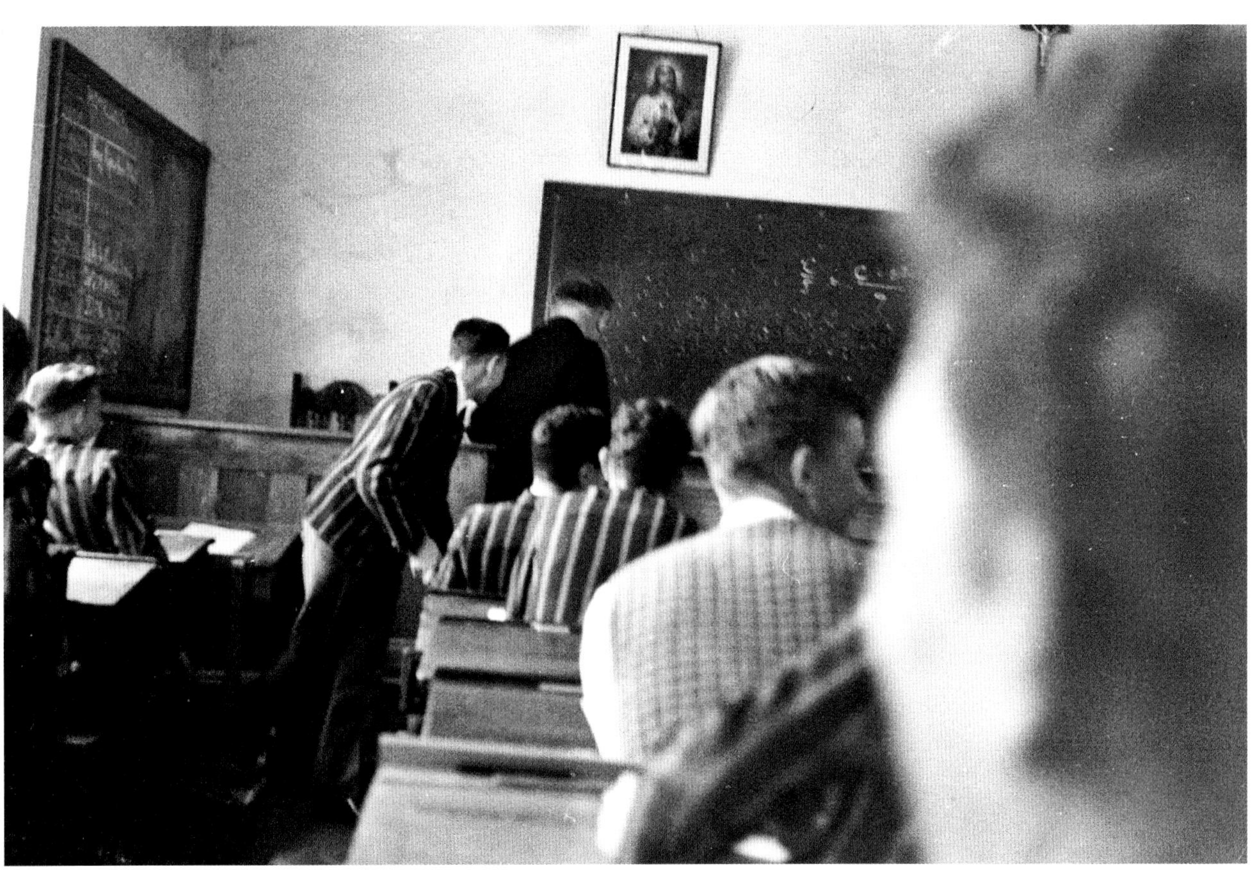

114   Harry Cartoulis (left) who was reputed to have had sex, the real thing.

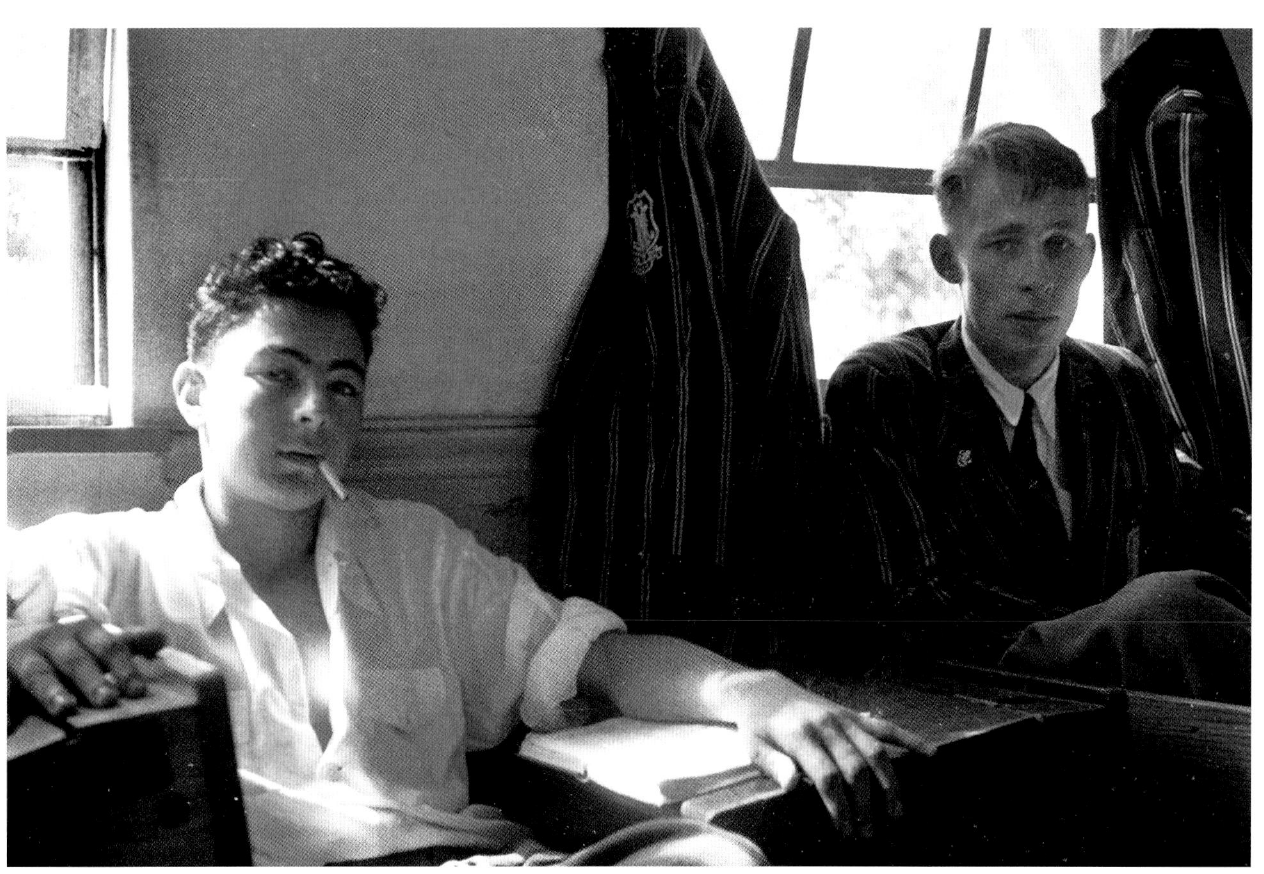

116   Nic Stathakis, my earliest and (as it turned out) most enduring friend. My

friends were mainly Jews and Greeks, hardly ever Anglos. Why, I wonder?

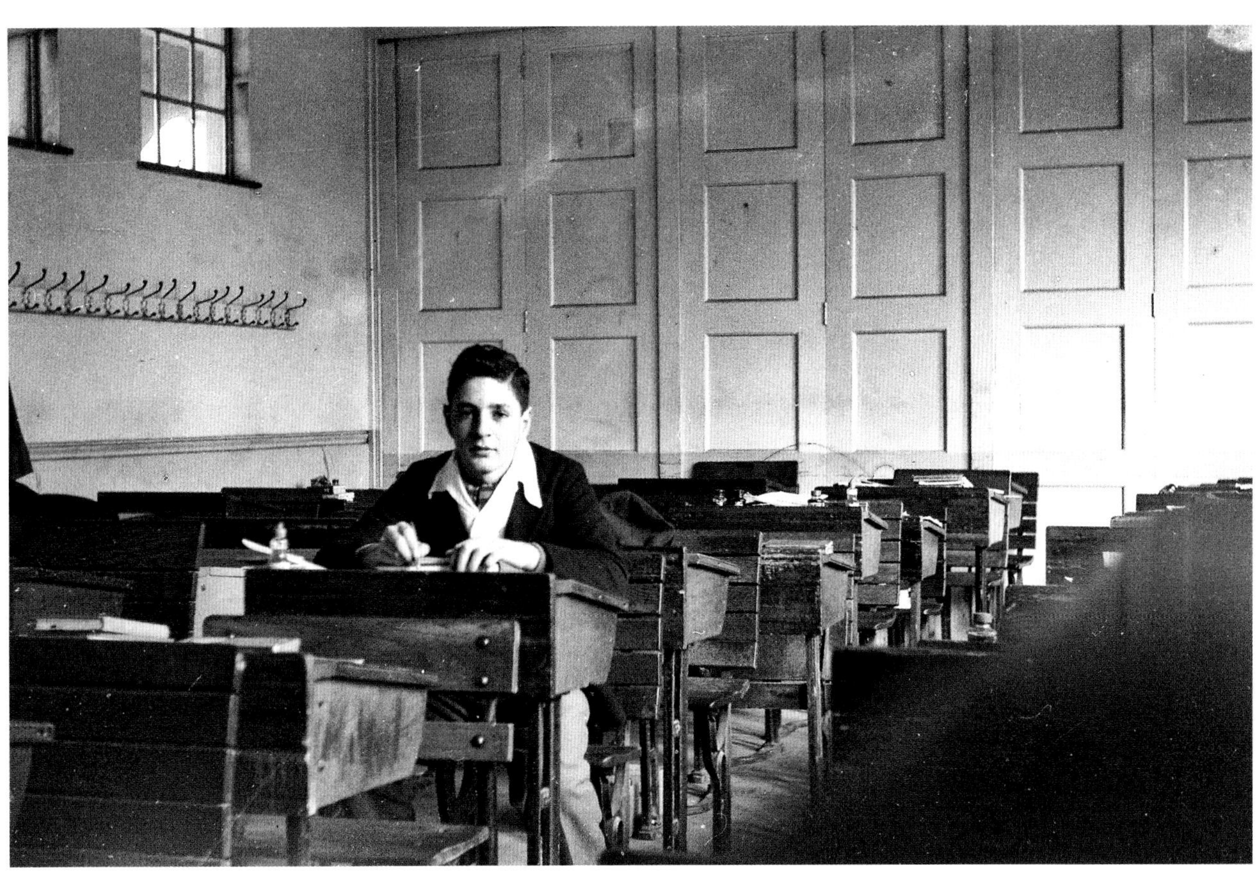

118 Nic Stathakis with the teacher's cane.

"Each of these canes has a personality, a character, which is known to the boys and talked about endlessly. In a spirit of connoisseurship, the boys weigh up the characters of the canes and the quality of pain they give, compare the arm and wrist technique of the teachers who wield them." (*Boyhood*, p. 6-7)

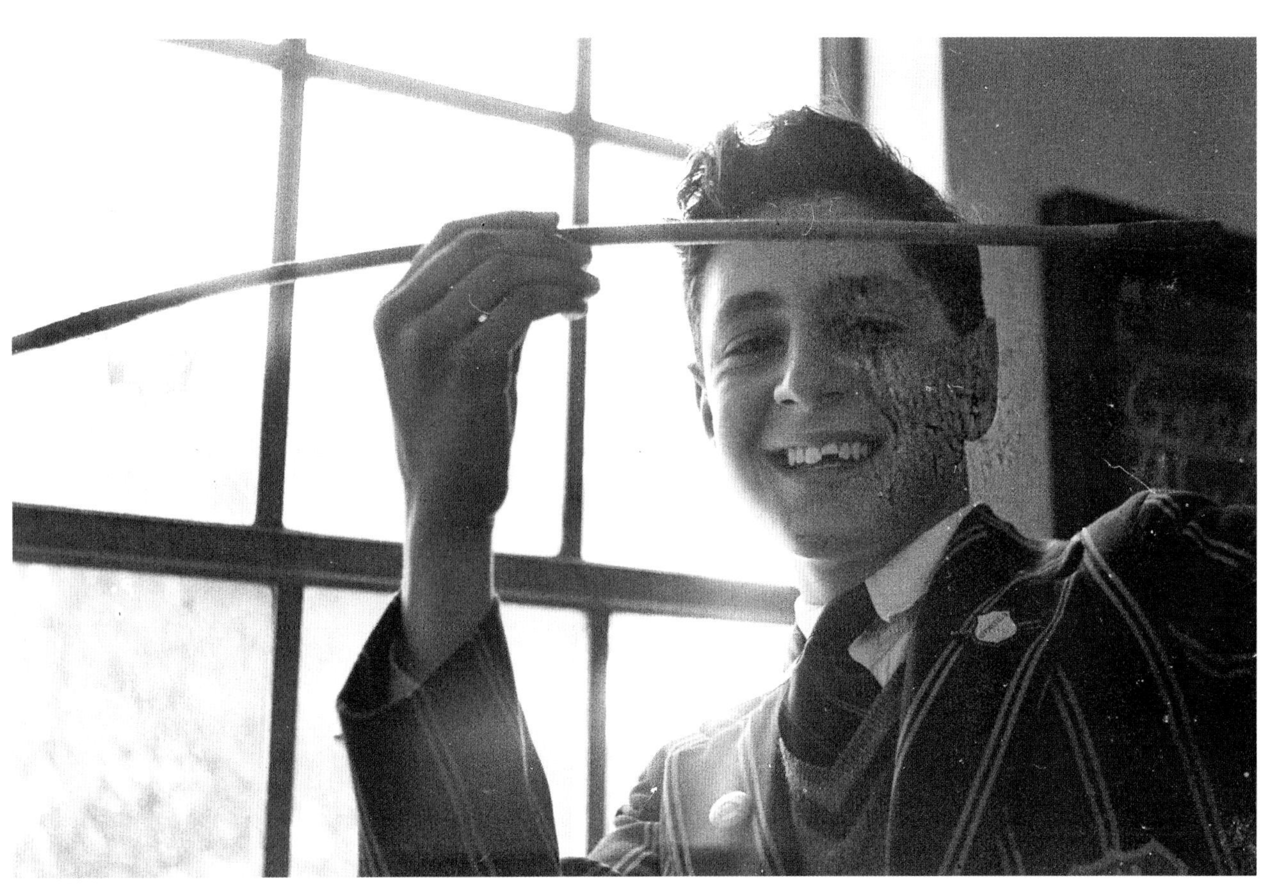

Rondebosch Station.

"To be in time for school at 8.30 he needs to leave home by 7.30: a half-hour walk to the station, a fifteen-minute ride in the train, a five-minute walk from station to school, and a ten-minute cushion in case of delays. However, because he is frightened of being late, he leaves home at 7.00 and is at school at 8.00."
(*Boyhood*, p. 137)

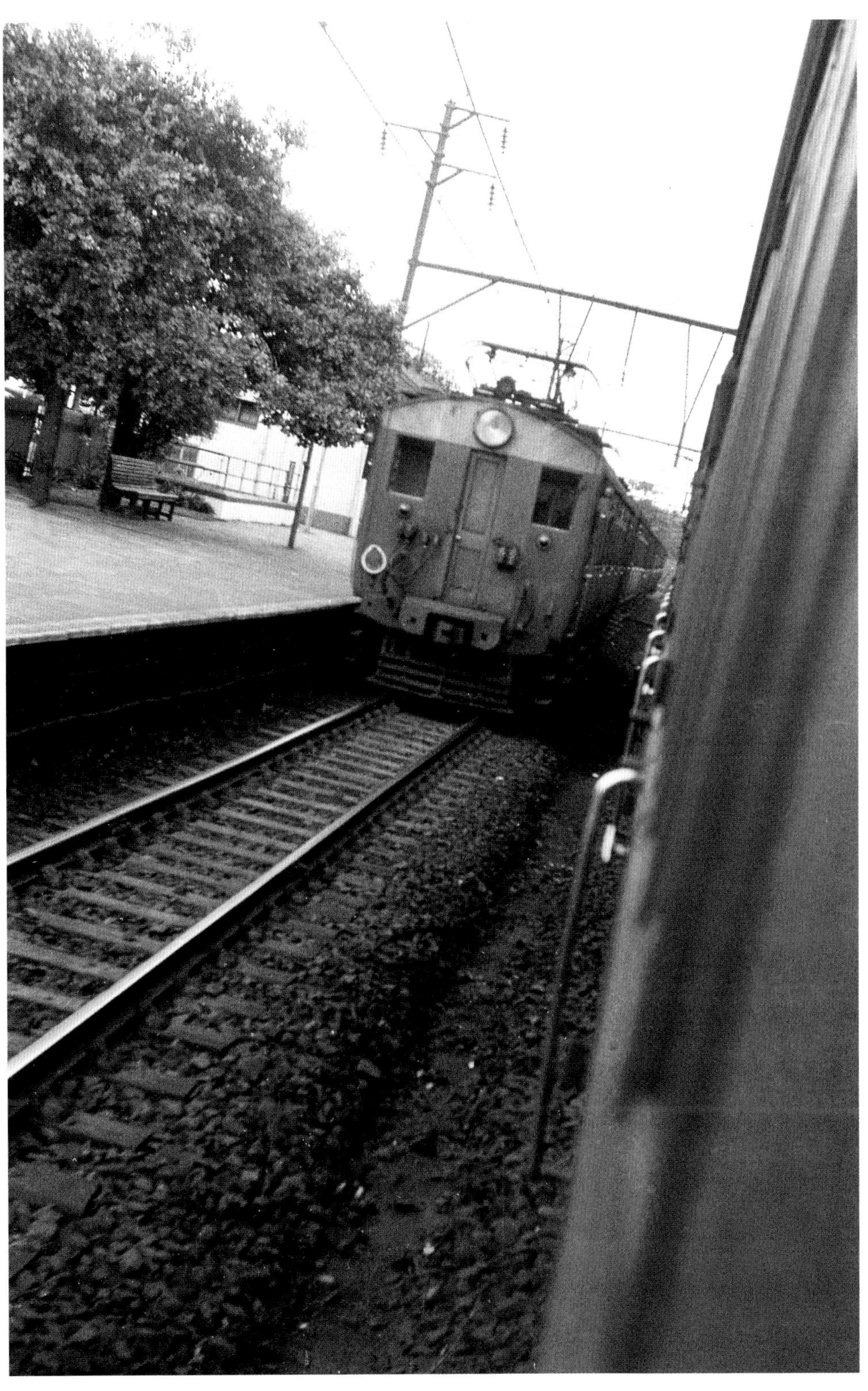

"The teachers at St Joseph's belong to the Marist order. To him these Brothers, in their severe black cassocks and white starched socks, are special people. Their air of mystery impresses him: the mystery of where they come from, the mystery of the names they have cast off." (*Boyhood*, p.137)

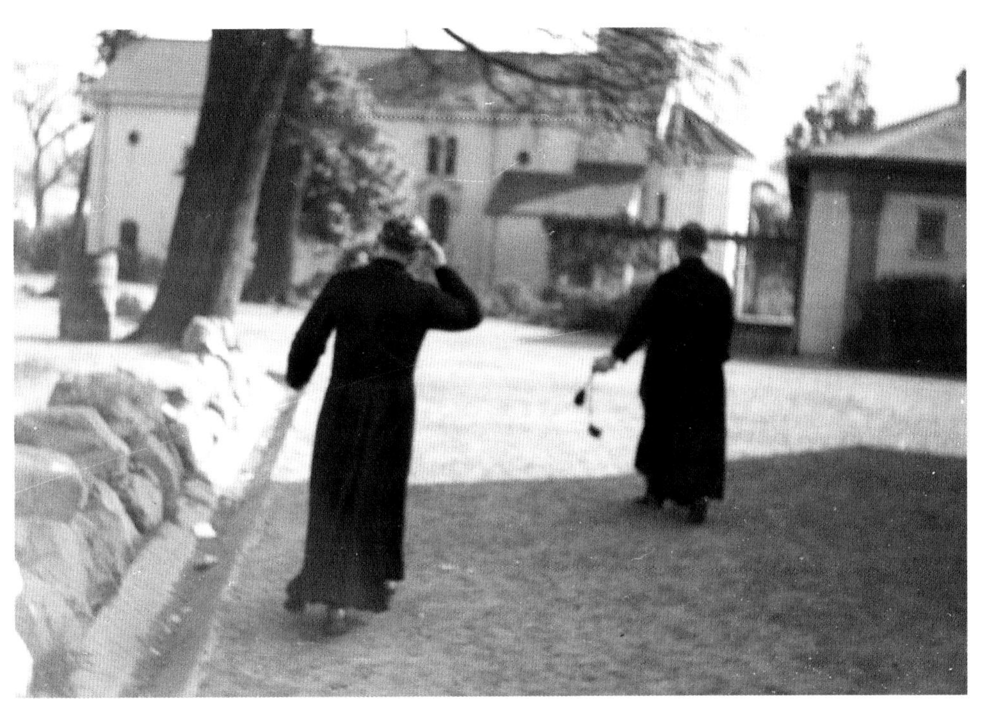

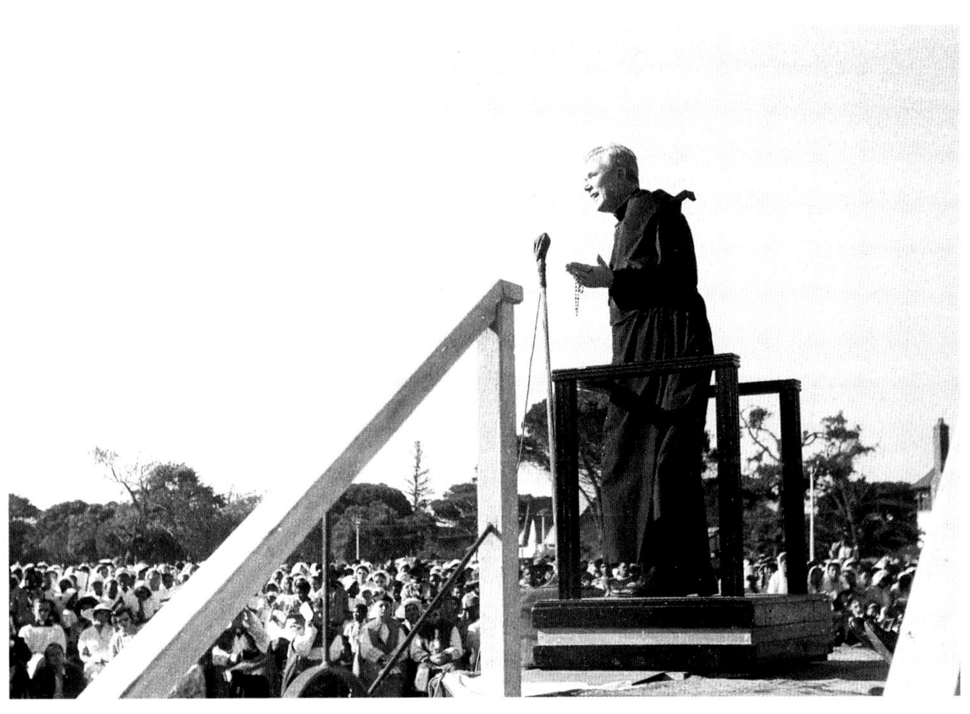

124   Brother Otto, who suffered for the faith in China (was even tortured, it was
rumoured), before being sent to the easier pastures of Africa.

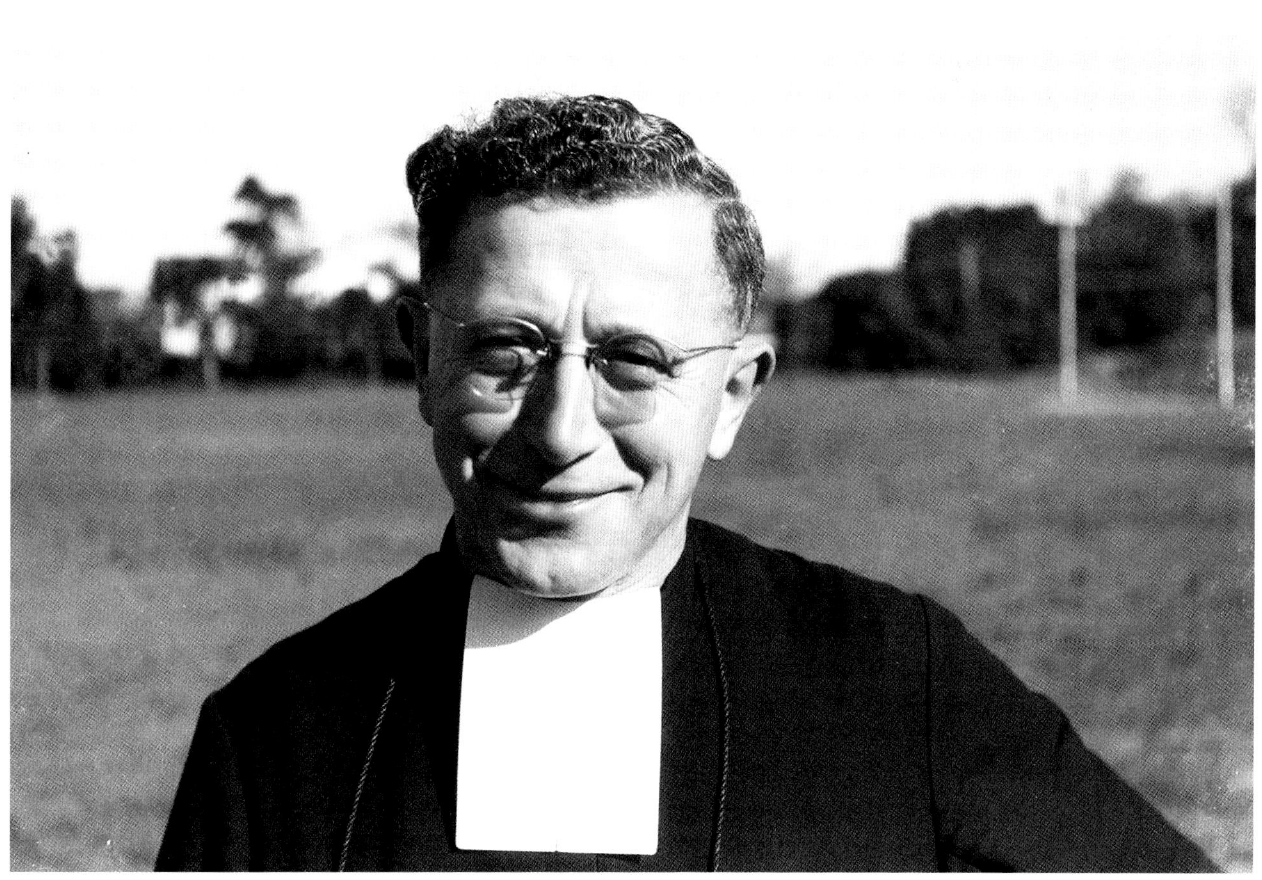

Mr Scully, on whom the benevolence of the Marist Brothers (who employed him to teach English) never quite rubbed off. A great hater of communists and of the English (he was an Irish Catholic); disdainful of Afrikaners, with their comically unpronounceable names.

"Mr Scully's first name is Terence. He wears a brown leather motoring jacket and a hat. When it is cold he keeps the hat on, even indoors. He rubs his pale white hands together to warm; he has the bloodless face of a corpse. What he is doing in South Africa is not clear. He seems to disapprove of the country and everything that happens in it." (*Boyhood*, p. 138)

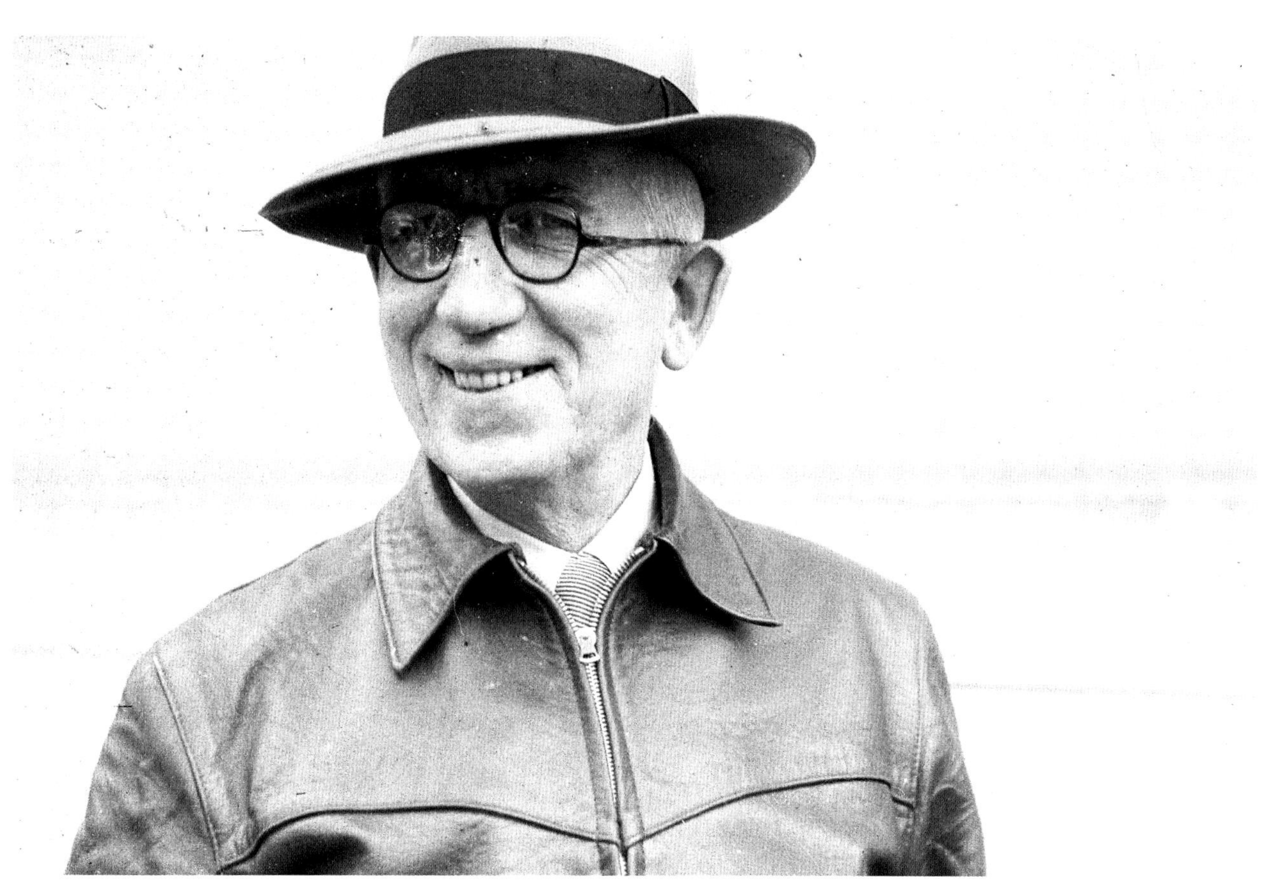

Brother Odilo, from Germany or Austria, a remote and admired figure. At the blackboard he would demonstrate what it meant to know mathematics or Latin: that and nothing more. How did he land up at this remote outpost, watching games of cricket that could have meant nothing to him?

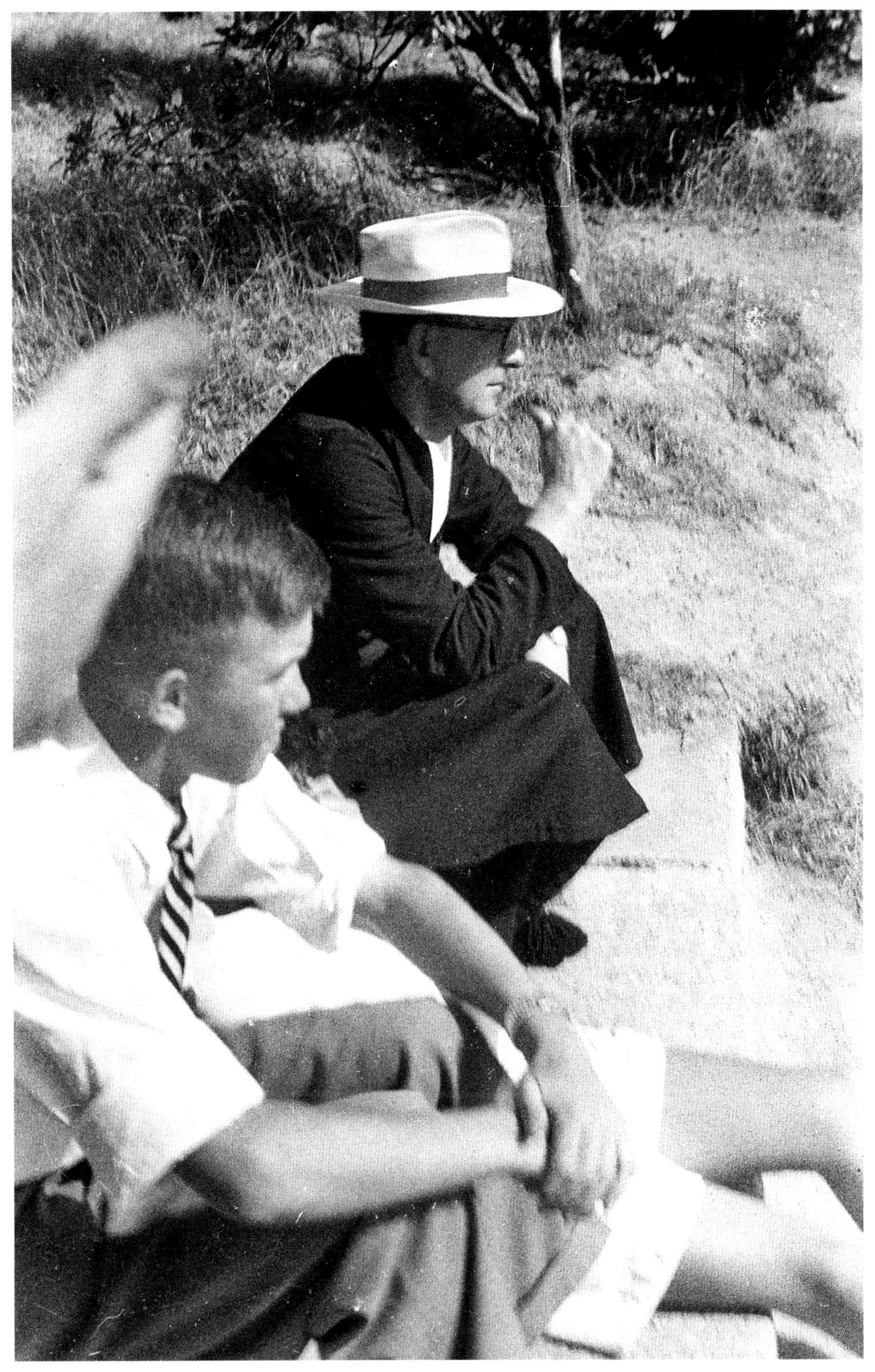

Sports fields, St Joseph's Marist College. In the background the British Union Jack is visible. In the 1950s it was still flown alongside the South African national flag on official occasions.

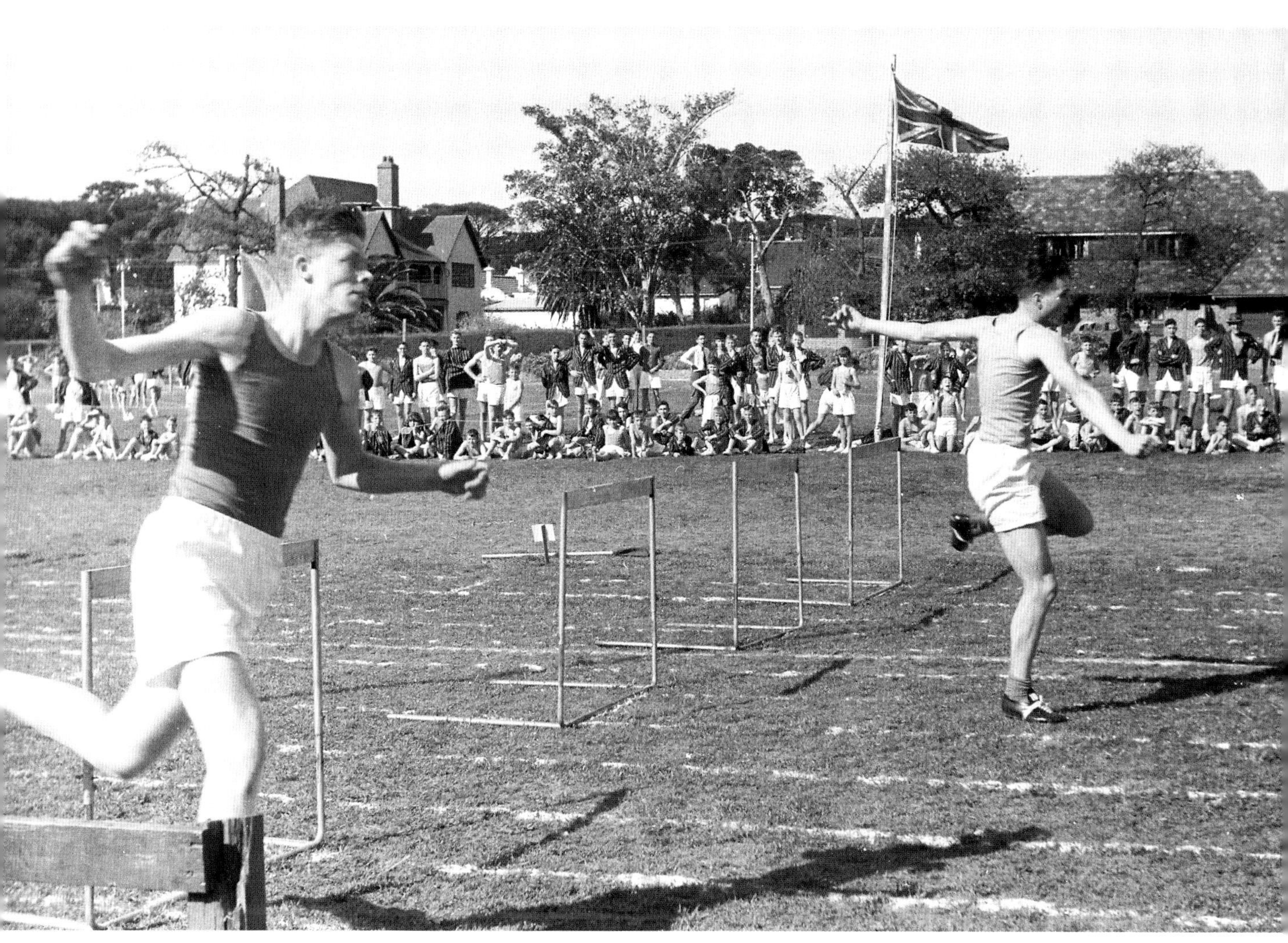

"The prospect of batting on a real pitch thrills him but fills him with fear too. He is particularly afraid of fast bowlers: afraid of being struck, afraid of pain. When he is playing real cricket he has to concentrate all his energies on not flinching, not giving himself away." (*Boyhood*, p.145)

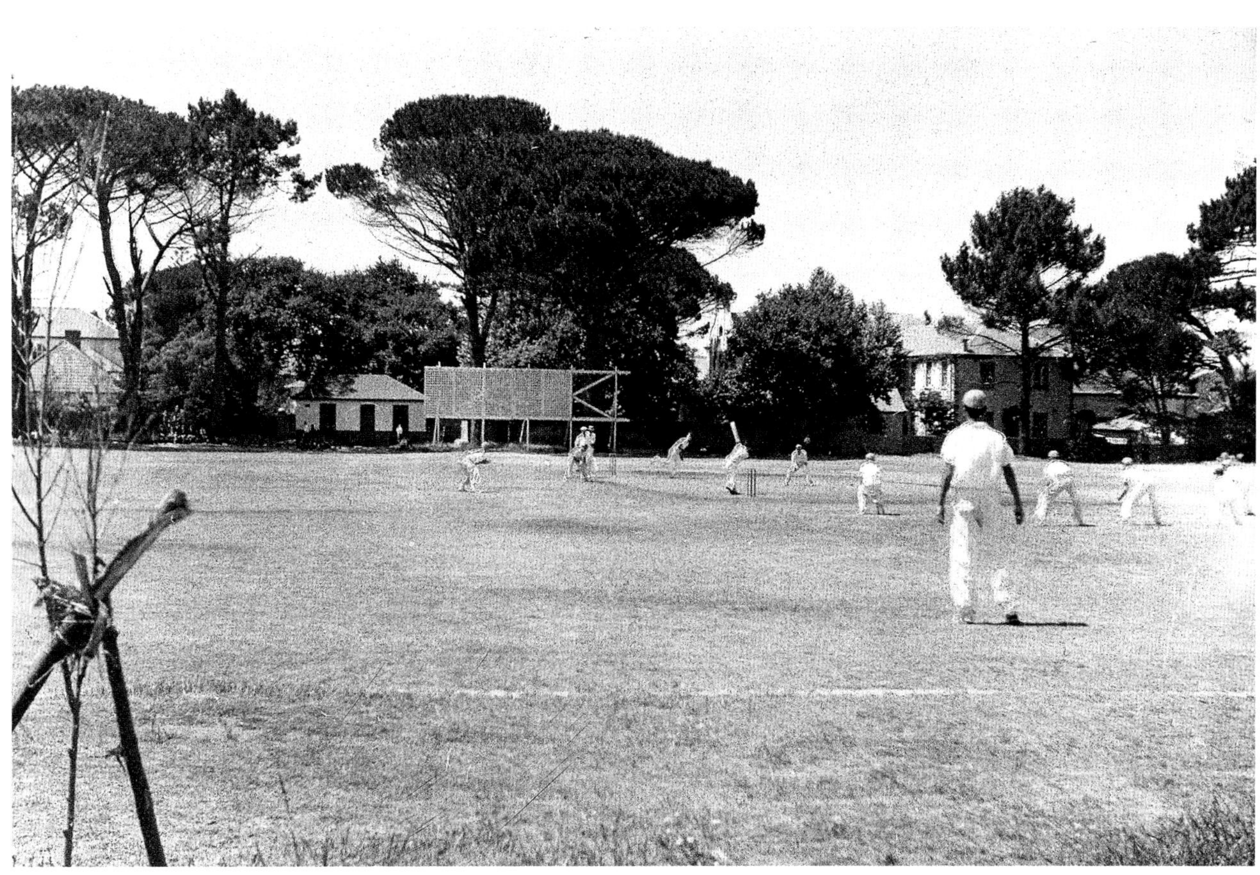

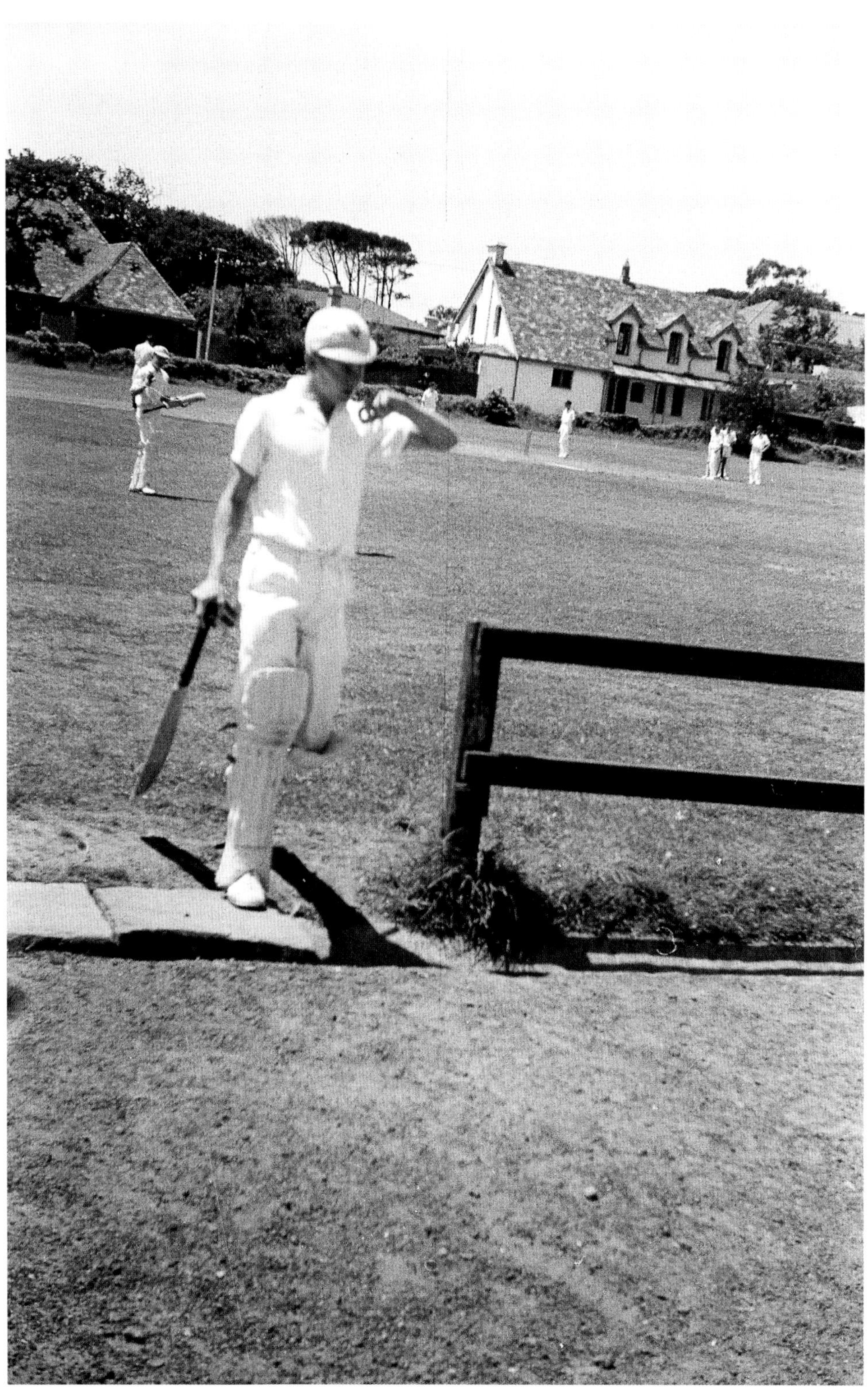

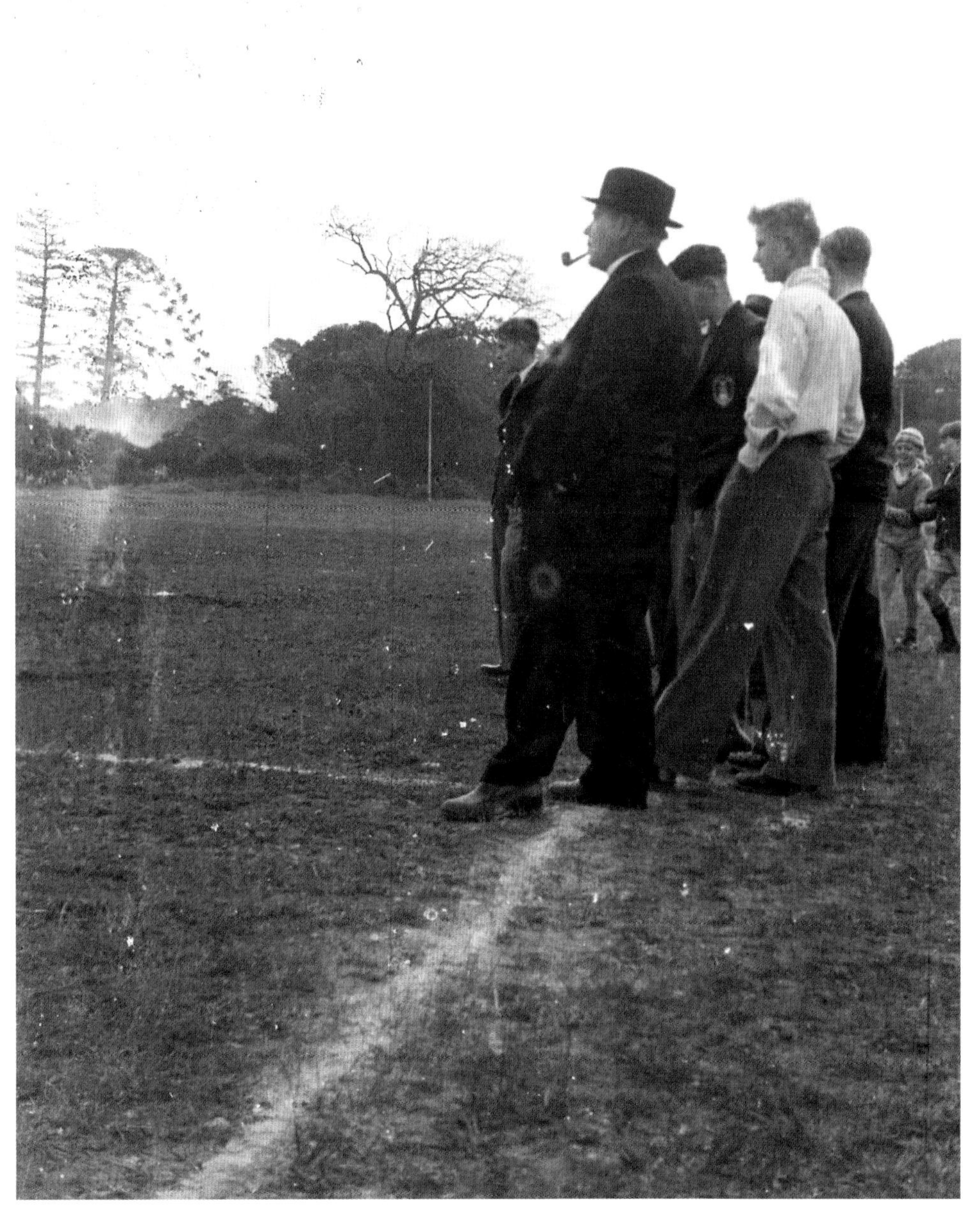

136   Rugby games at St Joseph's. The first two photographs are of the school's
First XV rugby team, whose jerseys had a double gold band around the middle.
The third photograph is of an under-15 game.

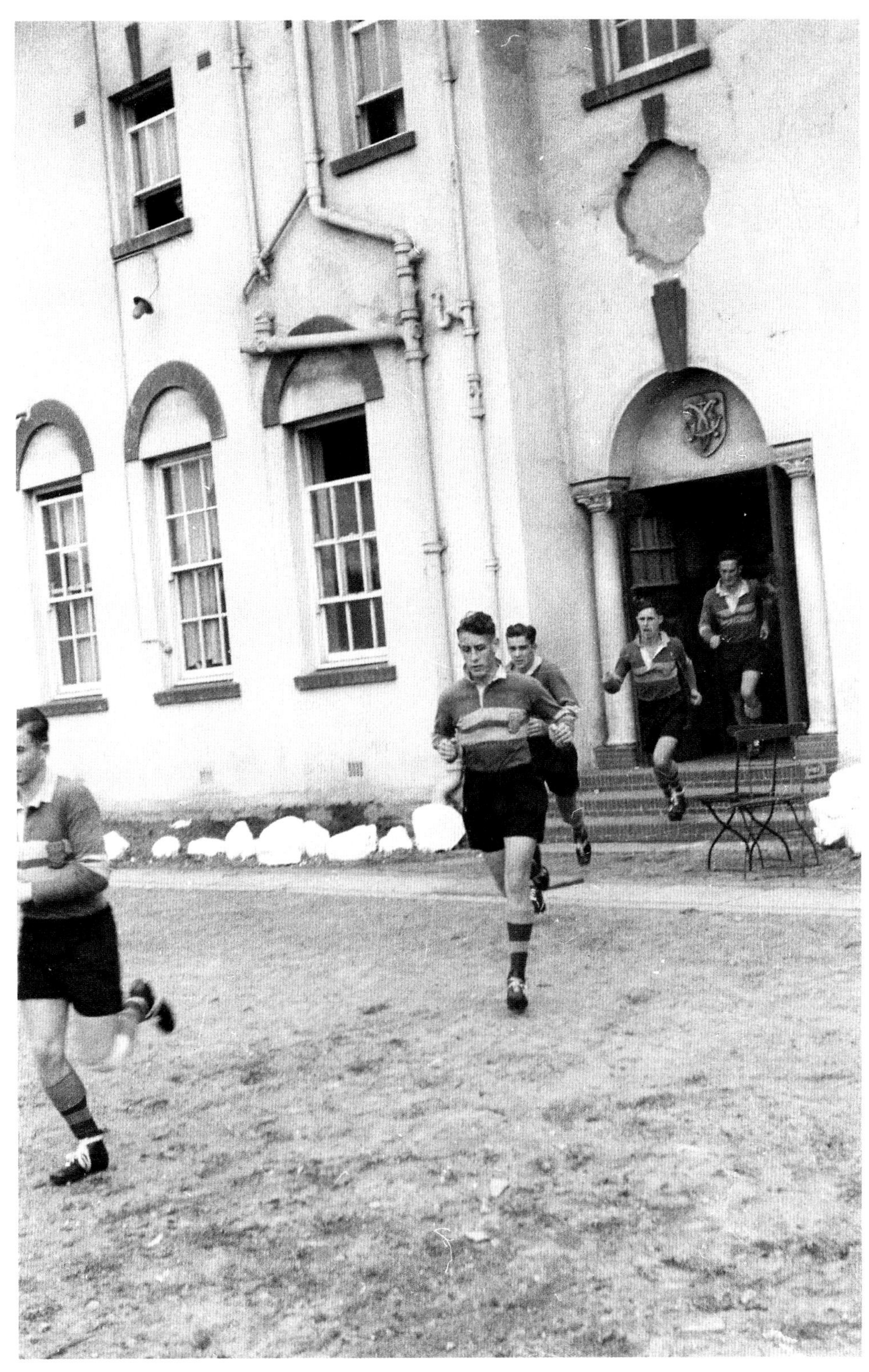

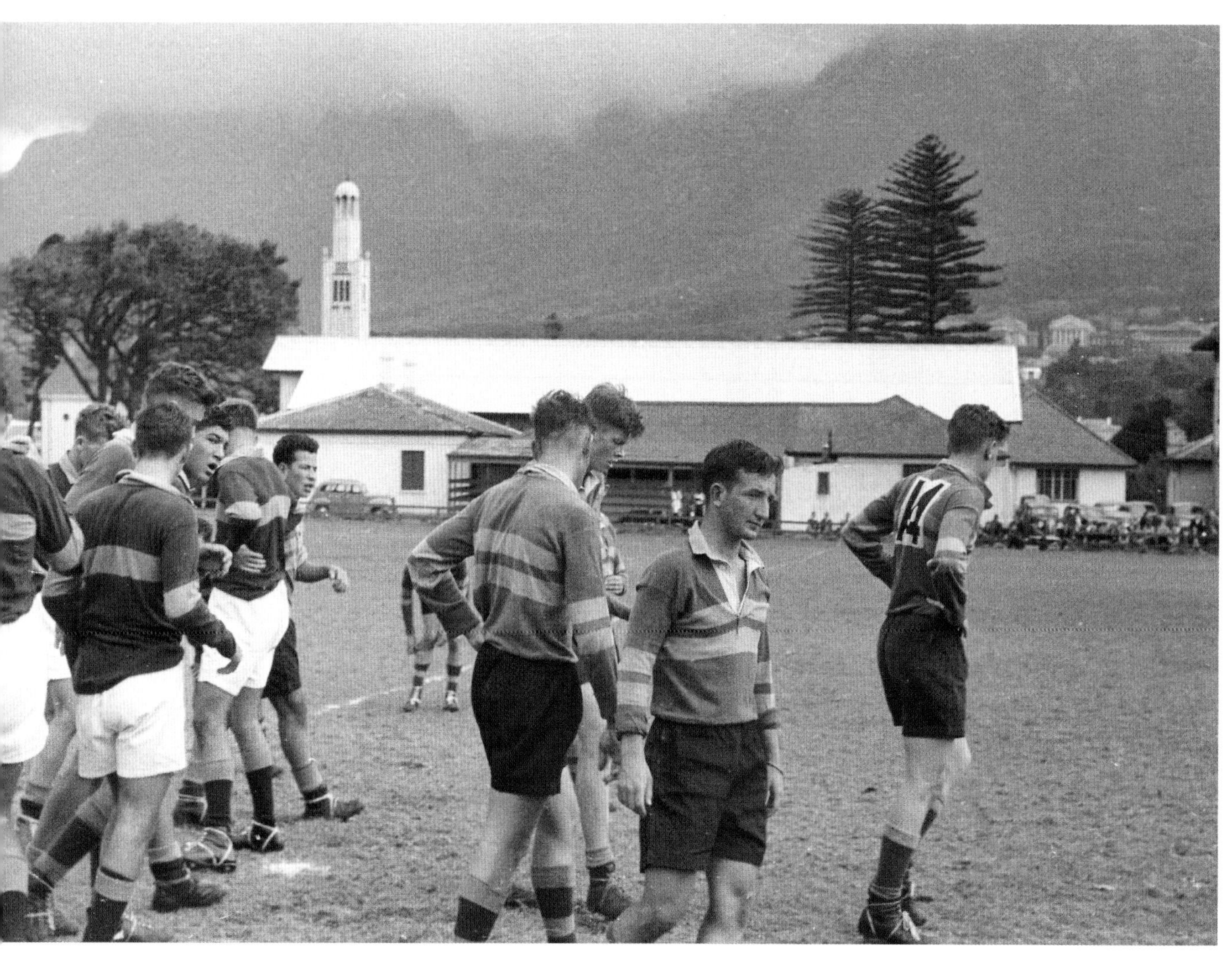

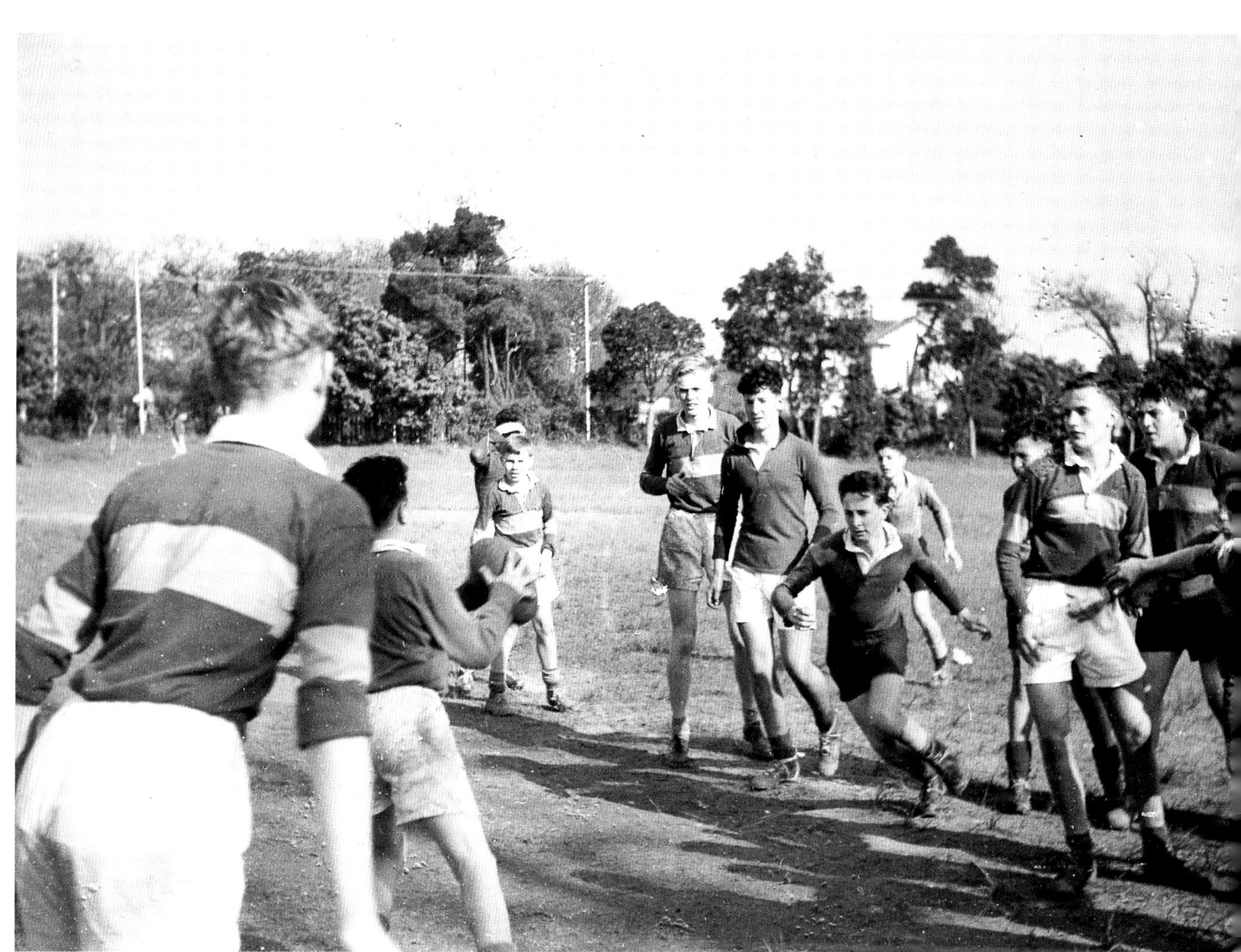

Experiments with Motion and Light

140   David Coetzee and Nic Stathakis. Shutter speeds on the Wega went up to 1/1000

of a second: almost professional.

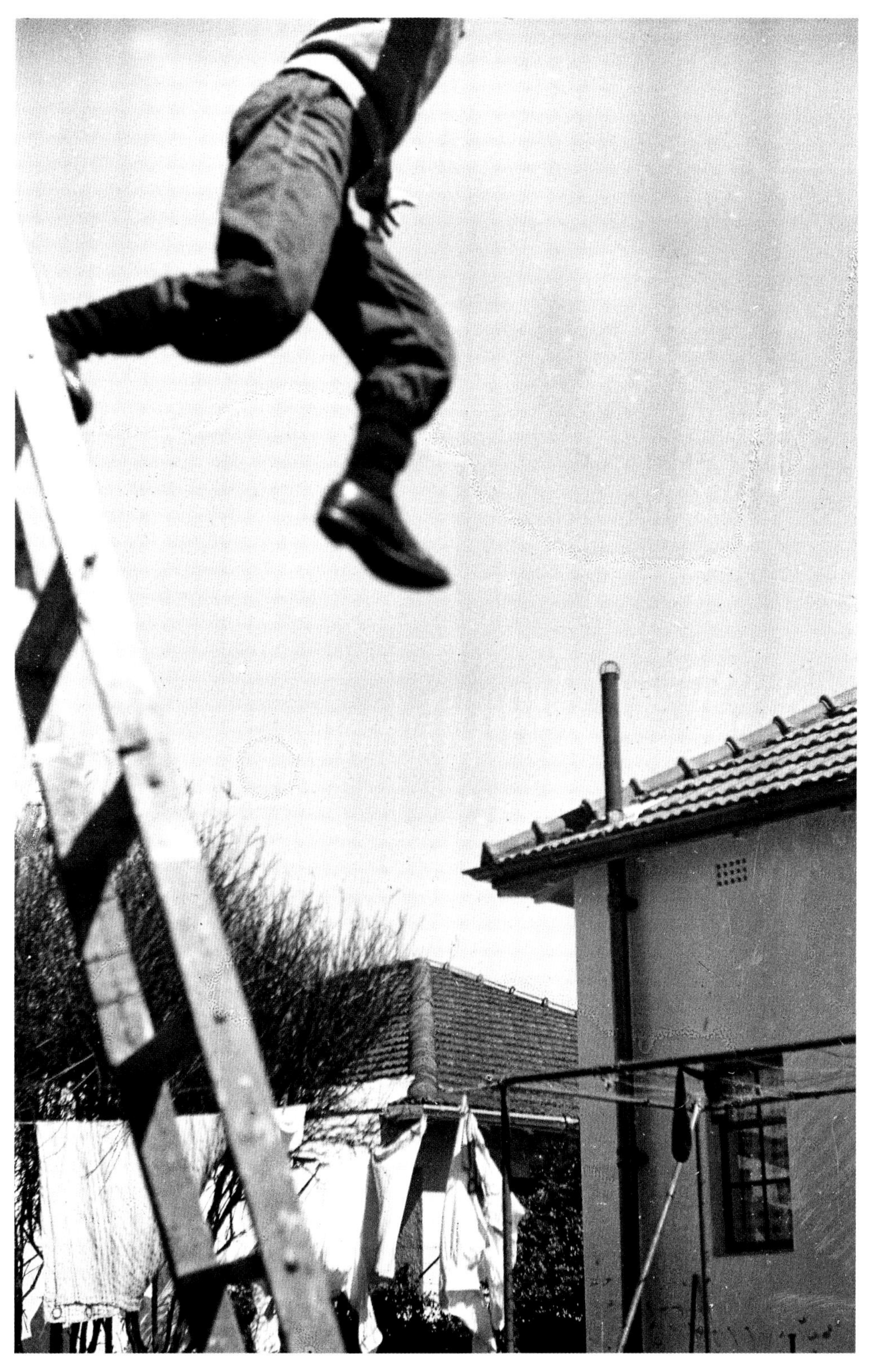

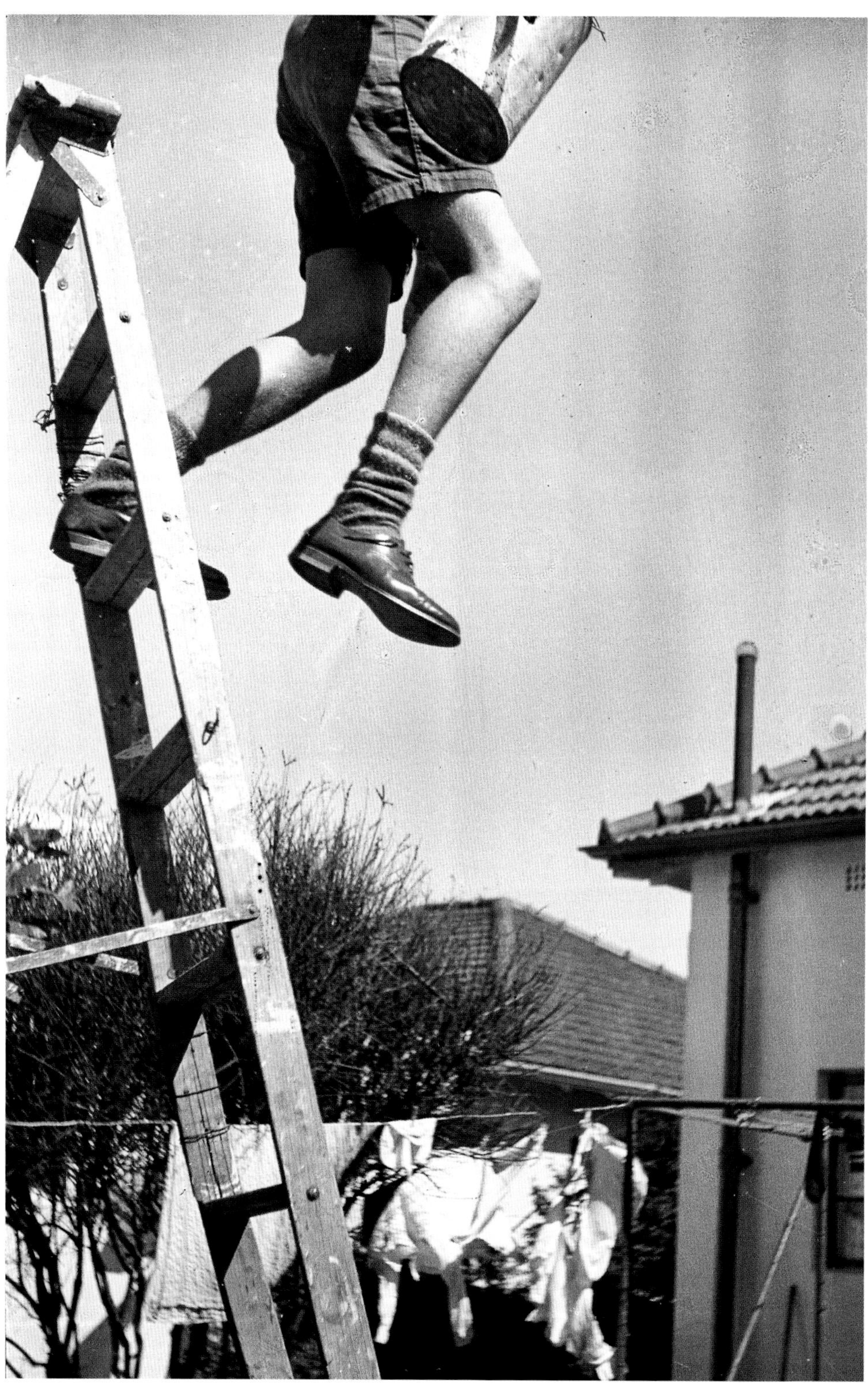

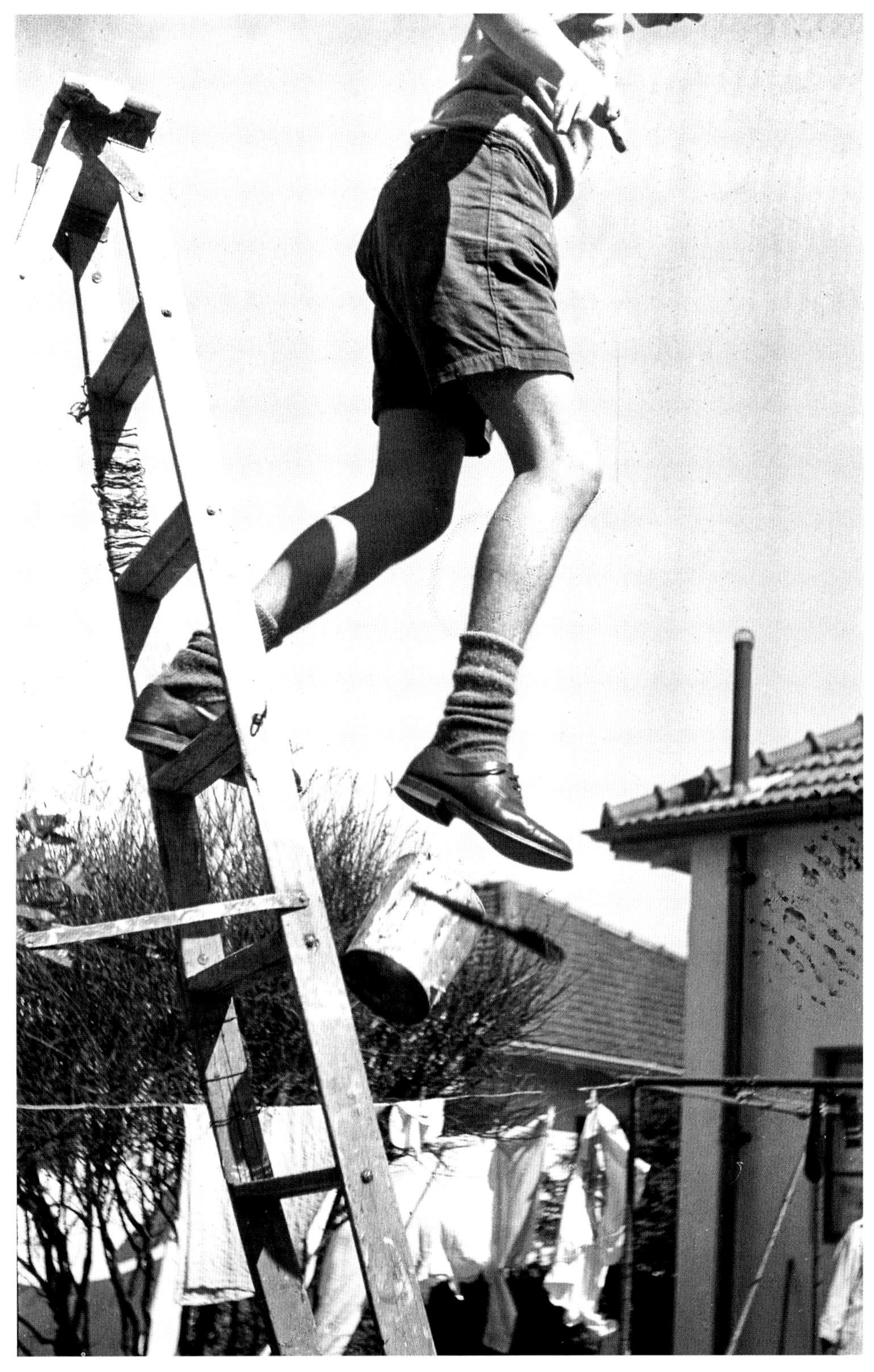

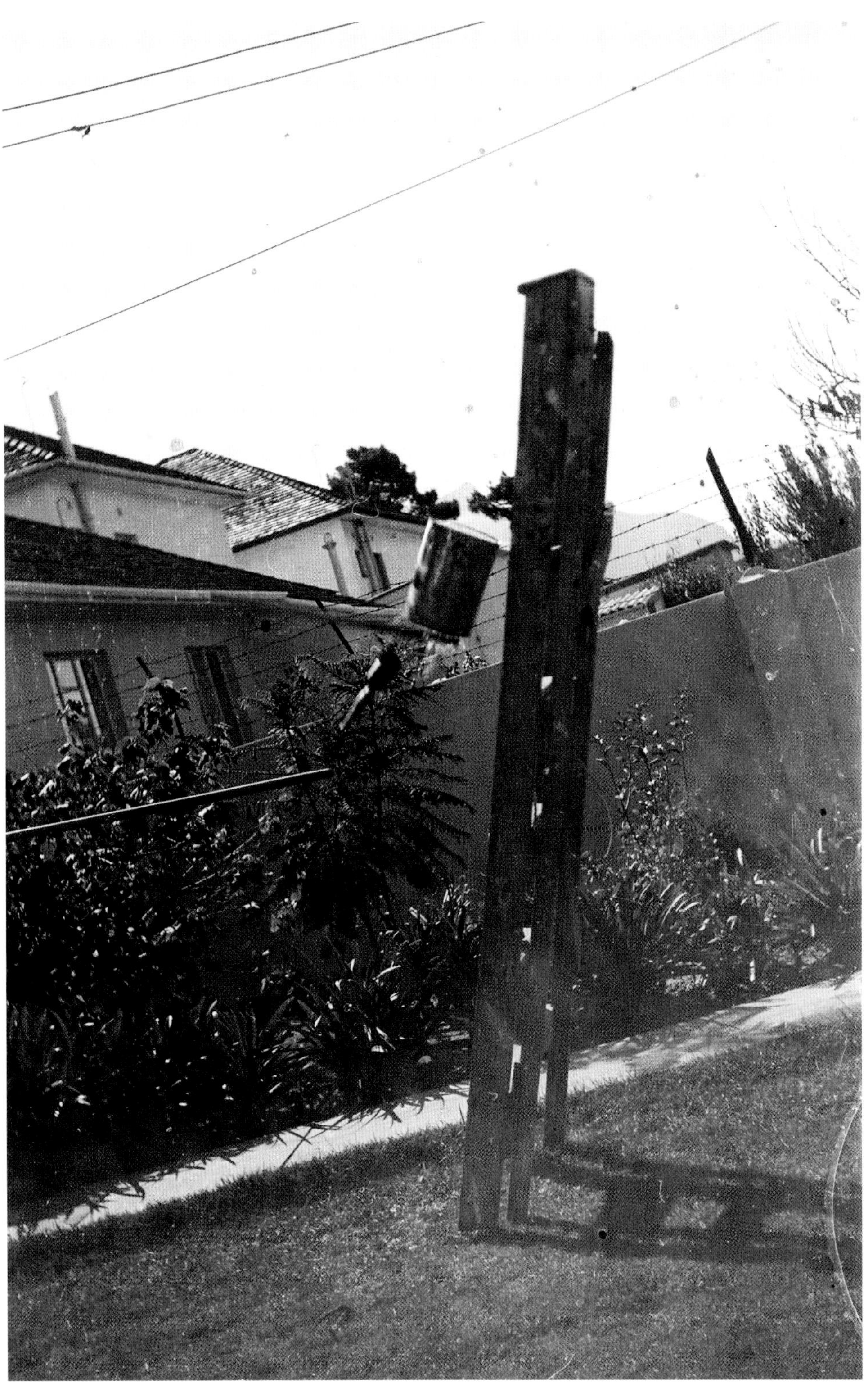

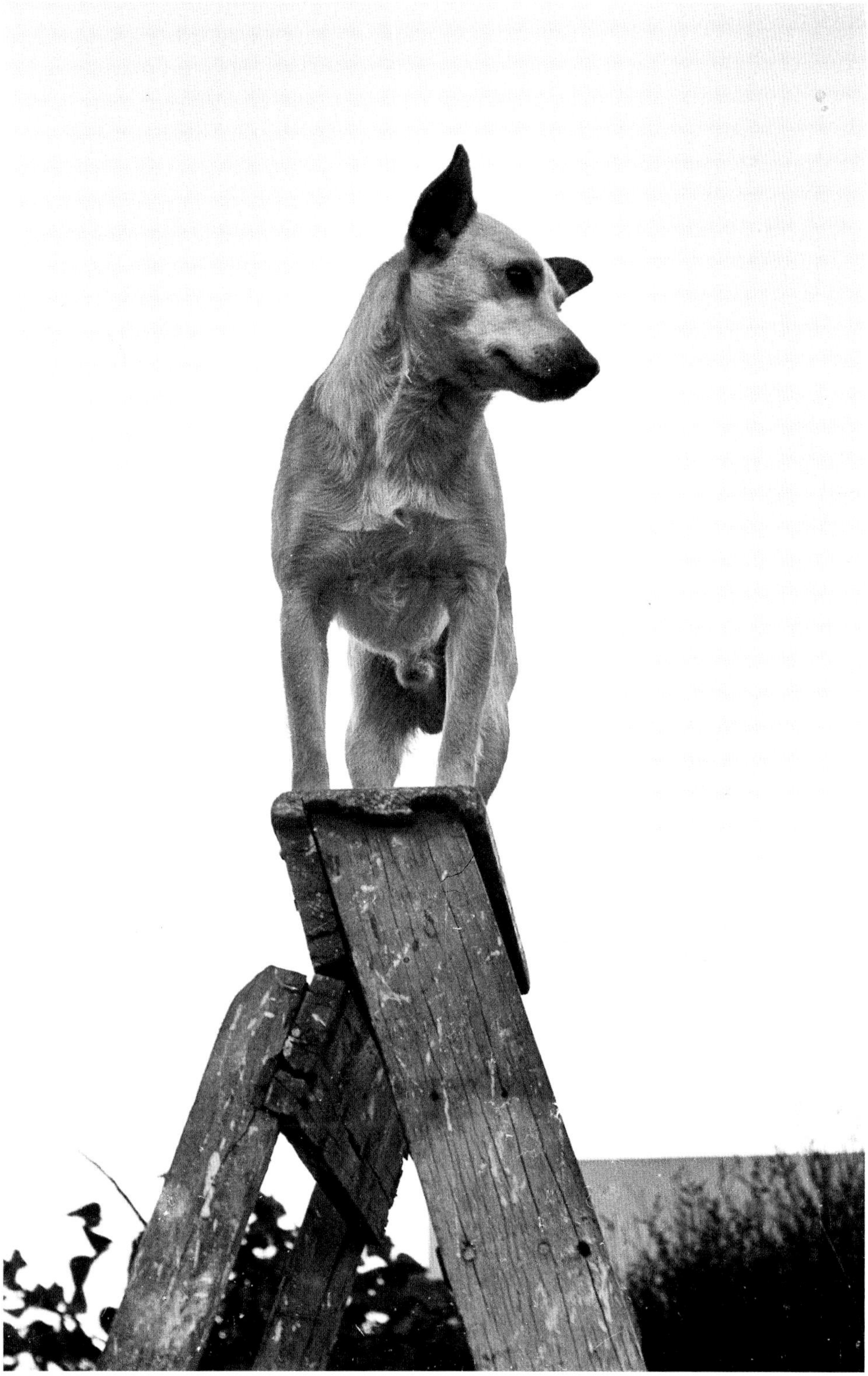

146   David Coetzee.

"There is nothing to match the elation of riding a bicycle, of leaning over and
swooping through curves." (*Boyhood*, p.55)

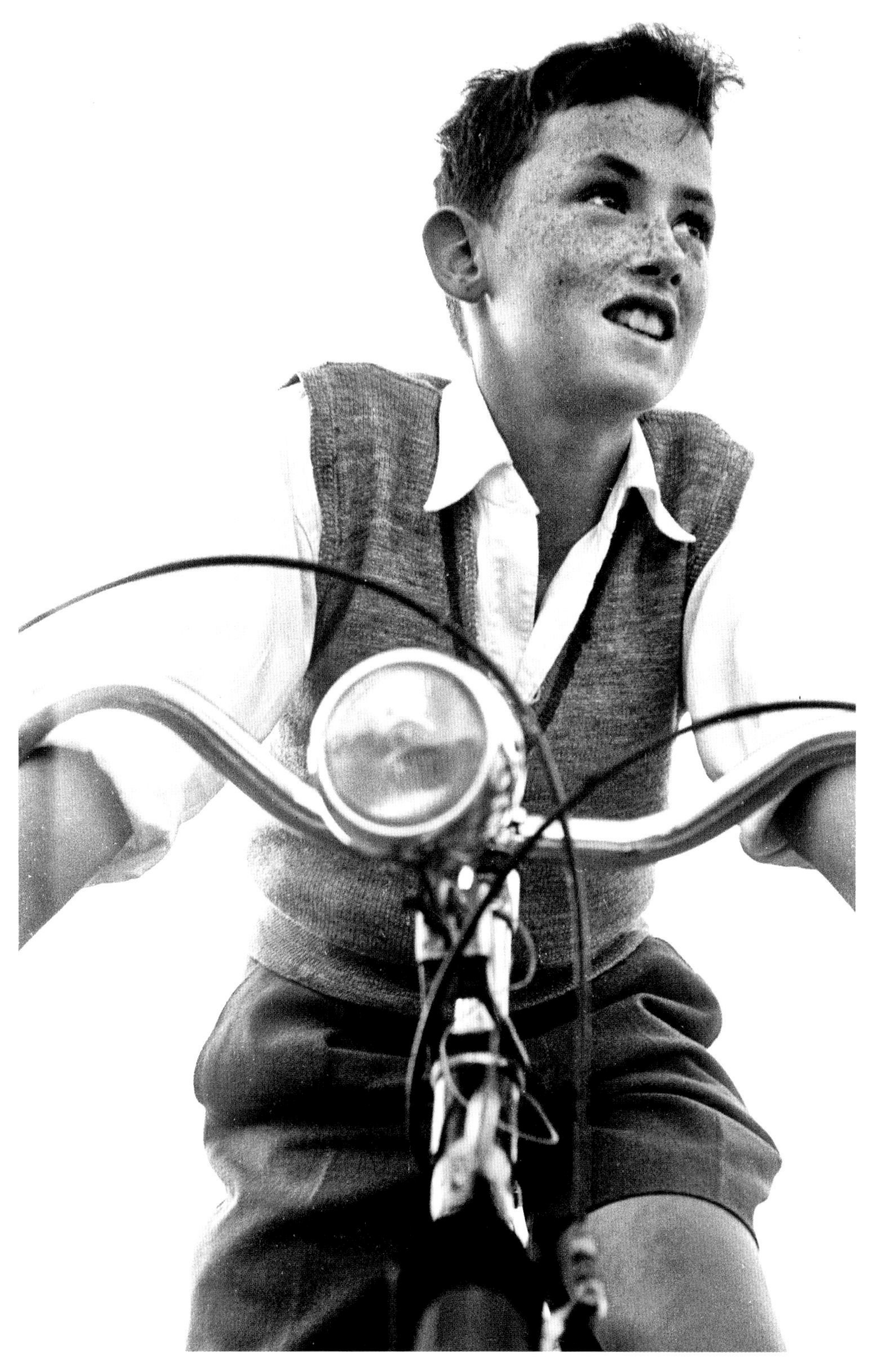

From these "experiments" in creating arcs of brilliant light I would emerge with a grey haze clouding my vision.

"John developed into a competent photographer and acquired a small camera, firmly convinced that it was intended for espionage. He converted a spare room into a darkroom to develop his photographs. Nic Stathakis, the friend who had been at school with him in Rosebank, now re-entered his life. Stathakis would recall, many years later, how they had between classes mischievously taken photos in secret of teachers and schoolfellows, and how they had one day almost blinded themselves by experimenting with sparks between two live wires."
(J.C. Kannemeyer, *JM Coetzee. A Life in Writing*, p. 62-63)

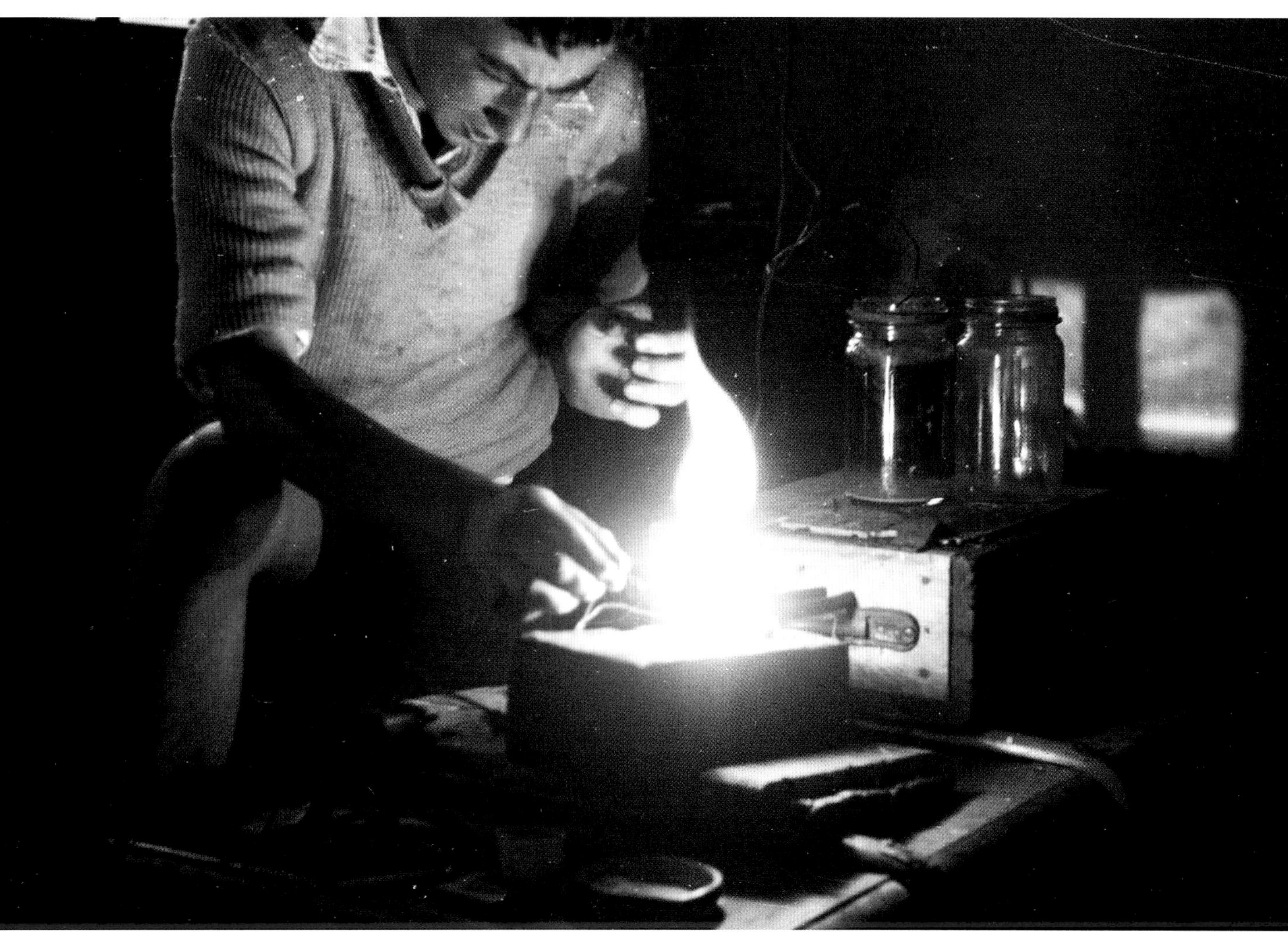

150   I photographed these strangers whizzing past (on the road up to the Rhodes

Memorial) by swinging the camera to follow them, so that the background

comes out blurred.

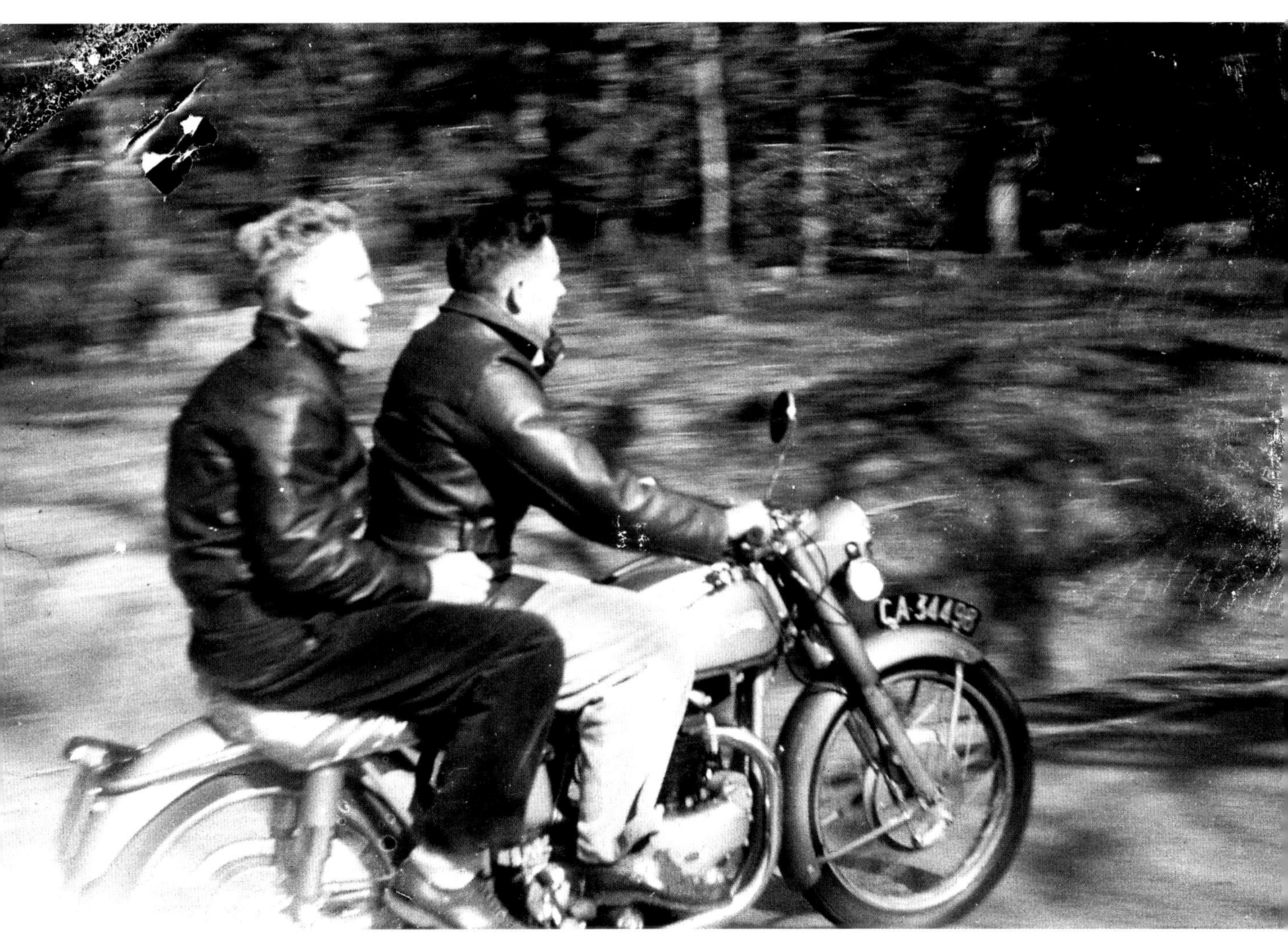

152   These photographs were taken at someone else's home. I had no particular

interest in the aeroplanes; I was there to photograph the models as if they were

flying in the air.

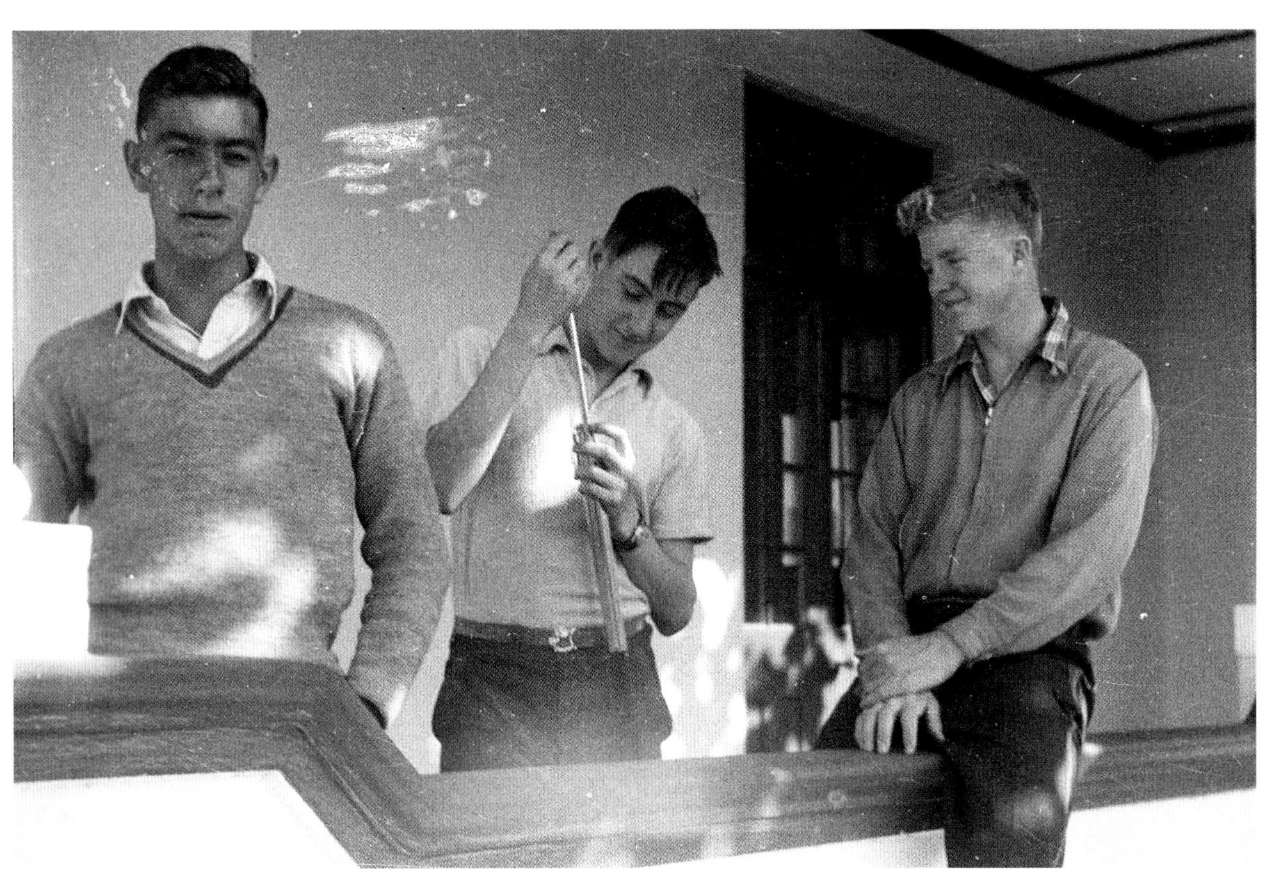

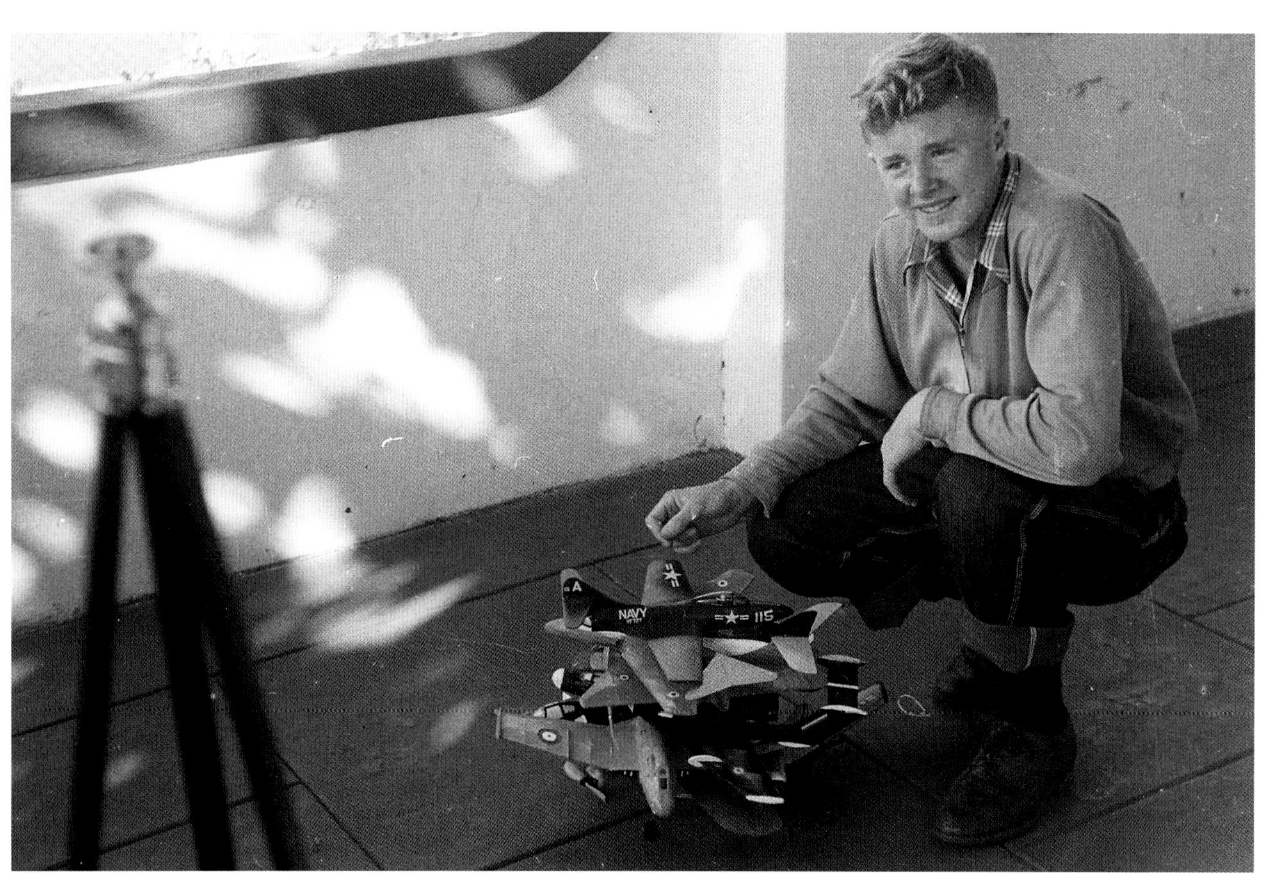

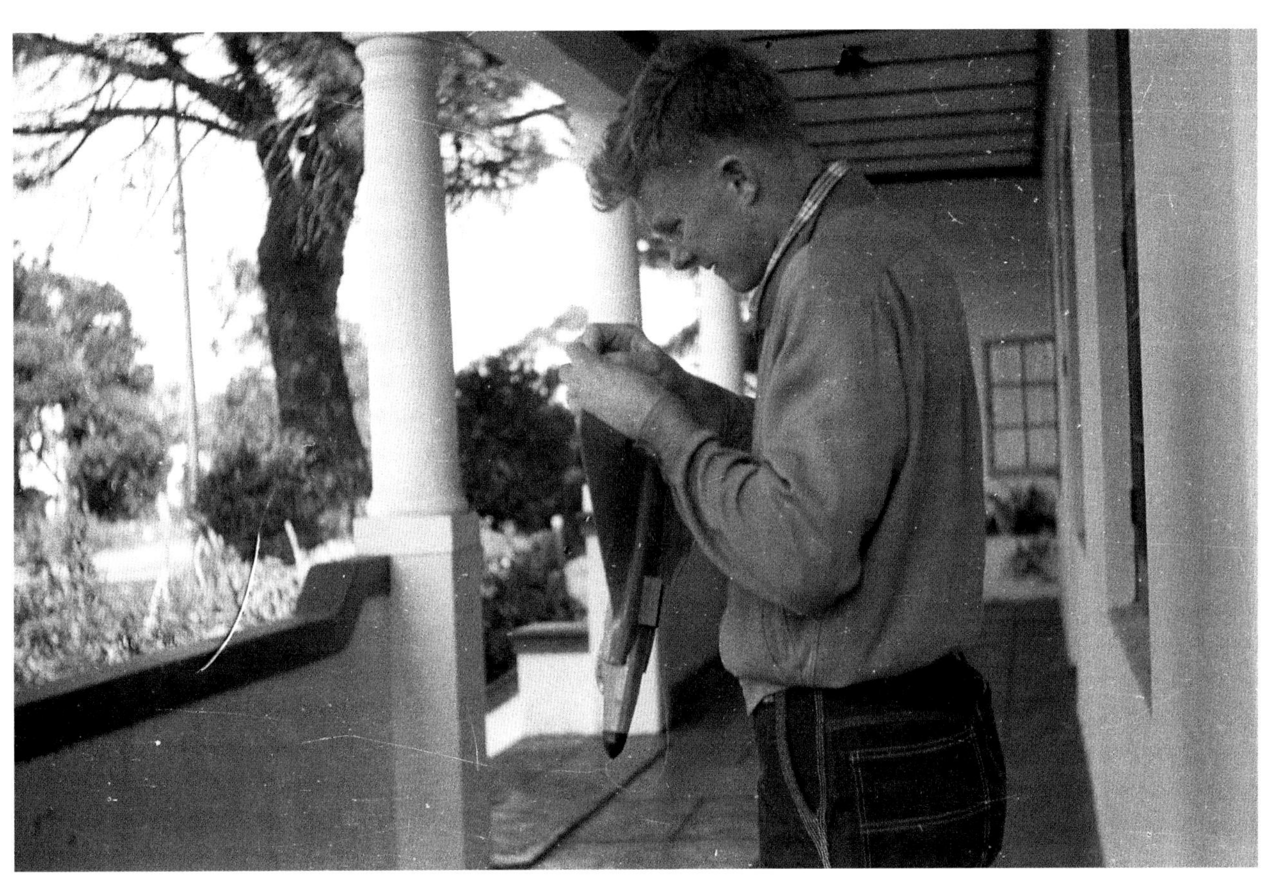

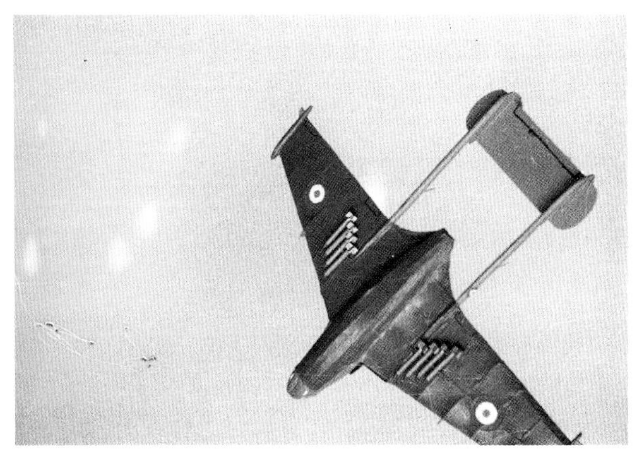
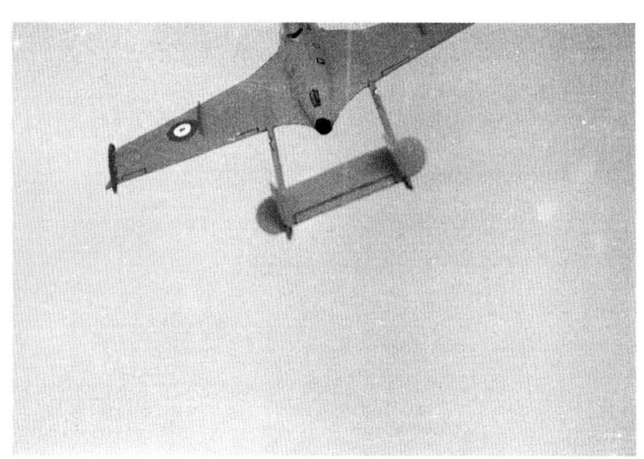
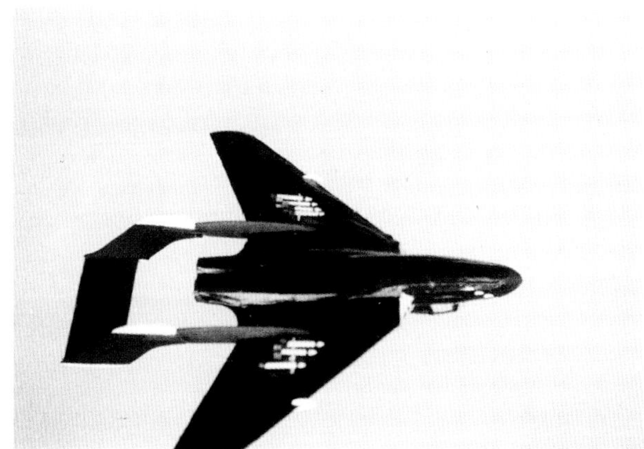
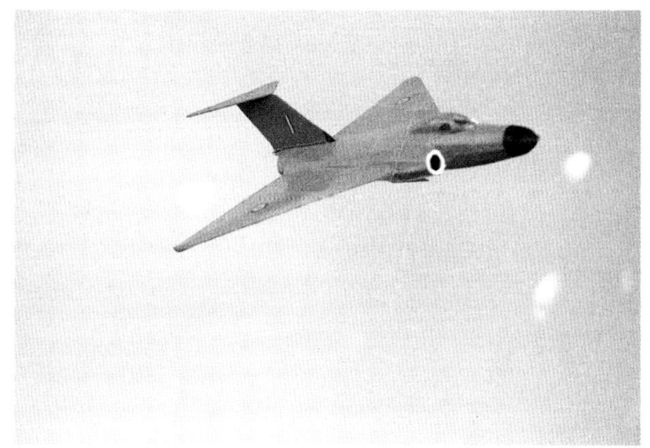

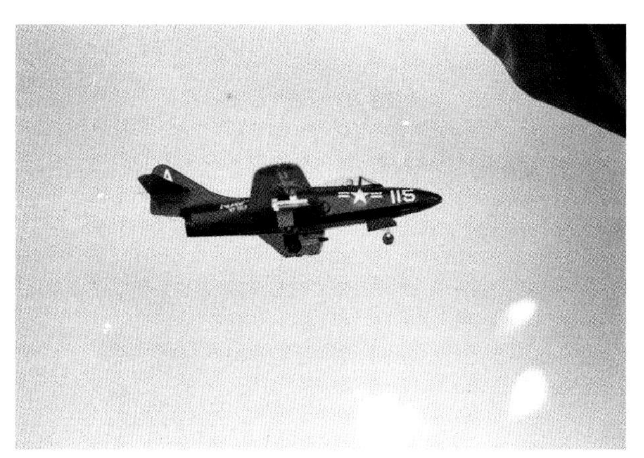

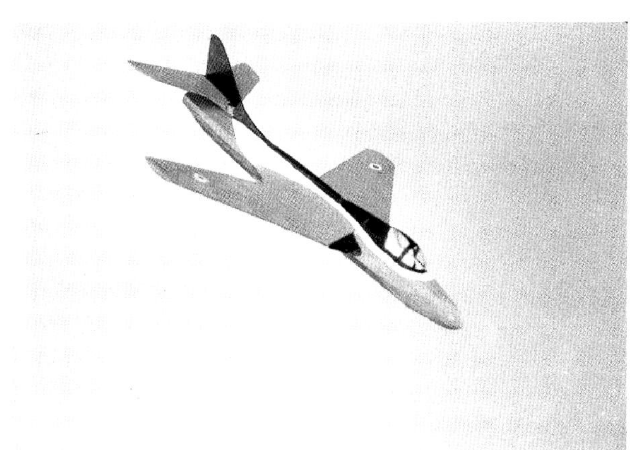

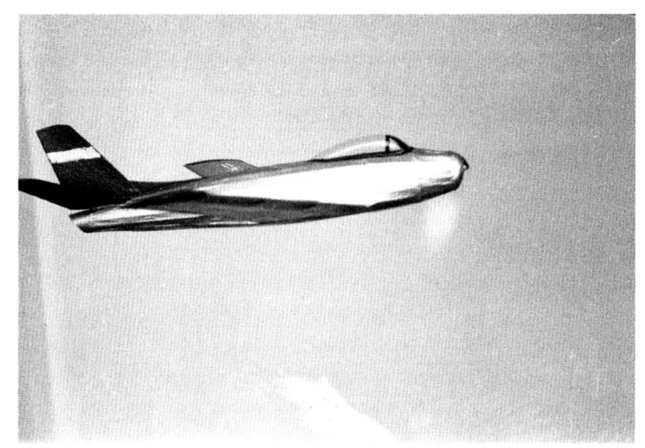

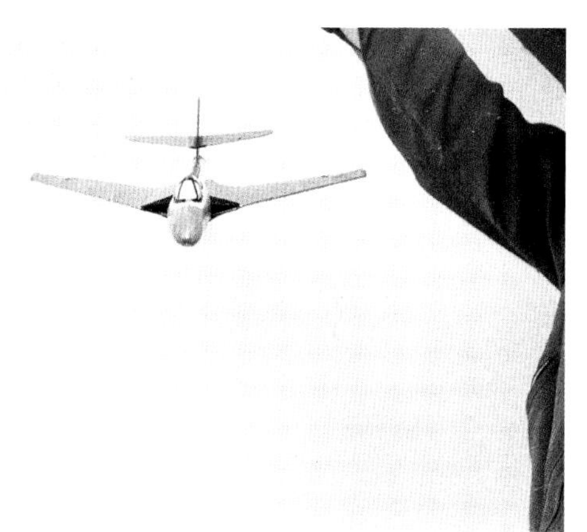

158   Main Road, Plumstead. Following pages: the construction of the Liesbeek canal in Rosebank.

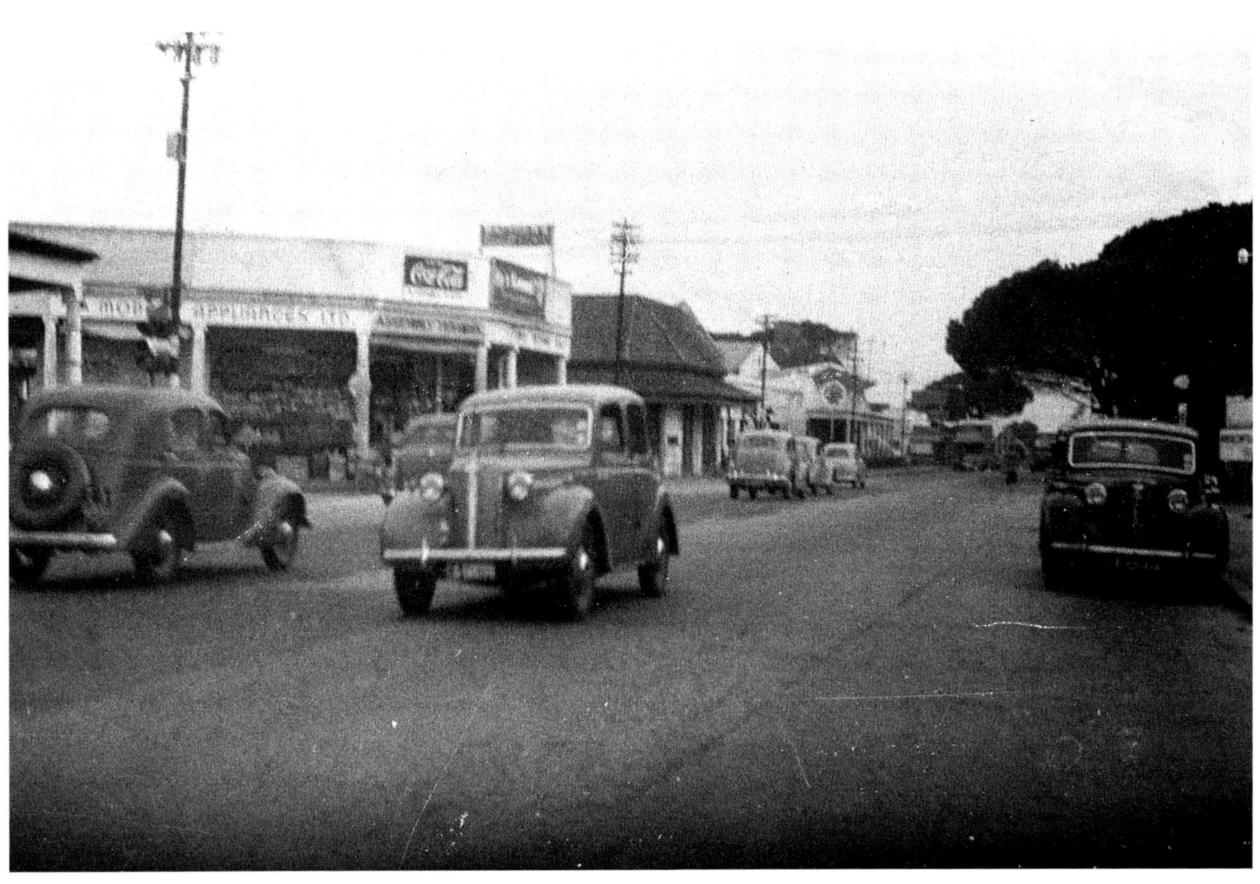

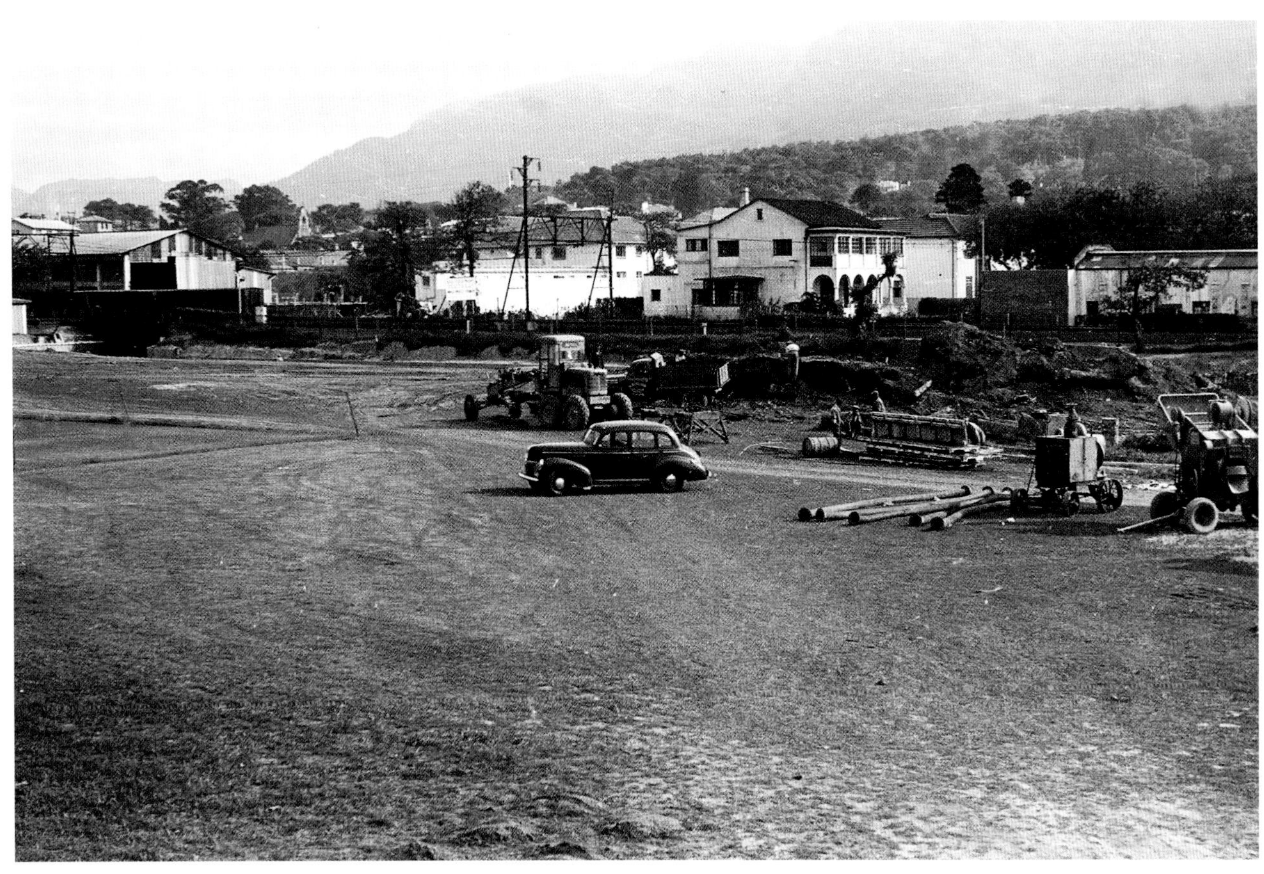

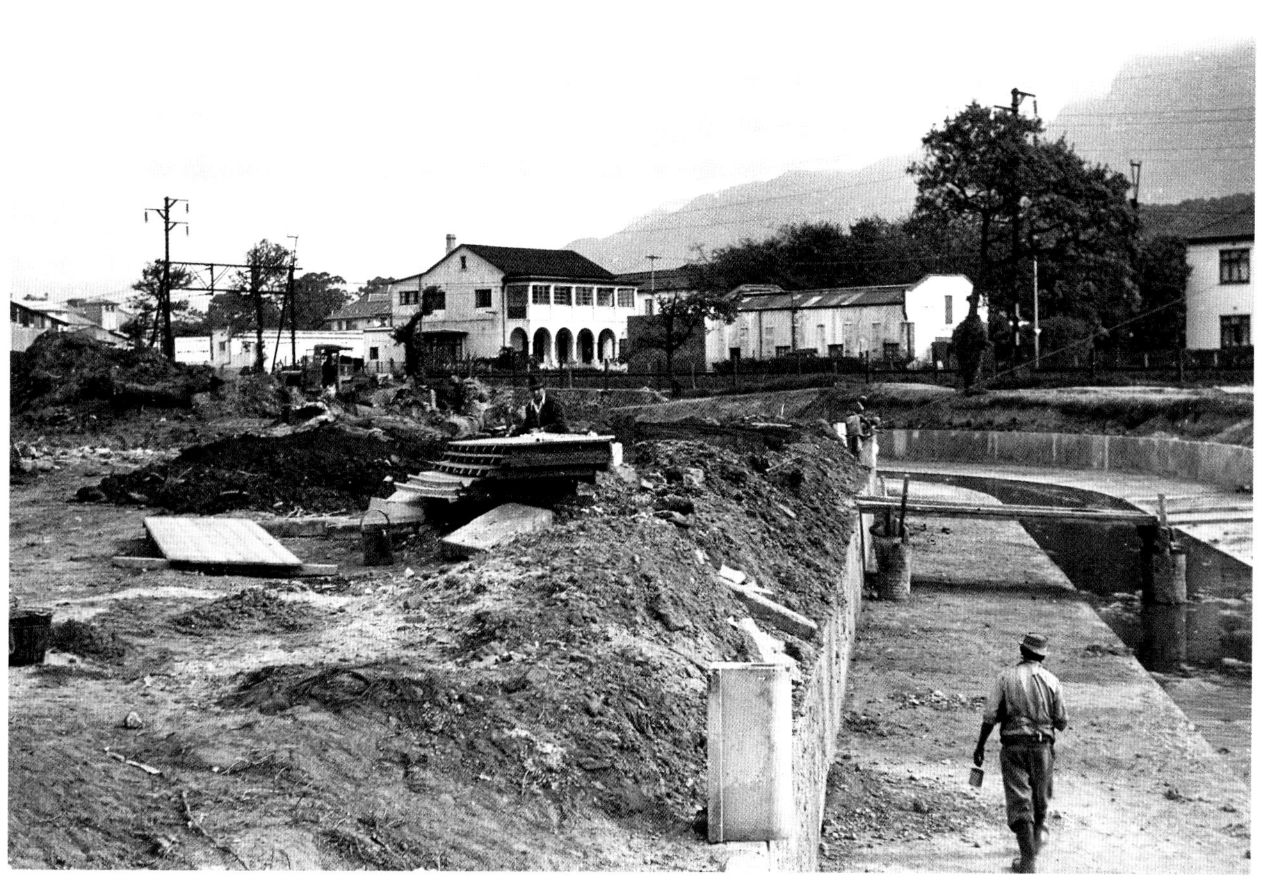

162   Taken from a train window on the suburban line between Salt River and
Cape Town.

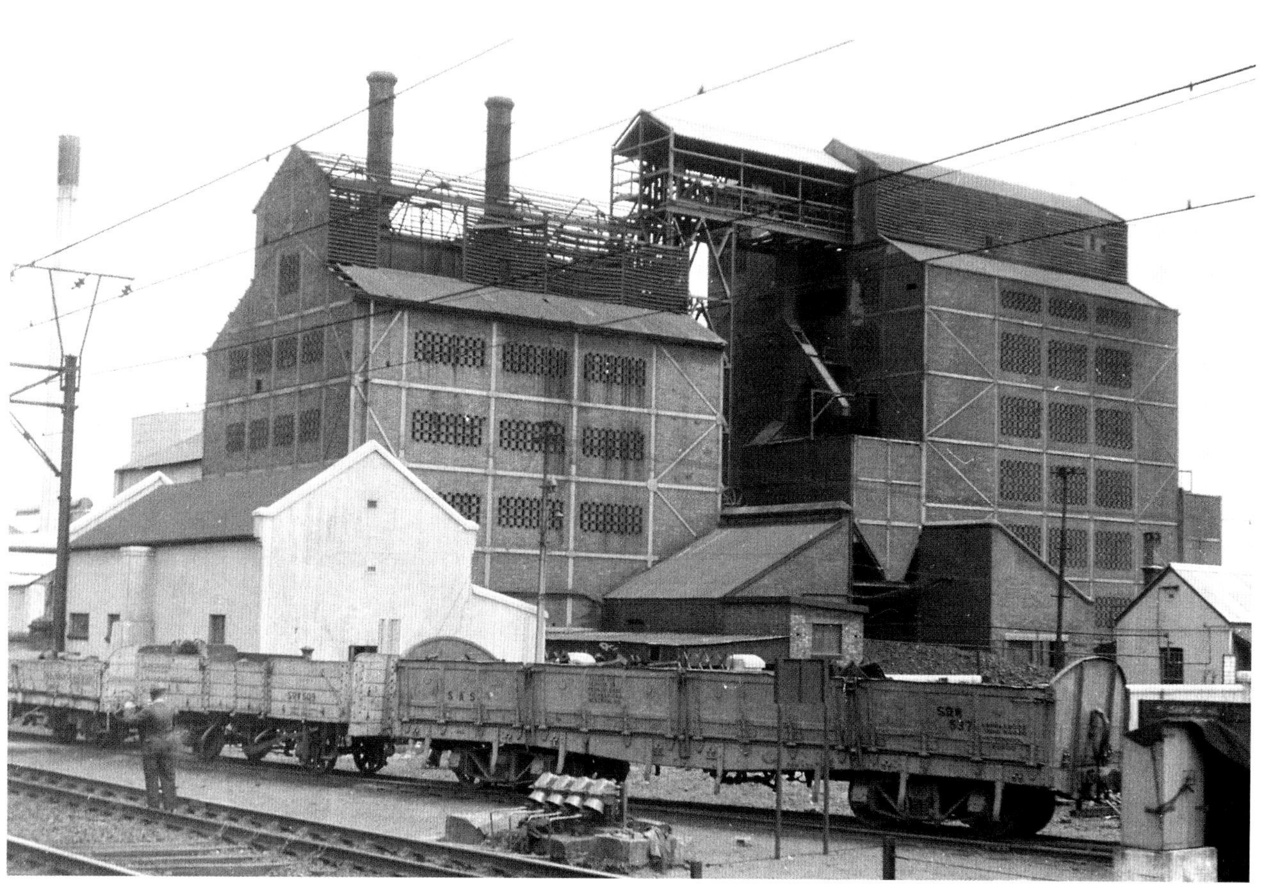

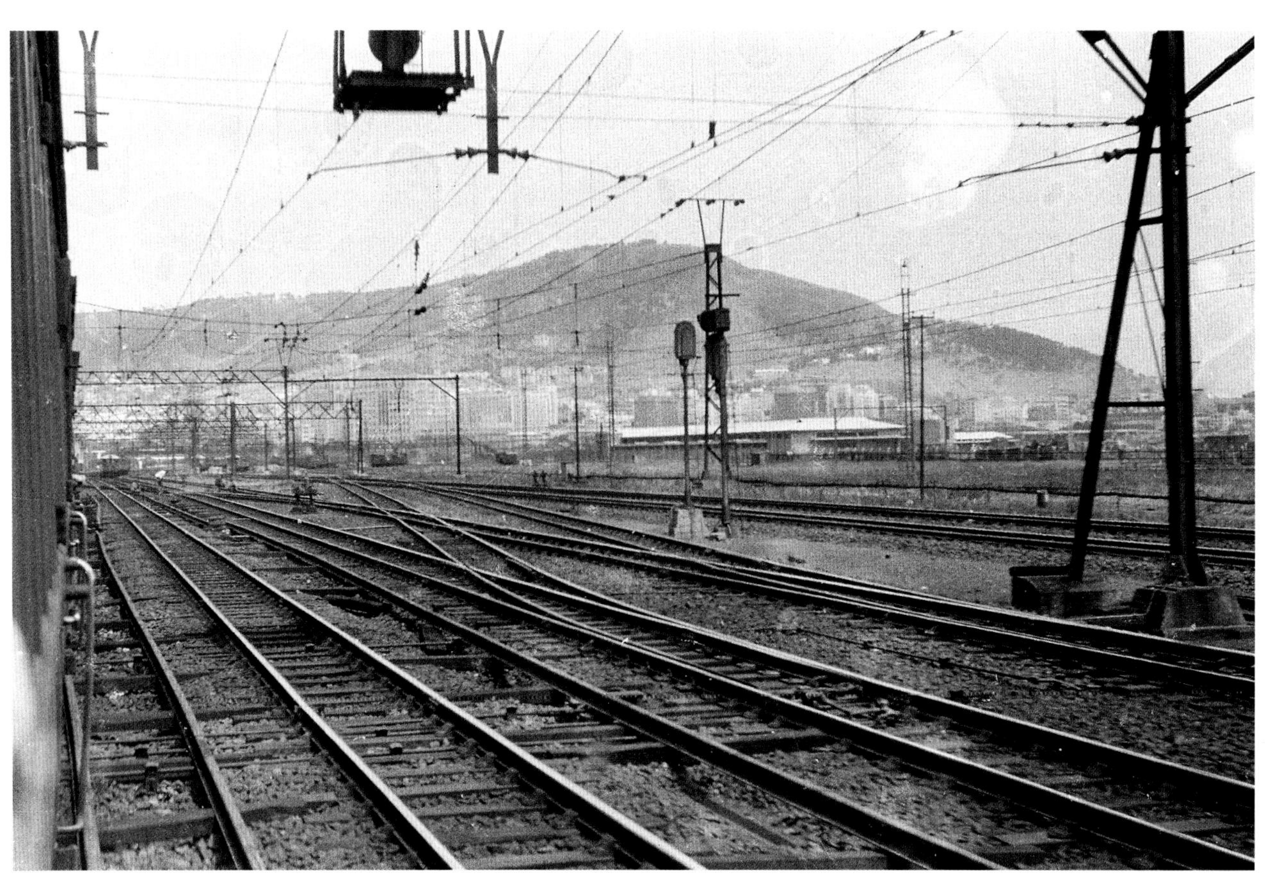

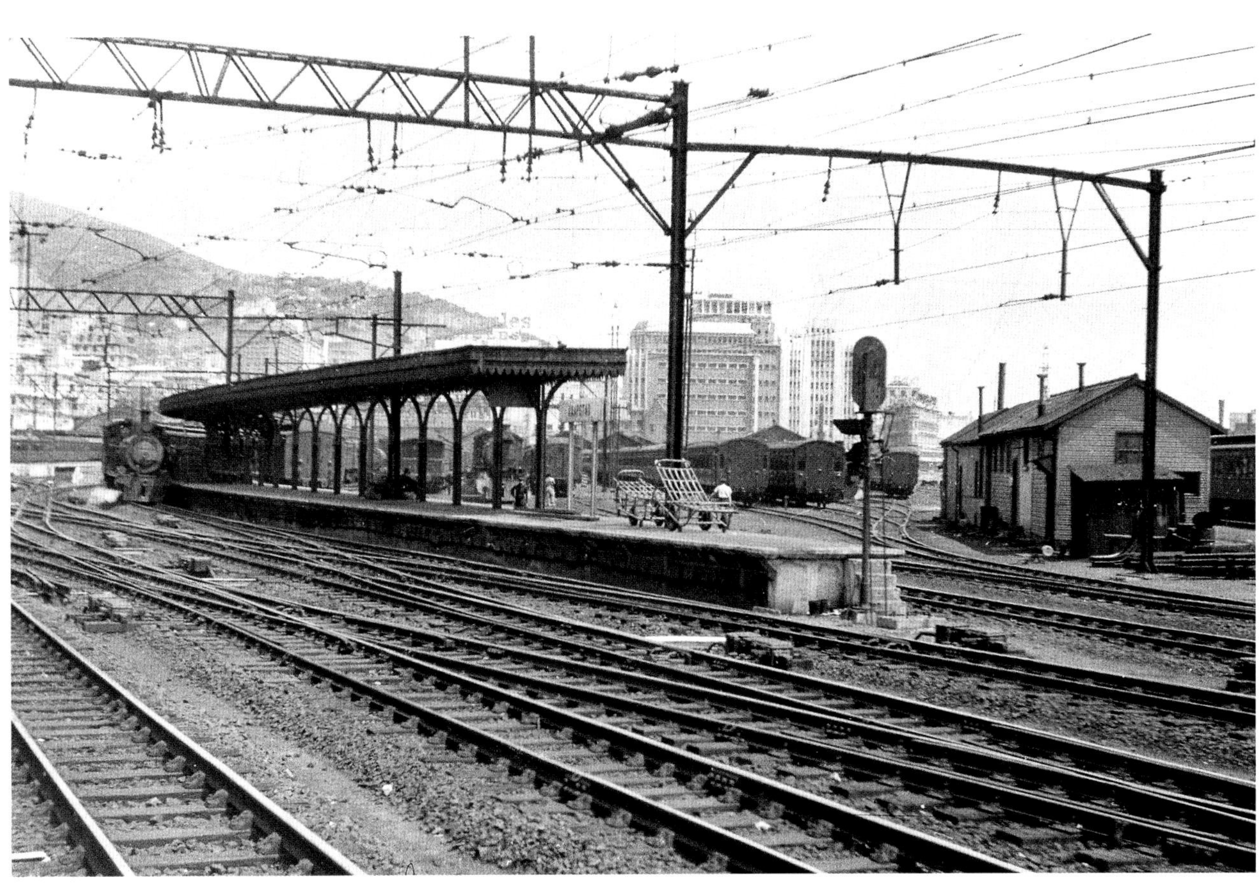

166   Along the False Bay coast between Muizenberg and Fish Hoek, taken during
winter.

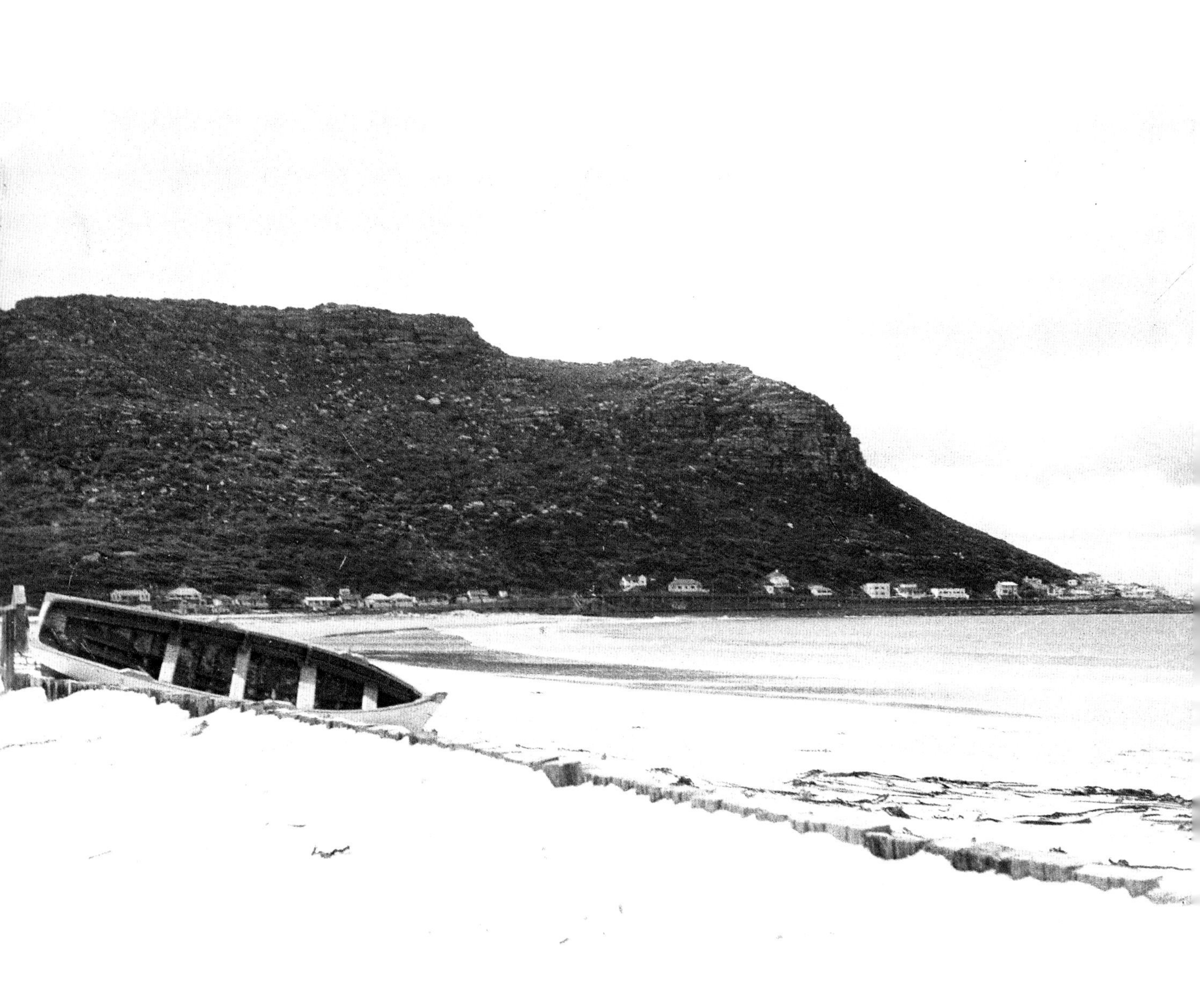

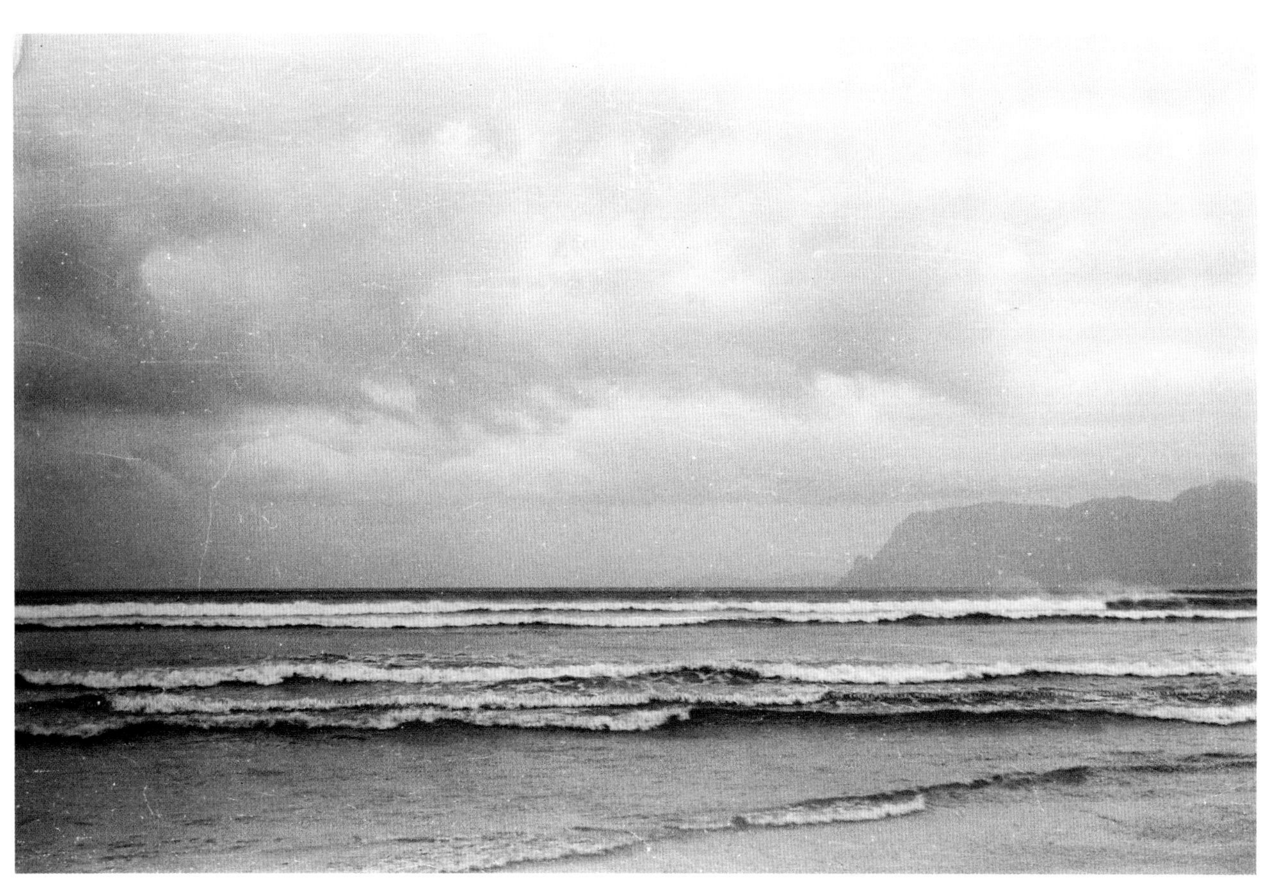

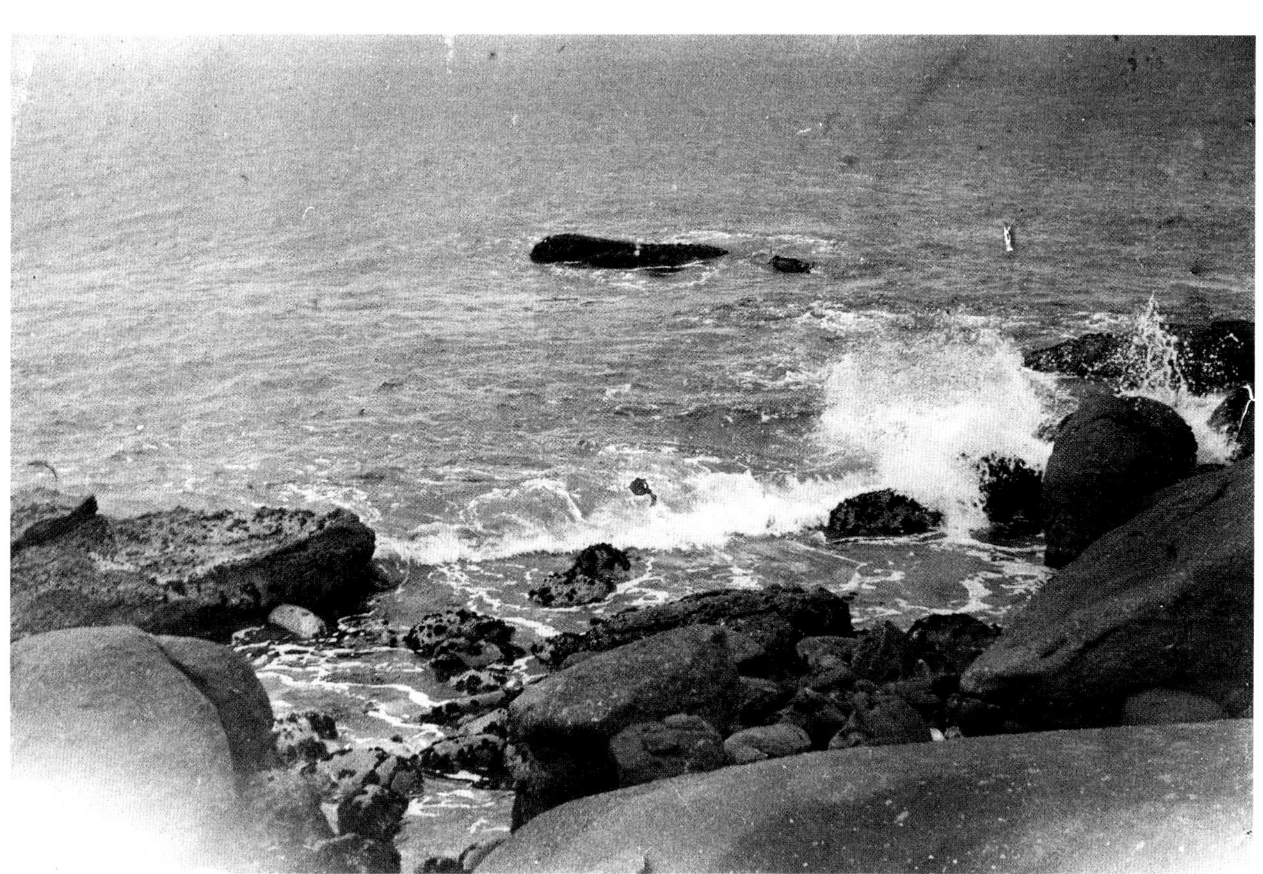

4

Remembering Photography

Interview with Hermann Wittenberg,
13 March 2017

HW: How did you come to photography? Was your mother, the family photographer, your first teacher? What cameras did you use?

JMC: *My mother bought a box camera before she and her brother went on their European tour in (I think) 1936. She recorded the Europe she saw in photographs which she later stuck in an album. Then, after her children arrived (1940, 1943), she documented their growth in photographs which in due course made up further albums. So taking pictures was part of our family culture, as it was of many other middle-class families. Through photo albums, families constructed a history for themselves, a past.*

HW: I am interested in the period of your life when you acquired an enlarger and set up your own darkroom. You would have invested considerable time (and pocket money) in photography. Is this the time when you got the Wega 35mm camera? What attracted you to pursuing photography seriously as a hobby?

JMC: *I bought my own first camera by mail order. It was a novelty, advertised as the sort of camera that spies used. It took images about 15 mm x 15 mm which had to be enlarged. There was only one shop in Cape Town that stocked film for it.*

The Wega cost me about forty pounds, much less than the Leica of which it was a copy. Buying the Wega plus darkroom equipment marked the moment when I began to take photographs "seriously." What drew me to photography? I am not in a position to diagnose the deeper reasons. Let me just say that in the 1950s "serious" photography carried considerable cultural cachet. It was also a manly activity, in contrast to such effeminate activities as composing poetry or playing the piano.

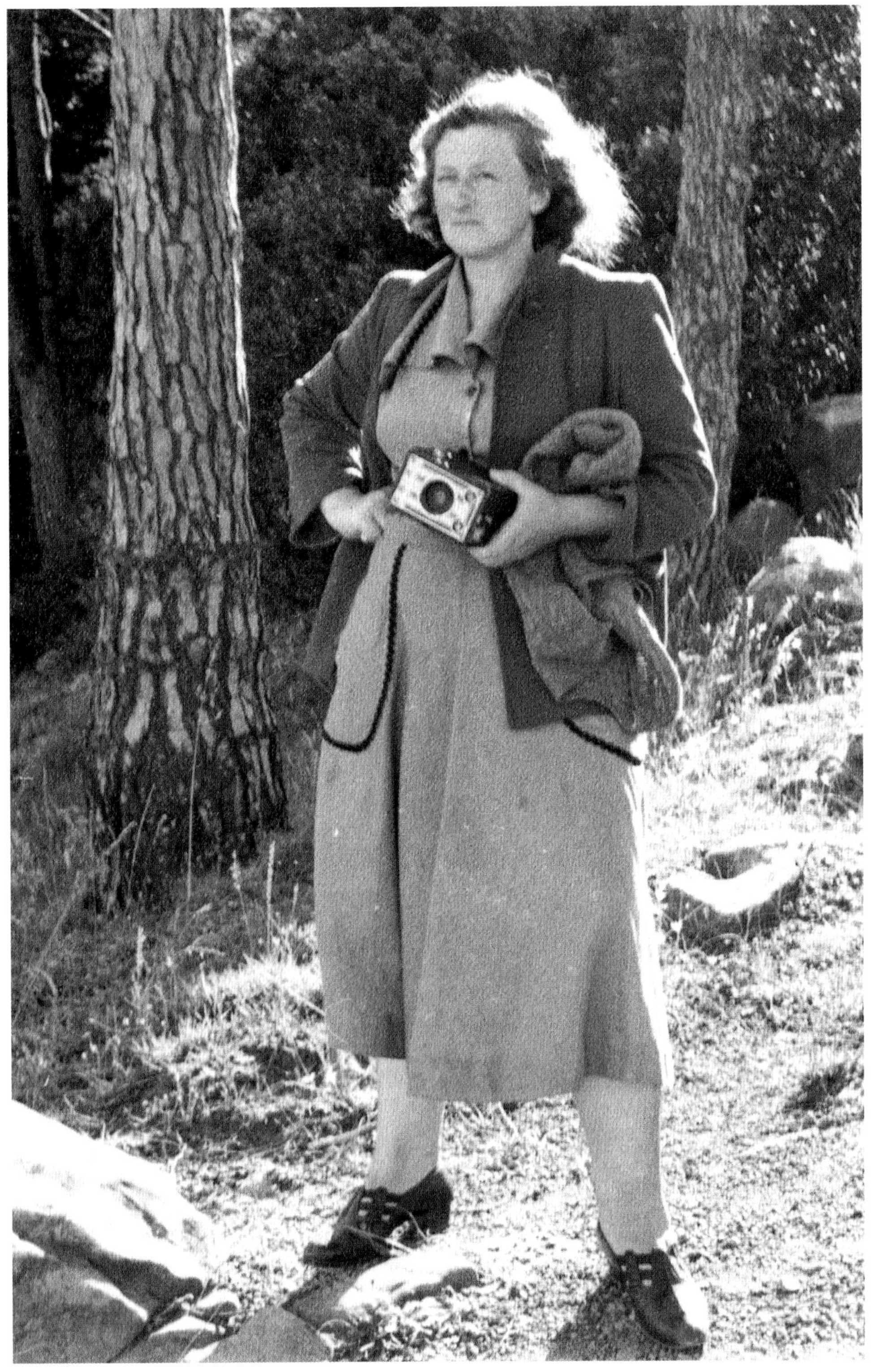

HW: You were member of a photographic club while at St Joseph's. Was this a school society? Could you say a bit more about these activities, the competitions, and exhibitions in which you took part?

JMC: *I was the driving force behind the photographic club at St Joseph's. For a while photography became a craze at the school, then some other craze took over from it. The Brothers allowed us to use the room where laboratory equipment was stored as a darkroom. We also had the use of a notice board to pin up our photographs. We ran a competition and invited one of the Brothers to judge entries.*

HW: You took a large number of images at school, at sports events, but also at formal occasions such as when class photographs were taken. Did you act in some way in an authorised role as a school photographer? In Kannemeyer's biography, your friend, Nic Stathakis, also recounts you taking surreptitious or unauthorised "spy" photographs. Could you say more about these images? You evidently used your Wega, but you also used a smaller, more discreet camera.

JMC: *The smaller camera was the so-called spy camera. The school used a commercial photographer for class photographs and so forth. My activities, and the activities of other members of the photographic club, were indulged rather than authorised.*

HW: The subjects of many of your photographs – Cape Town scenery, domestic life and school activities – are not in themselves remarkable, but many images reveal a care of composition, and an awareness of the techne of taking pictures in difficult conditions (for example shooting

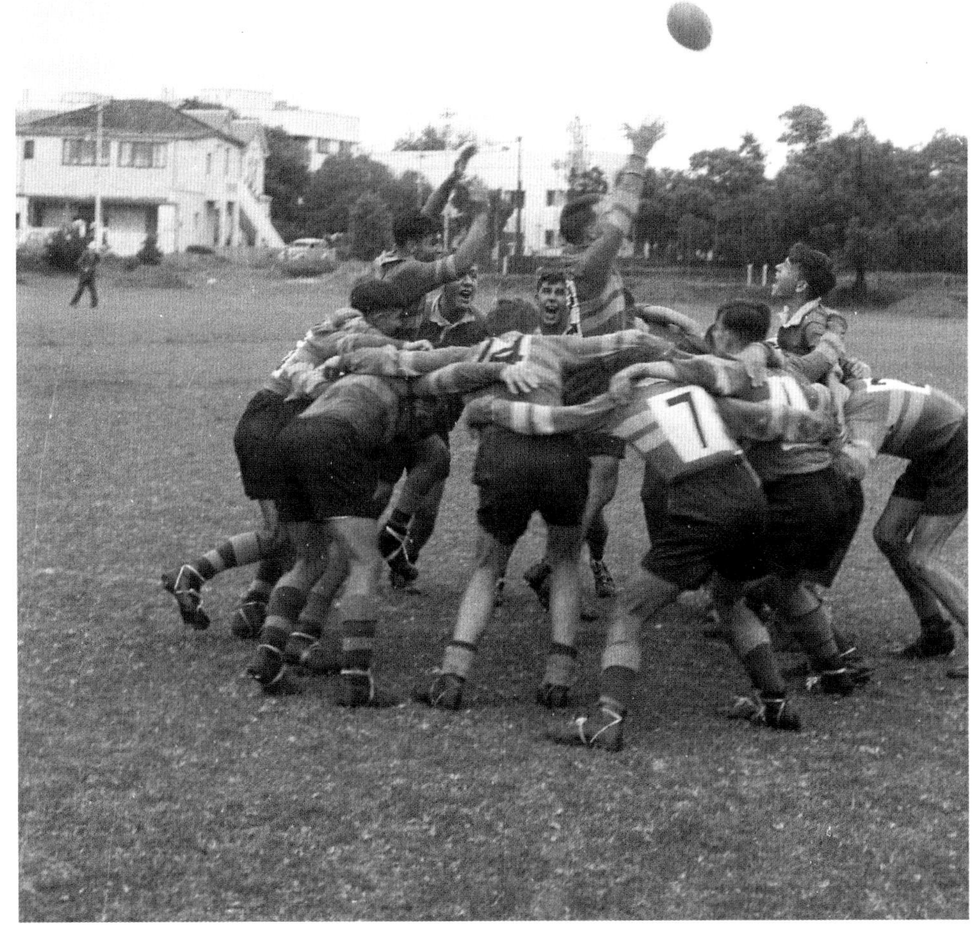

into the light, photographing in darkness, capturing fast movement).
There is a creativity, an experimentalism and a pushing of boundaries
in these images. There are some several carefully composed images, but
the majority of the photographs appear to be taken in an unplanned,
improvisational manner. Could you comment on your approach to the
medium?

JMC: *I read books about photography, imitated as best I could the kind of
photographs I saw in* Life *and other magazines. I believe I was interested in
being present at the moment when truth revealed itself, a moment which one
half discovered but also half created. This was, I think, the aesthetic behind
the practice of photographers like Cartier-Bresson. What I discovered over
the course of time, unfortunately, was that I didn't have the eye of an artist-
photographer. For a while I told myself that this was because I wasn't taking
enough pictures: the photographers I read about thought nothing of taking a
whole roll of 36 of a single subject, while I had to ration my shots. But the truth
was that I was never open enough to the world, particularly to other people's
experience. I was too wrapped up in myself. Which is not unusual at that age.*

HW: An "Opinion" in *Diary of a Bad Year* refers to Samuel Beckett's
hunted look in front of the intrusive photographer. One of the striking
features of many of your photographs is that they appear to be taken
without the subjects being aware of you and the camera. Or if they were
aware, they did not consciously pose. Was this a deliberate mode of using
the camera?

JMC: *One needs a certain inborn narcissism to flourish under the gaze of the
camera lens.*

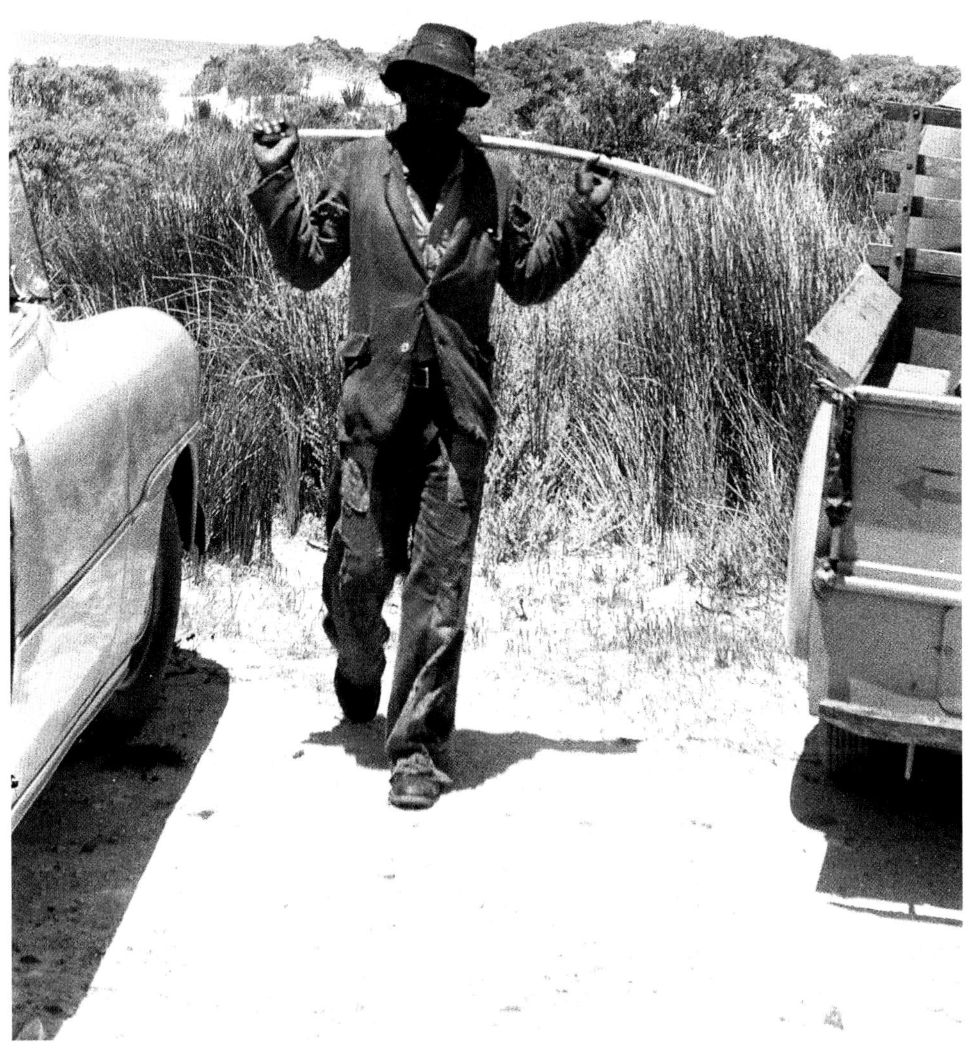

HW: In several of your novels there is an explicit engagement with photographs, from *Dusklands* (the 24 war atrocity images that Eugene Dawn is fascinated with) to *Slow Man*, whose protagonist was a professional photographer. How did photography, and your deep immersion in it, shape the way you would see the world, and would later write it? This is a large question, but how did photography play an enabling role in crafting the novels?

JMC: *The marks of photography (and of the cinema – for present purposes we need not distinguish the two) are all over my work, from the beginning ("The Vietnam Project"). It's not my job to join up the dots.*

5

The First Library

Top Shelf (from left to right)

Thomas Hobbes, *Leviathan* (Everyman,
    No. 691)
Spinoza, *Ethics and De Intellectus
    Emendatione* (Everyman, No. 481)
Jean Jacques Rousseau, *Social Contract
    and Other Essays* (Everyman, No. 660)
Malthus, *On the Principles of Population,
    Vol. 1 & 2* (Everyman, No. 692 & 693)
John Locke, *An Essay Concerning Human
    Understanding, Vol. 2* (Everyman, No.
    984)
St. Augustine, *The City of God, Vol. 1 & 2*
    (Everyman No. 982 & 983)
Unidentifiable (Penguin)
Plato, *The Symposium* (Penguin)
Bertrand Russel, *Mysteries and Logic*
    (Penguin)
Unidentifiable (Penguin)
Marcus Aurelius, *The Thoughts of Marcus
    Aurelius Antoninus* (Oxford World
    Classics, No. 60)
Thomas a Kempis, *Of the Imitation of
    Christ* (Oxford World Classics, No. 49)
Jean Jacques Rousseau, *Emile* (Everyman,
    No. 518)
Emmanuel Kant, *The Critique of Pure
    Reason* (Everyman, No. 909)
Henry Newman, *Apologia Pro Vita Sua*
    (Everyman, No. 636)
Swedenborg, *The True Christian Religion*
    (Everyman, No. 893)
Descartes, *Discourse on Method*
    (Everyman, No. 570)
Bishop Berkeley, *Principles of Human
    Knowledge, New Theory of Vision*
    (Everyman, No. 483)
Pascal, *Pensées* (Everyman, No. 874)

Bottom Shelf (from left to right)

Gordon Dean, *Report on the Atom* (Knopf)
Karl Marx, *Capital, Vol. 1 & 2* (Everyman,
    No. 848 & 849)
Jean Jacques Rousseau, *Confessions, Vol. 1
    & 2* (Everyman, No. 859 & 860)
Herbert Read, *The Meaning of Art*
    (Penguin)
Unidentifiable (Penguin)
Unidentifiable (Penguin)
Euclid, *Elements* (Everyman, No. 891)
E.T. Bell, *Men of Mathematics Vol. 1 & 2*
    (Penguin)
Dostoevsky, *Crime and Punishment*
    (Penguin)
Voltaire, *Candide* (Penguin)
Voltaire, *The Age of Louis XIV* (Everyman,
    No. 780)
Caesar, *The Conquest of Gaul* (Penguin)
Unidentifiable (Penguin)
Unidentifiable (Penguin)
TS Eliot, *Selected Prose* (Penguin)
Oscar Wilde, *Plays, Prose Writings & Poems*
    (Everyman, No. 858)
Unidentifiable (Penguin)
Tolstoy, *War and Peace* (Oxford)
TS Eliot, *Collected Poems 1909-1935* (Faber
    & Faber)
Unidentifiable (Penguin)
Unidentifiable (Penguin)
Unidentifiable (Penguin)
Unidentifiable
Keats, *Poetical Works*
Tennyson, *The Poems of Tennyson*
Wordsworth, *The Poetical Works of
    Wordsworth*

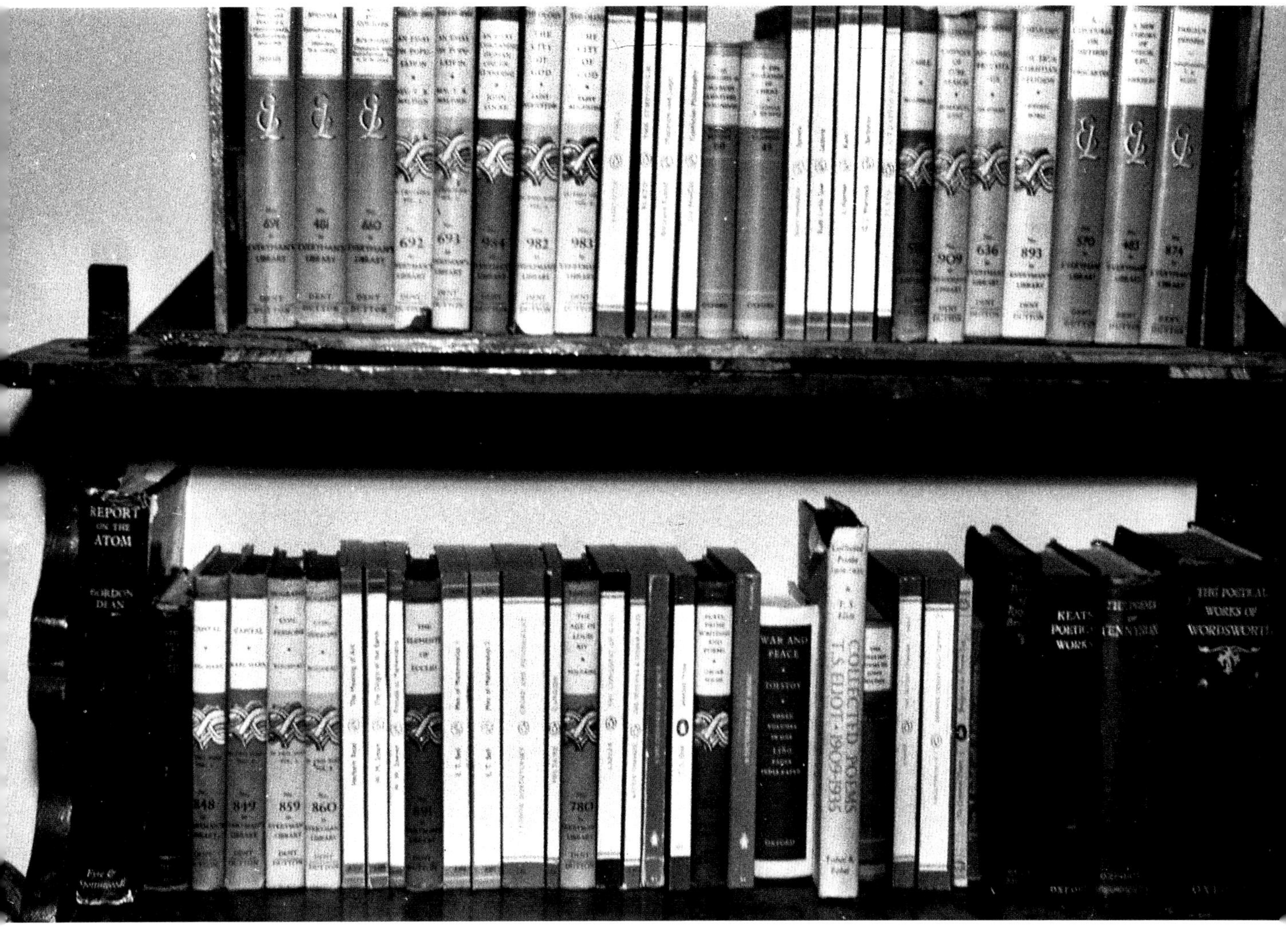

For readers who have followed Coetzee's literary career unfolding over the last 50 years, one of the most interesting images in this collection is a photograph of his first library. The photograph gives us insight into the beginnings of his authorship, a literary career that would in time absorb all his creative energies and displace the camera as the primary medium through which he engaged the world. The image of the first personal library, a collection of some 45 books arranged carefully in a wooden bookcase that stood in his bedroom in the Cape Town suburb of Plumstead, was taken when he would have been about 16 years old.

The collection of books marks a key moment of the young artist's development, showing a decisive break with his earlier literary tastes. As we learn from *Boyhood*, the first fictionalised memoir, the "books he likes best are the French Foreign Legion stories of P C Wren", and for a while he thinks that P C Wren is "the greatest writer in the world."[29] The young John also voraciously read the Enid Blyton mysteries, as well as Hardy Boys and Biggles stories, so much so that his mother found it difficult to keep up with the quantity of books that the boy consumed: she "had to visit the library twice a week to take out books for him: two on her cards, another two on his own."[30] Reading "with great speed and with total absorption" was a habit he established early in life. But the memoir also registers his early ambitions to read beyond these books, and *Treasure Island* and *Swiss Family Robinson* fare: "He knows that if he wants to be a great man he ought to be reading serious books."[31]

The "serious books" that the boy chose for himself mark a shift in his reading tastes towards a more mature, intellectual trajectory. For a teenager, it is a highly ambitious library of poetry, philosophy and translated classics, mostly affordable Everyman, Oxford and Penguin editions, those early twentieth-century projects in the democratization of knowledge. The photograph is not well lit, but the large Everyman numbers on the spines allow the identification of several volumes. The key writings of Plato, St Augustine, Hobbes, Spinoza, Rousseau, Locke, Kant and Descartes are represented, as are Russian classics such as Dostoevsky's *Crime and Punishment* and Tolstoy's *War and Peace*. There are no English novels, nor is there any Shakespeare, but there are collected works of poetry by T.S. Eliot, Wordsworth, Tennyson and Keats. Books such as Euclid's *Elements* point to his ambitions to become a mathematician, and the presence of Marx's *Das Kapital*, a book that was to be banned by the apartheid state, suggests an early interest in questions of inequality and social justice. Several of these books would leave their mark on the later fictions, if we for example consider the influence of the classics more generally on *Age of Iron*, the direct engagement with Dostoevsky in *The Master of Petersburg*, and the pervasiveness of Platonic thinking in *The Childhood of Jesus*. But we also need to note that important future influences such as Pound, Beckett and Kafka are not as yet present.

The bookshelf also speaks to another key moment in Coetzee's complex and evolving relationship to the European classical tradition. In the essay "What is a Classic?", he describes how he was transfixed by the sounds

of Bach's 'Well-Tempered Clavier': "As long as the music lasted, I was
frozen, I dared not breathe. I was spoken to by music as music had
never spoken to me." As he recounts it, the scene occurred in the
backyard of the Plumstead home, one "Sunday afternoon in the summer
of 1955, when I was 15 years old."[32] The Bach moment was a key event,
marking a reorientation in intellectual development and cultural
taste in which he was "symbolically electing high European culture."
Retrospectively though, Coetzee questioned whether his passionate
response was triggered by the "inherent quality of the music" or whether
Bach did not represent "a way out of a social and historical dead end" in
provincial South Africa at the time.[33] The library that the young Coetzee
then began to assemble was in this sense a consequence of these
aspirations.

In a letter to Paul Auster, Coetzee reflected on this period, singling
out his purchase of *War and Peace*: "When I was sixteen, having some
money to spend, I bought ten or so books that were going to constitute
the foundation of a personal library. They included *War and Peace* in the
translation by Aylmer Maude, published by Oxford University Press,
a bulky little book printed on thin India paper." Coetzee appears to
have formed a deep and lasting relationship with this book, recounting
that the volume, which in its "original cream and maroon wrapper has
accompanied me through half a century's moves from continent to
continent."[34] In the photograph, Tolstoy's novel is visible on the lower
shelf, a short, fairly thick book near the middle.

184

The well-thumbed book next to it is similarly significant. It is a post-war Faber & Faber edition of T.S. Eliot's *Collected Poems 1909-1935*, complemented by a Penguin edition of Eliot's prose. In Youth, the second memoir, Coetzee writes about Eliot as the poet "with whom he had his first overwhelming encounter while he was still at school."[35] And writing in the essay "Homage", Coetzee confesses that he "found Eliot's example highly seductive" and that he "wrote poems in the manner of T.S. Eliot."[36] The double initials of his self-effacing authorial stylisation (J.M., standing for John Maxwell) are likely to be an acknowledgement of Thomas Stearns Eliot's controlling influence.

It is also possible to trace the provenance of some books on the shelf. *The Poetical Works of Wordsworth*, for instance, is likely to have been given to him by his father, if we trust the account from the memoir. Throughout *Boyhood,* John's complex relationship with his father is described as awkward and even hostile, but there is a rare moment where the father attempts to reach out to the son: "One day his father comes to his room with the Wordsworth book. 'You should read these,' he says, and points out poems he has ticked in pencil."[37] When he later returns to discuss 'Tintern Abbey' with his son, the embarrassed boy professes ignorance and lack of interest. Its presence in the photographed book shelf though shows that the young Coetzee had evidently valued Wordsworth enough, and had only feigned lack of interest to fob off the father. Or perhaps not, since the fictionalising strategies of the memoir cannot take us to what really happened. Coetzee's relationship with the Romantic tradition would in any case be an ambivalent one, if we recall the ironic treatment of David Lurie's Byronic obsession in *Disgrace* (1999).

The photograph of the early library, and the traces of these books in Coetzee's comments in various fictions and essays, allow insight into the key influences on the writer as he attempted to cast off a provincial and colonial culture and began to claim a literary and philosophical heritage associated with a European intellectual tradition he would later go on simultaneously to use and subject to sustained interrogation. Reflecting on his reading in this formative period Coetzee notes in "Homage" that this was "a time of life when one begins, almost inevitably, to define or at least demarcate an identity for oneself" and where one reads "with a degree of absorption and intensity that deserts us as we grow older."[38] If these early feelings slackened, other, more self-conscious and self-critical attitudes took their place, leaving their mark on every book since *Dusklands* (1974).

Notes

1   J.M. Coetzee, "Remembering Photography". Interview with H. Wittenberg, reproduced in this publication.

2   J.C. Kannemeyer, *JM Coetzee. A Life in Writing*, Johannesburg, Jonathan Ball, 2012, p. 62-3.

3   J.M. Coetzee, *Slow Man*, London, Secker & Warburg, 2005, p. 64.

4   "Remembering Photography"

5   Ibid.

6   Ibid.

7   Ibid.

8   Ibid.

9   Ibid.

10   J.M. Coetzee, *Boyhood*, London, Secker & Warburg, 1997, p. 27.

11   Ibid, p. 149.

12   Ibid, p. 91.

13   J.M. Coetzee, *Summertime*, London, Harvill Secker, 2009, p. 225.

14   J.M. Coetzee, "Arthur Miller, The Misfits", *Inner Workings: Literary Essays 2000-2005*, London, Harvill Secker, 2007, p. 226.

15   J.M. Coetzee, *Doubling the Point: Essays and Interviews*, ed. David Attwell, Cambridge (Massachusetts), Harvard University Press, 1992, p. 391.

16 *Boyhood*, p. 85.

17 Ibid, p. 86-87.

18 *Summertime*, p.346.

19 J.M. Coetzee, *Dusklands*, Johannesburg, Ravan, 1974, p. 13.

20 For a closer analysis of photographic and cinematic modes of narration, see H. Wittenberg, "Film and Photography in J.M. Coetzee's *Life & Times of Michael K." Texas Studies in Literature and Language*, Vol. 58, No. 4, Winter 2016, pp. 473-492.

21 *Boyhood*, p. 34.

22 Ibid, p. 90.

23 Ibid, p. 40.

24 Ibid, p. 140.

24 Kannemeyer, p.136.

26 *Slow Man*, p.175.

27 "Remembering Photography"

28 Ibid.

29 *Boyhood*, p. 104.

30 Ibid, p. 103.

31 Ibid.

32 J.M. Coetzee, "What is a Classic?" *Stranger Shores: Literary Essays, 1986–1999*, London, Secker & Warburg, 2001, p. 9.

33 Ibid, p. 10-11.

34 J.M. Coetzee & Paul Auster, *Here and Now: Letters, 2008–2011*. Letter to Paul Auster, 10 August 2010.

35 J.M. Coetzee, *Youth*, London, Secker & Warburg, 2002, p. 20.

36 J.M. Coetzee, "Homage." *The Threepenny Review*, No. 53, Spring, 1993, p. 5.

37 *Boyhood*, p. 105.

38 "Homage", p. 5.

Photographs from Boyhood – J.M. Coetzee

Published in its original edition as

De foto's van Jongensjaren in 2020 by

Uitgeverij Cossee BV, Amsterdam

First edition, first impression in 2020 by Protea Book House

PO Box 35110, Menlo Park, 0102

1067 Burnett Street, Hatfield, Pretoria

8 Minni Street, Clydesdale, Pretoria

info@proteaboekhuis.co.za

www.proteaboekhuis.com

ISBN: 978-1-4853-1146-1